Also by Robert C. Daniels

1220 Days: The story of U.S. Marine Edmond Babler and his experiences in Japanese Prisoner of War Camps during World War II. 2nd ed. AuthorHouse, 2011

Published at www.militaryhistoryonline.com

Hell Ship - From the Philippines to Japan
Hitler, Germany's Worst General
MacArthur's Failures in the Philippines
Failures during the Spanish Civil War
Muslim Invasion of Iberia
The Failures at Spion Kop
Combatants in the Black Hawk War
WWII Veteran Interview – Charles and Nova (Wagner) Vellema
WWII Veteran Interview – Walter Riel

WORLD WAR II IN MID-AMERICA

EXPERIENCES FROM RURAL MID-AMERICA DURING THE SECOND WORLD WAR

By Robert C. Daniels

authorHOUSE®

AuthorHouse™
1663 Liberty Drive
Bloomington, IN 47403
www.authorhouse.com
Phone: 1-800-839-8640

Published by AuthorHouse 7/31/2012

ISBN: 978-1-4772-3684-0 (sc)
ISBN: 978-1-4772-3683-3 (hc)
ISBN: 978-1-4772-3682-6 (e)

Library of Congress Control Number: 2012911737

Dedication

This book is dedicated to all
those who personally experienced
the World War II era.

Preface

By all accounts, the Second World War was one of the most singular world shaping events of all time. Never before had such a war been fought by and effected so many differing nations; over fifty countries or dependencies were involved in one way or another. The casualty rates were staggering by all accounts. Estimates on the military and civilian death toll vary from sixty million to around seventy-five million, and this does not include the millions upon millions that were wounded, injured, or displaced.

Like the First World War, the United States was a relative latecomer to the Second World War, not fully becoming engaged in the conflict until after the 7 December 1941 Japanese surprise attack on Pearl Harbor, Hawaii, and other Allied Pacific outposts. Once engaged, however, the United Stated entered the war with everything it had, eventually fighting in every theater of the conflict and sending over sixteen million of its sons and daughters to the fight. Over three hundred twenty thousand of these would be either killed or wounded.

Unlike many of the previous wars, however, and even the wars since—the Korean War, the Vietnam Conflict, and even the first Persian Gulf war (1991), as well as the current wars in Iraq and Afghanistan—the Second World War did not just involve the military. In World War II the entire country went to war, with those that stayed home full-heartedly supporting the war effort in any way they could throughout its *entire* duration. There were no anti-war riots, and very few, if any, anti-war protests. There were very few draft dodgers; for that matter, it was considered nearly a disgrace for any able bodied man of service age to be seen on the streets throughout the United States not in uniform. Many of the disabled even attempted to enlist, sometimes more than once, to 'do their part'; some would eventually be accepted. Others lied about their age to enlist, some actually being in their mid-teens. It was also a time when movie actors, directors, and producers, professional athletes, politicians, and sons of presidents and congressmen flocked to the recruiting stations—not to do so would have been considered unpatriotic.

Those who were not able to serve in the military due to their gender, age, or health, or, in some instances, where the need was greater for the individual to serve in factories or on farms for the nation's and the war effort's good, including the parents, grandparents, wives, sisters, brothers, girl friends, and even children of the servicemen and women, eagerly and unwaveringly served their country's war effort in other ways. They not only stood firmly behind the war effort, they also endured rationing, many times going without such staples as sugar, new clothes, new shoes, tires, gasoline, silk stockings, and new cars. Even old cars often sat idle for months and sometimes years on end when repair parts or replacement tires became non-existent. These Americans gathered and donated, without expecting any reimbursement, *anything* the government requested for the war effort. They also helped and supported each other, many times without even being asked to do so, and they seldom if ever grumbled about their difficulties and shortages—because it was for the war effort.

What follows is their story, many times quoting their own words using the exact dialect and idioms in which they related them, representing *their* thoughts, *their* views, and how *they* experienced the war, with no apologies made nor intended to conform to the modern concept of political correctness. These accounts are not from a politician's view, or a military leader's view, or even a historian's view, but the view of the everyday citizen, soldier, sailor, and airman who lived through the World War II era. Although it is a story that centers around one small, rural, mid-western community, this community can easily be considered indicative of nearly every small, rural community in the heartland of America. The area of the country for this narrative was chosen simply because it is the town and community the author grew up in; it is a community he is familiar with. But it is also a community that readily represents many thousands of other rural, small American towns throughout the country.

Although it is in fact a story about the Second World War, it is not intended to be in itself a history of the war. Instead, it will only cover the theaters and battles of the war that were experienced—and then only to the extent that they were experienced—by those individuals included within these pages. It is the story, however, of the honest, hard working, patriotic American of that generation. It is the story of the soldier, the airman, the Marine, and the sailor; why, how, and where they fought in the war, as well as how the war affected their lives—including many of their pre-war as well as post-war experiences. It is also the story of the housewife, the factory worker, the farmer, the girlfriend, and the children of the era. The story of how they too willingly sacrificed to win the war against Japan and Nazi Germany; and how the war changed their lives, as well as how they lived their lives before, during, and after the war. In short, it is a study of how rural small-town America contributed to and fared during the Second World War through the eyes of some of those who witnessed and lived it.

Our story begins in the mid 1930's, since this is when most of those featured grew up struggling through the Great Depression, a time when many did not even have electricity and running water in their homes and country schools. A time when youngsters walked a mile or more to and from school—in all forms of weather. It was also a time when one out of every four adults was out of work, and had been for quite some time due to the Depression. We then move onto that fateful day in December of 1941 when the United States was suddenly and shockingly forced into World War II, and then follow our featured characters from year to year as the war progressed and finally came to an end.

Acknowledgments

In writing this book I owe a great personal debt of gratitude to many people. First and foremost is my wife Becky, who not only stuck by me throughout the long days and nights of research, writing, and rewriting, as well as my being away for periods of time conducting interviews, but also gave me constant encouragement. Her keen eye also helped catch some of my overlooked editing errors.

A great thank you also goes to Mr. James Laird of the Waupun Historical Society in Waupun, Wisconsin, without whose assistance the completion of this book would not have been possible. Jim was the backbone in helping set up the numerous interviews I conducted as well as opening up the Historical Society's archives for my use. He was also always there when additional information was needed, which he quickly supplied, as well as sat in on and assisted with several of the interviews.

In addition, a large thank you goes out to Colleen Kottke and DiAnna Mueller of the Fond du Lac, Wisconsin, *Reporter* and the Beaver Dam, Wisconsin, *Daily Citizen*, respectively, both of whom were kind enough to print several articles in their respective newspapers getting the word out about my research and encouraging their readers to consider allowing me to interview them. I also wish to thank the Reverend Mike Bausch and the congregation of the Union-Congregational Church of Waupun for graciously allowing me to use their facilities to conduct many of my interviews, along with Mrs. Lynn Adams, the church secretary, who patiently put up with and assisted me by ushering several of the interviewees through the church to the room I was using.

A thank you also goes out to Elif Guler, David Winkelsas, Shannon Peer, and Elizabeth Berry who took the time to conduct the tedious transcriptions of my interviews from DVD format into written text . . . not an easy task!

And, of course, these pages could never have been written without all of those who allowed themselves to be interviewed or submitted written correspondence, whose life experiences made this book possible. A great thank you goes out to you all of you.

– Robert C. Daniels

Table of Contents

Prologue

The 7 December 1941 Japanese sneak attack on the United States military installations and ships at Pearl Harbor, Hawaii, literally shocked the nation. As U.S. Marine Edmond Babler, stationed outside of Manila on the Philippine island of Luzon, recalled, "On December 8th [7 December Hawaii time] the air raid sirens began blowing. After several minutes we heard the Japs had bombed Pearl Harbor."[1]

Charles Vellema, in the U.S. Army stationed at Fort Bragg, North Carolina, heard the news of the attack on that same day around 4 p.m. local North Carolina time over the radio in his barracks. As he remembered, "[I]t was hard to believe that something like that could happen."[2] Like many others, Doris Bohnert, along with her co-workers at the National Rivet and Manufacturing Company in the small Wisconsin town of Waupun, became scared when she heard it, recalling, "We thought it was terrible. We were sort of scared, you know."[3] In the neighboring small village of Brandon, Wisconsin, Nova Wagner was also "Scared! I just knew it would mean more young men would be called on, and I had brother-in-laws, my sisters were married," who would be part of that call-up.[4] Besides, Charles Vellema, the man she was dating, was already in the army.

The next day, President Franklin Delano Roosevelt made his famous "Day of Infamy" speech, and two days later German Dictator Adolf Hitler declared war on the United States. The nation was suddenly plunged into war, and, as has been commonly written and stated, a sleeping giant was about to awaken. That sleeping giant would not only come out of the nation's large cities, it would also come from the everyday farmland and small community. The small, rural town of Waupun, Wisconsin, was one such community, and like all other American communities, small and large, it, its citizens, and its surrounding communities would unflinchingly, unwaveringly, and enthusiastically play its part in this war.

Waupun, in many ways, was very similar to nearly all other small, rural, mid-American communities, with a long history of patriotism and national support. The area, near the head waters of the Rock River, had been inhabited for centuries by numerous Native American tribes, including the Potawatomis, Winnebago, and Menominees, prior to the Europeans entering the area. The first white settler, Seymour Wilcox, arrived in 1839. At the time, there were only trails made by the Indians and the animals; no roads or bridges existed. Streams needed to be forded, trails and roads needed to be blazed. Since horses were a luxury that few could afford, most of the settlers would arrive on foot or sometimes in wagons hauled by oxen. The village of Green Bay was a three day trip, if one was lucky.[5]

Early settlers described the area as having "broad prairies and pleasant openings."[6] One settler would write:

> Beautiful indeed was the panorama which greeted my sight. The landscape was then covered with a luxuriant growth of vegetation, the greater part of which was new and strange to me. Wild flowers of every shade and color that fancy could paint or imagination conceive were blooming on every hand, richly contrasted by the tall prairie grass, which in wild luxuriance was waving in the gentle breezes of that balmy summer afternoon.[7]

Another wrote:

> The country where Waupun stands was what is called 'Oak Openings'.... Rock River was, at that time considerably larger, affording good water power, and was a rapid boisterous stream, abounding in fish, with many pools where the wild fowl congregated in large numbers. Along the river, where the same passes through the present town, there was heavy timber of oak, ash, hickory, elm, and scattering trees of other kinds. To the west and south was the prairie with deep black soil. The woods were full of game and no one to molest it but the Red Men. It was a beautiful country with its forest columns capped

with leaves, opening onto park-like prairies, dotted with flowers of every color.[8]

With the arrival of more settlers, the community soon began to resemble a town, with a water powered saw mill appearing in 1841 and then a grist mill in 1842. By the end of 1845, the village had two hotels, and in 1851 the State of Wisconsin decided to locate the State's prison in the town. Within five years of this decision, the first railroad train also began making regular stops in Waupun. One year later, in 1857, the township was officially incorporated with the name of Waupun, which was a misspelling in the official documentation of the word Waubun, meaning Dawn of the Morning or The Early Day, depending upon which translation one wishes to abide by.

In that year, an anonymous writer would pen:

> Look at the little village now and see what a contrast it presents. It is set off with beautiful dwellings, cultivated gardens, and shaded streets. There are five dry-goods stores, five grocery stores, three clothing stores, four hotels, three drug stores, five physicians, two lawyers, two hardware and tinning establishments, two grist mills, one planing mill, one pump factory, two printing houses, three wagon shops, several lumber merchants, cabinet-makers, stone-masons, and painters. There are two banks—the Waupun Bank and the Corn Exchange, two school houses, and four churches.[9]

Over the years Waupun would grow into a well established farming and light-industrial town boasting of several shoe companies, a knitting company, several canning factories, and an umbrella factory (the later which would eventually evolve into Shaler's National Rivet and Manufacturing Company), as well as the State's maximum security prison and the State's Central State Hospital for the Criminally Insane. Local farming would change with the times from a strong wheat producer in the settlement's early days—at the outbreak of the American Civil War, Wisconsin was the number two wheat producing state in the nation, just below Illinois[10]—to dairy production, with the surrounding counties, Dodge and Fond du Lac, being some of the nation's leading dairy producers.

Waupun has always had a strong patriotic spirit, sending her sons and a few of her daughters off to fight in every major national conflict since the time of her founding. Even as early as 1858, Waupun's first settlers boasted fourteen War of 1812 veterans, and the American Civil War saw over 225 of its sons fight for the Union; thirty-one volunteered for service in the Spanish-American War, and 296, along with four of her daughters who volunteered as nurses, went to fight in the First World War.[11]

With the outbreak of World War II, Waupun would again send many of its sons and some of its daughters off to war. According to a picture of the Roll of Honor that once stood on Main Street in front of the town's city hall, 862 of Waupun's men and women served in uniform during the war. In addition, seven Gold Wives and fifteen Gold Mothers were also listed; gold representing wives or mothers that had lost husbands or sons in the war. Therefore, according to the Roll of Honor, twenty-two of those that served from the Waupun area never came home from the war.

To put this into perspective, Waupun today has a population of just over ten thousand souls, with an excess of two thousand of these as inmates in the town's three correctional institutions. Therefore, it can be easily assumed that a good ten percent to fifteen percent of the 1941-1945 population of Waupun went off to the war.

What is different during World War II, however, is that like every other small and large community throughout the United States during this war, every citizen of the Waupun, Wisconsin, area, fully, even enthusiastically and unwaveringly also fought the war in any way they could . . . unflinchingly supporting not only the troops, but the United States president and government in *every* effort requested by both the president and the government. As such, the citizens did not question the president, or his motives. They did not question the various government bureaus' or agencies' requests, or their motives. They just blindly supported, and did so willingly. Not to do so would have been unthinkable since it would have been considered un-patriotic, possibly even considered aiding the enemy.

In addition, local factories and industries quickly changed from making shoes to making combat boots, from making aluminum coffee pots to making aluminum aircraft parts, from making washing machines to making shell casings, from making rivets for toys and automobiles to making nearly every rivet that went into literally every military aircraft produced in the nation, and from building ships designed to ply the waters of the great lakes to building submarines and large troop and tank landing craft for ocean going use. Local farmers also stepped up to the task, growing not only their normal feed crops for their dairy and hog farms, but also additional grain, sweet corn, and peas to help feed the troops, and, in some cases, hemp for the making of rope. Others, including children, willfully scavenged the countryside for both unused items for re-cycling and raw materials for the war use: rubber, metals, paper, even a weed that grew wild along country roads—the milkweed plant. Anything that had a military use was collected and *donated* to the war effort without expectation of compensation.

World War II was a war that the *nation* was to fight, not just the military, and it was a war that the citizens of Waupun, Wisconsin, as the citizens of all of the United States communities, were determined to win regardless of the sacrifices that would have to be made.

Map of Wisconsin

Difficult Yet Peaceful Times

Nazi Germany's 1 September 1939 invasion of Poland signaled the beginning of war in Europe, a war that would eventually engulf all of Europe, North Africa, and a good portion of the Middle-East. Although this act plunged Europe into war, the United States, under the tutelage of President Franklin Delano Roosevelt, maintained its strict policy of isolationism and neutrality. This same timeframe saw the Western Pacific, specifically China, also in turmoil. Even before the 1 July 1937 'China Incident,' in which Japanese soldiers of the Kwantung Army opened fire on Chinese National troops,[12] the Japanese had been encroaching into the Asian mainland, not hesitating to use military force when the need arose. On 12 December of the same year as the China Incident, the *USS Panay*, an American naval gunboat flying an oversized American flag, was bombed by Japanese Imperial Navy bombers on China's Yangtze River, killing an Italian journalist and two American sailors.[13] Within a year, most of the fertile portions of China had fallen to Japan.[14] As a result, although maintaining its isolationism and neutrality in the European war and overlooking the Panay incident, by the end of the 1930's, with Japan's push for their Greater Asia Co-Prosperity Sphere in nearly full swing, diplomatic relations between the United States and Japan were increasingly deteriorating to the extent that if things did not change, and soon, war in the Pacific might very well be imminent.

Throughout the 1930's, cities and villages in the United States had been reeling from the 29 October 1929 stock market crash, commonly referred to as Black Tuesday, which touched off the Great Depression, nearly devastating the country. Not only the United States was affected by this crash, but nearly the entire world had been suffering as well. People, hard working people, were out of work, some having been so for years. It was estimated that in the United States alone, nearly one in four adults of working age—twenty-five percent of the working population—were

1

out of work at the height of the Depression. The respective governments tried to help, but with limited success. Only Germany, under their Nazi Dictator, Adolf Hitler, of all of the free-market societies, seemed to be showing any type of real signs of progress.

The mid-western American town of Waupun, Wisconsin, was no exception. By 1938, Waupun, situated in the southern-mid-eastern portion of the state along the headwaters of the Rock River, was a relatively small farming community typical of many other small, mid-western American farming communities. The three real main differences offsetting it from the other communities of its size was the fact that the State's maximum security prison, the State's Central State Hospital for the Criminally Insane, and the National Rivet and Manufacturing Company were all three situated within the town's small city limits. Even with these three institutions, however, the Waupun area was still suffering from the Depression. Jobs were hard to find and money was scarce to purchase even the needed goods, much less any luxuries. Children of the era were growing up poor, yet many never realized it at the time since it was all they had really known, it was all they had been used to.

Due to the Depression and lack of work, Joseph "Joe" and Linda (Paskey) Bohnert and their four children were forced to move from time to time throughout the decade following the stock market crash. But somehow, with the exception of a short move to South Dakota, they always managed to remain within a ten mile radius of Waupun. Linda had been born in the town in 1896 to German immigrants. Joe, twelve years older than Linda, had, himself, emigrated from Switzerland in 1914. With Joe being forced to regularly seek new employment upon the termination of numerous short-lived jobs, and since new jobs became more and more scarce as the decade progressed, the family was forced to move even more often than before due to the lack of availability of work within walking distance—cars were a luxury the family could ill afford.[15]

Prior to the market crash, Joe had worked for the Central State Hospital for the Criminally Insane, commonly known simply as the Central State Hospital or Central State, located on the outskirts of Waupun. He had also worked for his father-in-law at the family owned tavern in town. But during the Depression jobs just became too scarce. He was eventually able to get assistance from the Works Progress Administration (WPA). The WPA was established in 1935 by presidential order and funded by Congress through 1943, when it was disbanded due to the World War II war boom.

The organization provided jobs and income for many of the unemployed during the Great Depression, and built roads and parks, as well as art, literary, and drama projects. Like many areas around the country, local projects were constructed by the WPA in the Waupun area as well. Two of these are still visible at the Fond du Lac County Park, just outside of the town. Both the park's band shell and the lining on the Rock River, where it flows through the park, were constructed by WPA workers.[16]

The organization required that individuals work for assistance, and, as one of Joe's daughters was to remember, "Many of the people refused to work, but dad did, and got on with the [Waupun] City Parks Department."[17] This job required Joe to get up before the sun every school-day morning and roll the tennis courts at the high school with a heavy roller to maintain the courts' flat, smooth playing surfaces. He was also a caretaker of the city's flower gardens.

To help the family, his wife Linda also worked for awhile at the local five and dime store. When Joe and Linda's children were old enough, they too pitched in to help. They would babysit and do other odd jobs; nearly anything for a little money. "I would babysit for Uncle Walter and Aunt Louise [Paskey]," reported Joe and Linda's oldest daughter, Doris, "and on the way home, I would stop off at the butcher's and buy 15 cents worth of cold cuts. That would be enough for each of us to have one or two slices of meat with our potatoes for supper." Like many of her generation, Doris was born not in a hospital, but at home in the family dwelling—in Waupun on 22 July 1923.[18]

Even with Joe working through the WPA and his other odd jobs, Linda working at the Five and Dime, and their children helping when they could, times were financially rough on the family. Money was scarce, and hand-me-down clothes were the sign of the times in the Bohnert household. Linda would use her treadle-powered Singer sewing machine to alter these hand-me-downs, as well as make clothes from scratch to fit her children. "Most of the girls had pretty dresses in high school. We didn't," recalled Doris. "I had one dress for Sunday and a couple for school. Everyone else had several skirts and dresses to wear."[19]

Lois, Joseph and Linda's youngest child, born in the family home in Waupun in 1925, recalled that "We didn't have a lot, but I think we had a lot more fun in our life, I think, in those days. . . . We went swimming, like I went swimming in the river [Rock River]." "China Hole," she called it. "I think everybody was in the same boat, kinda, except for like doctors

3

or lawyers or someone. Other than that we were all in the same boat, we didn't have a lot. But what we had we shared and had a good time."[20]

In emphasizing how they would share, Lois went on to tell a story of how, when one of them would get a nickel, she and her brothers and sister would gather the neighborhood kids and they would all go to a nearby small neighborhood store where they would "see what we could get the most for our penny. You know, two for a penny, always something like that. . . . And then we go home and spread it out on the blanket, and then we'd divide it up."[21]

Although very little money was available, the family of six, which also included Ralph, born in South Dakota on 6 September 1924, and the oldest, Alfred "Al," who was born in the family home in Waupun on 11 December 1921, nonetheless, always seemed to have had enough food, never having had to go hungry. According to Doris, the local butchers would give away beef bones for soup, and "We always had a big garden, and we ate a lot of vegetables. Mother cooked bread, and because there wasn't such a thing as a freezer back then, she canned a lot of vegetables."[22] The family also received a monthly stipend of oatmeal, cornbread, sugar, flour, and one pound of butter from the government. In addition, for a period, the farmer from whom they were renting a home from would give them a gallon of milk every day.

Like many of her fellow school age friends, including her good friend Lois Bohnert, thirteen year old Dorothy Bal and her family were also having a rough time. Dorothy was born on 25 November 1925 in St. Agnes Hospital in Fond du Lac, Wisconsin, the county seat about eighteen miles north-east of Waupun, to Martin and Bessie Bal. As she was to state, "[W]e didn't have a lot of material things, but what we had we appreciated. . . . [I]n winter time we ice-skated on the [Rock] river and went sledding and skiing and . . ., I mean, we had good times."[23] She also recalled walking home with her father from his place of work each day. He would give her a penny, which she would take to the corner drug store where, she stated, "there was a big table there, and boy, there was really a decision to make up your mind what you are gonna buy for that penny, because it was twenty-five or fifty different candies. . . . So, every day it was a decision what you were gonna get for that penny."[24]

Like her schoolmates Lois and Dorothy, in 1938 thirteen year old Joan Laandal was living in Waupun and attending the town's large Lincoln Elementary School. Having been born the youngest of four children to

Melvin and Mae Laandal on 19 July 1925 in the family home in Merrill, Wisconsin, about 100 miles northwest of Waupun, the family had moved to Waupun where they opened and ran a restaurant and tavern called *Laandal's Lunch*. "It was a combination restaurant-tavern. A kind of a family place, you know," Joan recalled. "We lived in the west side of it. It was next to the Catholic Church, but it's been torn down now, so that area is [now] all parking lot."[25]

Young six year old Shirley Karmann was also attending Lincoln School in Waupun; however, her family, like the Laandals, was not as bad off as the Bohnerts or the Bal's. Born in Milwaukee on 17 November 1930, her father, John, had been a successful bookkeeper and accountant there, but due to the Depression had lost his job. So John, after being hired on at the Maximum Security Prison in Waupun as a guard, had somewhat recently moved his wife, Clara (Igowski), and their family to Waupun. As Shirley recalled about her father getting the job at the prison and the family moving to Waupun, "I remember him saying there were over a thousand taking the test, and fortunately he passed the test and was hired, they only hired ten new men to work there. He started the job, and when he found a rental for Mom and I, we moved there too."[26]

In moving to Waupun, however, the family left behind all of their extended family and relatives, who still lived in Milwaukee, including both her paternal and maternal grandparents who "were born in Germany, Poland, and Luxembourg."[27] In contrast to their conditions in Milwaukee, times in Waupun for the Karmann family were rather good, even during the Depression. After his salary from the State had increased from $90.00 a month to $100.00 each month, which, during the Depression was rather good money, her father had been able to have a home built in town for $3,700.00. Shirley did state, however, that with the family that would grow to include a total of six children, money was still in short supply.[28]

Other children living in Waupun at the time were to attend Waupun's second elementary school, the South Ward School. Among these were Josephine Aarts, who grew up poor as well. But, as she recalled, we "probably didn't know any better, I suppose. But we were satisfied." Like many others of her generation, she had been born in the family home—in Waupun on 28 March 1927. The second oldest child of Joseph and Ella Aarts, Josephine would attend school only up through the eighth grade, which would be the highest her education reached. Her father, Joseph, worked at the nearby Libby plant in Waupun making tin cans.[29]

By that same year, 1938, fourteen year old Emil Hopp was already done with his schooling, having completed only the sixth grade at Lincoln School. Born on 24 August 1924, he was one of three children of Manus and Hattie Hopp. His father was a painter by trade, and the family lived in town on West Jefferson Street. Done with his schooling, Emil would work for local farmers in the area until he was able to get on with Shaler's National Rivet and Manufacturing Company.[30] Next to the state prison and state hospital, Shaler's factory was the small city's biggest industry and employer.

Others lived in the surrounding rural areas on farms. Although many of these farm children would attend Waupun High School upon coming of age, through the eighth grade they would attend one-room country schools, which, prior to today's school bus era, they would be required to walk to and from in all forms of weather, even the harsh Wisconsin winters. Edward Theodore Uecker was one of these. One of four siblings, Edward was born in the family farmhouse in the township of Alto, Wisconsin, just three miles west of Waupun, on 29 December 1927 to Fred and Gladys Uecker. His mother, as he was to state, was assisted in Edward's birth by a midwife who "was a full blooded Oneida Indian. . . . And she walked . . . a mile and a half on the prairie to be there. And she stayed there at the house until I came into the world. Yeah. Her name was Leona, Leona Tetzloff. She's gone many years [now]. Her maiden name was Dakota."[31] Edward fondly spoke of Leona, stating that she would always say, "'Yeah, yeah, you were worth that half of pig that we got.' My dad had a lot of pigs, and that's what he paid for the delivery, half a dressed pork."[32]

In 1938 Edward was attending a one-room country school about a mile and a half from his home. As he recalled, it was "Named after a President Harrison [either William Henry Harrison or William's grandson Benjamin Harrison]. There was . . . most times about thirty-four of us in the one-room schoolhouse."[33] In relating what it was like having to walk to and from his school, Edward was to state:

> We'd get in some snow storms coming home sometimes.
> One time we got lost, big bunch of little kids following us.
> We walked right through the fields. St. Valentine's Day. . . .
> And the fences were covered, you know, and it was one of
> these whiteouts, you know what I'm talking about? Well,

of course, we were the older boys, and the little kids were crying and all. . . . We come and walking in this field, and Milt Kastien had a big oak tree in the middle of the field for shade for the [cows]. I says, "I know where we are." He [Milt] had a stone pile on the south side. We made a beeline, headed for the school fence, and we caught to the second to the last post of that schoolyard fence. If we had missed that we would have walked right into an eighty acre field into a woods. But we got there, yup. But that's. . . . It wasn't easy, it wasn't easy. But we made it.[34]

When not in school, Edward worked on the family farm. As he recalled:

I'm gonna tell you right out it was hard. Born and raised out in the prairie. We walked to school; rain, snow, shine, anything, we walked to school and back. And we lived in a house, no furnace, just heat your own, you know, with coal . . . we always were cold.

We had enough to eat. My dad, you know, being a farmer we had chickens, eggs, and all. We always had enough to eat. That's the only time that city relatives would come and see us is time when they're butchering and all like that. But it wasn't easy.[35]

Getting to and from these country schools were not just difficult at times for the students, but also for the teachers. In 1938 Nova Wagner was teaching school at one of the many one-room country schools not far from Waupun. As she recalled, she would get help at times from the local farmers:

In the winter times, sometimes the roads wouldn't be cleared for me to get through. And I can remember getting the chains out of my car and lying on the ground putting the chains on . . . so I could get through the snow. And one time I had to walk the rest of the way, and by the end of the day my car was there. I left the keys in it and one of the good people along the road brought it up to me. They were wonderful people, all of them.[36]

Nova was no novice, however, when it came to country one-room schoolhouses. She attended one herself when she was young. Born on 19 August 1920 on a farm in Green Lake County, Wisconsin, approximately twenty miles northwest of Waupun, she recalled that "We always walked to country [elementary] school.... My mother was so much for education that she wanted her girls to all get an education, and my dad saw to it.... I walked to high school too.... We walked to school on the snow banks in the winter." Like many of Nova's neighbors, her walk to the schoolhouse encompassed between two and three miles each way. However, although her experiences in grade school were quite similar to other farm children living in the country, unlike many of her neighbors, her father's heart was not really into farming. As she related, "I had a good family, but we were very poor. My dad farmed only because that's what my mother wanted him to do. That 'The only place to raise a family was on a farm,'" her mother would say.[37]

Upon her mother's death when Nova was sixteen years old, her father gave up farming and moved the family to the small Wisconsin farming community of Brandon, which is located about ten miles northwest of Waupun, and became an insurance agent. In Brandon, Nova would attend and graduate from Brandon High School. She then attended the Green Lake County Normal School to become a grade-school teacher.[38]

Normal schools, based on and named after the French concept of *École Normale* (normal school), which in turn was based upon German teacher schools, were first created in the United States during the nineteenth century. They were designed to train teachers to teach in the primary, or elementary schools (first through eighth grade), and, as such, were normally only two-year schools, as was Nova's. Some normal schools, most all of which were located in rural areas, would eventually go on to evolve into four-year teacher colleges, some even eventually evolving into full universities.[39]

After graduating from the normal school, Nova continued to live with and keep house for her father in Brandon as well as began teaching grade school at Monroe Country School, a one-room schoolhouse outside of Alto. As a teacher, she would receive $90 a month. According to Nova,

"[T]o me it was a lot of money, because we grew up without money, and then to think you could earn your own."[40]

The first year that she taught the class consisted of eleven children of differing ages and grades, comprising first through eighth grades. Although her one-room country schoolhouse had electricity, it did not have running water. As Nova remembered, "[T]he water had to be carried. Some farmer would bring the water to school. And you had these big earthen water coolers, and that's what you put the water in." Without running water, there were also, of course, no indoor toilets. The toilets were essentially outhouses located out back, one for the boys and one for the girls. That first schoolhouse Nova taught in also did not have a telephone, and it was heated only by a stove, which stood in the back corner.[41]

As with the farmers assisting by bringing in the water and helping her get her car to school, Nova was also assisted by other people in the area as well. "I was real fortunate," she stated, "to have young men living across from the school, and they would go over and build the fire for me on cool days before I got there." The parents of her students would also "take turns making the hot dish for the school for the children at noon when it was so cold, and we would heat it on the top of the stove in the building because there was no way to plug in anything. That was appreciated."[42]

Elva Drews was another farm girl that had attended one-room country schools during her grade school years. Having attended the Lake Emily Country School through her eighth grade, in 1938 fifteen year old Elva was now attending Randolph High School at Randolph, Wisconsin, about fifteen miles west of Waupun. Elva had been born the middle of eleven children—six girls and five boys—on 18 November 1923 to Herman and Elsa Drews on the family farm on Lake Emily Road outside of Fox Lake, a small town about ten miles west of Waupun. About her childhood years Elva recalled that it was "Hectic. But we didn't know we were poor during the Depression because we always had enough to eat." Growing up on the farm she wore hand me down clothes and went barefoot in the summer. As she related:

> You had to work. You'd go out and hoe and pull mustard out of the grain and shuck corn and shuck grain, milk cows. I did it all. Now it's all done by machinery. Well, we worked hard, but we had a lot of fun because there were

a lot of us. We were the hub of the neighborhood. All the kids came to our house to play—play ball. We made our own fun. Played kick the can and run my good sheep run, and we made sticks to play a game we called cricket, which isn't nothing like the English cricket. But we had fun doing it. Rode horses.[43]

Much like Elva, sixteen year old Tillie Dykstra also had to work on her family's eighty acre farm to help her family, which included her parents and her ten surviving siblings. As she recalled concerning her brothers and sisters, "[T]here were thirteen of us. Well, really eleven, one was still born and the other one . . . died when she was a couple of weeks old. . . . We always figured eleven, but there really were thirteen." Nonetheless, with such a large family, Tillie, born to Jense and Nellie Dykstra on 22 April 1922 in the family's country home near Cambria, Wisconsin, approximately twenty miles west of Waupun, was forced to help with the family's support at a young age. As such, between attending the one-room Ross School in the countryside by Cambria and a school in the nearby village of Friesland, Wisconsin, like Josephine Aarts, she was only able to finish her formal schooling through the eighth grade. Tillie recalled that I "went out and helped neighbors and everything work, and so on, and I remember [I] milked cows and all of that, you know. . . . [I] worked out in the field picking up potatoes and things like that."[44]

Living on a farm on the other side of Waupun near the small village of South Byron, Wisconsin, ten miles east of Waupun, was young five year old Marshall McLean, along with his parents Evan and Fern and his brother and sister Douglas and Jill. Having been born in 1933 in Granton, Wisconsin, about 110 miles northwest of Waupun, the family had moved to their present home, where, in 1938, Marshall was beginning his grade school years at the South Byron Grade School.[45] Also living on a farm, but much farther from Waupun than Marshall, was sixteen year old high school student Carl Manthe. His paternal grandmother and aunt and uncle had taken him in on their farm outside of Milwaukee, Wisconsin, approximately sixty miles southeast of Waupun, when he was only two years old. As Carl's future wife was to record, "He was not on the 'Head Start' program" when he was young. Having been born in Milwaukee on 29 November 1922, his parents soon split up, separated, and left Carl with his grandparents. His grandmother, uncle, and aunt would end up raising him as their own on their farm.[46]

Although the Great Depression was rough on many, it did not affect others as deeply. For example, things were a little better than for most for ten year old Cora DeMunck in the small Iowa town of Alton. Born on 10 October 1928 to Cornelius, who emigrated from the Netherlands, and Bessie (Bell) DeMunck in a hospital in the nearby town of Le Mars, Iowa, she was the youngest of three siblings. Both of her brothers were quite a bit older than her, Bob, being ten years older and Glen twelve years older. Cora's father operated a garage where he repaired cars and radios, even selling radios at one time as well as storing cars for the highway department on another occasion. Cora's mother, who had had one year of college, played the organ in church and was the bookkeeper for Cora's father's business. Her mother was also very active in different organizations, usually taking a leading role in many of them. With her father's somewhat booming business, the family had enough money to finance college for both Bob and Glen, while young Cora attended grade school at the Alton Public School.[47]

Not far from the DeMuncks lived her best friend Pauline Hoeven, whose father, Charles Bernard Hoeven, would soon become a United States Congressman, serving as such from 1943 to 1965. Another of her neighbors was Robert Schuller, who would go on to become the Reverend Robert Schuller of the Hour of Power Crystal Cathedral in Garden Grove, California. As Cora stated, "[W]e always thought that was pretty good for coming from a small rural farm area."[48]

Like Cora, the depression didn't have as much effect on seventeen year old Robert Van Alstine and his sister Lucile as it did on most others. Living in Kenosha, Wisconsin, along the Lake Michigan shore and just north of the Wisconsin-Illinois border, in 1938 Robert was attending high school. The son of Frank and Elsie Van Alstine, Robert was born in the Milwaukee suburb of Waukesha on 5 July 1921 in the family home. His father, Frank, was the manager for a dairy co-op, so the family had a yearly salary to depend upon. Although money was still pretty tight because his father did not know from one year to the next if he would be rehired by the co-op, as Robert summarized, "[B]asically I had it pretty good, I think, compared to looking back on what other kids had, and so on. We were not wealthy by any means, but wealthier than a lot of the other people."[49]

Like most of the school systems in the area, due to the Depression, Robert's school was hurting for money and was understaffed. As he explained:

> There was nothing in the school system, there was no money, you know, as for sports—*nothing*, music—*nothing*, you know, things like that. The classes were obviously oversized for what the teachers were capable of handling. But in spite of that, I think probably I got a pretty good education compared to what a lot of these kids are getting today.[50]

Also seventeen in 1938 was Howard Boyle. Having been born on 2 July 1921 in Fond du Lac to a rather well to do family—his father, John Boyle, and Uncle, Henry Boyle, had started a large local telephone company—Howard was attending a Fond du Lac high school, and, for the most part, like Robert, not being wholly affected by the Great Depression.[51]

Young thirteen year old grade school student Theron Alva Mickelson also did not have it as bad as many others since his father was at least employed. Living about four miles west of Neenah, Wisconsin, in the small Wisconsin village of Larson, about forty-five miles northeast of Waupun, Theron was attending Larson School on State Highway 150. Born on 27 July 1925 in a hospital in Oshkosh, Wisconsin, approximately twenty-five miles northeast of Waupun, and raised in Larson, he was one of three children born to Veronica and Thomas Mickelson.[52] Theron was the middle and only boy of his three siblings. As he recalled:

> We walked to school everyday for eight years I was in grade school. And after that I went to Neenah High School. Which . . . back then there was no buses or anything. My dad worked in Menasha for a machine shop. He had to be there at 7 o'clock, so I would get up in time to ride with him, and he would drop me off in downtown Neenah. And I would walk to the Neenah High School, which was maybe another two miles or better. And after high school then I would walk over to the machine shop and doodle-

berry around over there, whatever I could . . . until he got done at 5 0'clock.[53]

Remembering of his youth growing up in rural Wisconsin, Theron was to state:

> I was a pistol. I was always into trouble, I guess. I loved where I grew up and I loved everybody in the town. A town with a population of ninety-three when I left it, and now I don't know how it is because they've put up some big, big, big houses in that little . . . town. While I was growing up I did farm work for the neighbor farmer and later on I did farm work for a farmer [near] Hortonville [Wisconsin].
>
> When I started out, the first place, the first farmer I worked for there [I] was planting cucumbers for him and for me. Well, I'd have to cultivate his cucumbers and my cucumbers. And when it come to picking cucumbers, he had to pick the cucumbers, and they were always four times bigger than what the store would take. Now they take the big ones too. Well, I loved every minute of my work.[54]

Still others were out of school by 1938 and beginning their working life or, for those from the more prosperous families, attending college. Gladys May Jolly was one of the former. Ripon, Wisconsin, located about twenty miles north of Waupun, housed several factories, both small and rather large. One of these was a knitting mill that made gloves—army gloves, driving gloves, "or any kind of a glove," as she recalled. At nineteen years old, Gladys was one of the workers at the factory. Gladys had been born on 26 December 1919 at the Lawson estate outside Green Lake, Wisconsin, about five miles west of Ripon, where her parents, Arthur and Rose Jolly, both emigrants from England, worked. Although the doctor was on the way, due to a severe winter storm with a heavy snow fall, Gladys was delivered in the family home by a midwife. Her younger brother was also born in the family home.[55]

Gladys attended both the Ripon and Green Lake high schools, and recalled that she "loved Green Lake . . . it was sort of a poor rent little village, and nobody had any money and all, so we gelled together." She also recalled that her life growing up was rather, "Scary. . . . The anticipation of, well . . ., did I do right or did I get mad enough to holler, 'How did I get into this mess in the first place?'" As she continued explaining, "I used to say to the Lord, you know, 'Lord . . . I got myself into this, now you get me out.'"[56]

That same year, 1938, also at age nineteen and also a high school graduate, Charles Vellema registered for the draft. He was also working for a living. Born in the Vellema family home in the Wisconsin township of Springvale, located approximately ten miles northwest of Waupun, on 15 May 1919, Charles spent his formative years living and working on the family farm and, like many farm kids of the time, attending country schools. When he was about eighteen years old, around 1937, he had gone to work in Waupun at the Ideal Shoe Factory, where he "Worked for room and board at home and worked in the shoe factory from 8:00 [a.m.] till 4:00 [p.m.]" for $13 a week.[57]

Gertrude, "Ges" (pronounced, Jess), Mintzlaff was also done with high school. But unlike Gladys and Charles, Ges was able to attend college, and, as such, in 1938 was well into her early college years at the University of Madison in Madison, Wisconsin. Having been born and raised in Grafton, Wisconsin, approximately forty-five miles east of Waupun, Ges had graduated from Grafton High School in 1936. Born at 4 o'clock on the 4th of July in 1918 to Charles and Matilda (Freyer) Mintzlaff, she was the oldest of four siblings. Her only brother, however, had died at age nine from the effects of polio. Her father, an electrician by trade, had worked for a time at a "record factory in Grafton, where they made records for Caruso, Bing Crosby, and all the famous guys," Ges was to state. "But, you know," she continued, "he never took us down there when they were here, and now I wish he had."[58]

In recalling her days in college, Ges stated, "Well, what a big change it was from Grafton High School with a class of twenty-four graduating onto being seat number one hundred twenty-first in my first economic class,"—Grafton at the time had only around 800 people. Remembering her childhood, Ges related:

> I think I had a very protected life. And my father's sisters
> lived and brothers lived within a few blocks. We were very
> family-orientated, and my cousins were my playmates,

and, of course, the girl next door. And I played with the boys too while my brother was living, because I got to be a tomboy. I learned how to play baseball and ride a bike and do those things because I didn't have any girl friends that had bikes.[59]

Also attending school at the same university was Leonard Schrank. Like Ges, Leonard was also born in 1918—on 13 March. Unlike Ges, however, he came from a large family of nine children, Leonard being the youngest, and grew up helping work the family farm near Brownsville, Wisconsin, which is located approximately fourteen miles east of Waupun. His older brother by six and a half years, Raymond, had already completed his studies at the university and was interning as a medical doctor in Akron, Ohio, at the Akron City Hospital.[60]

South of Wisconsin, in Illinois, life for Elmer Rigg in 1938 was quite good as well. Having attended McHenry College near St Louis, Missouri, and the University of Illinois, where he received first a bachelors and then a masters degree in chemistry, respectively, he was currently teaching chemistry and physics in a high school in Vandalia, Illinois, as he had been for several years. In addition, just the year before, he had married Gertrude Etheridge. Born on 13 July 1906 to Charlie and Mary (Grismer) Rigg in the family home in Alvin, Illinois, Elmer attended Conway Grade School, a country school, and Alvin High School. Recalling his childhood during the early 1920's prior to the Great Depression, Elmer related that it was "Just fun. Worked on the farm all the time. We didn't have much of a chance to do anything except for what we developed ourselves."[61]

At this same time, on the other side of the Atlantic Ocean, seven-year old AnnaMarie Kretzer was attending grade school in her hometown of Geisenheim, Germany, on the banks of the Rhine River. She had been born in 1931 in the family home to Johann and Philippine Kretzer. As a German of the Arian stock, life, under the Nazi Dictator Adolf Hitler, was going quite well for AnnaMarie and her family in 1938.[62]

With the Great Depression still affecting many in the United States, along with the WPA, President Roosevelt, on 19 March 1933, had established the Civilian Conservation Corps (CCC). It was a federally funded work release program for young men designed, like the WPA, to alleviate the unemployment and poverty. The CCC established camps around the country to house the men as they built roads and parks and conducted other outdoor construction work. Several of these camps were set up throughout the Wisconsin area.

One of seven children of Ferdinand and , Edmond "Ed" Babler was one of the many young men who would find employment at these CCC camps; spending a six-month period at the Star Lake, Wisconsin, camp and another six-month period at a camp at Blue Lake, Wisconsin. Born on 14 December 1913 in the small, rural Wisconsin village of Maplewood, located east of Green Bay, Ed spent several years after graduating from the Door County, Wisconsin, Brussels High School working in his father's blacksmith shop making horse shoes and building wagons and buggies, as well as working on the family's several farms not far from Maplewood. Along with his two stints at the CCC camps, he was also an avid boxer, competing in approximately thirty fights at state fairs and Golden Glove tournaments throughout the state and the Upper Peninsula of Michigan, once even 'riding the rails' to San Diego, California, and back where he won several boxing matches. However, in late 1938, with the Great Depression on and not being able to make a decent living, he decided to join the United States Marine Corps. As he was to write:

> December of 1938 saw the depression at its peak. I wasn't going anywhere as a boxer, having just lost my last two fights, and, in reality, the $30 worth of boxing purses I made every month or so just wasn't enough. So, although I hated to leave home just before Christmas, I enlisted in the United States Marine Corps in Chicago, Illinois, on 20 December 1938. I recall the recruiting sergeant telling me that anything could happen during my tour of duty, including a war. Nonetheless, I told him that I was ready to go.[63]

Just under a year later, on 10 December 1939, the transport ship *SS Henderson* arrived at the Bund in Shanghai, China. Onboard, as a new member of the 4th Marine Regiment, was U.S. Marine Private Ed Babler. Commonly called the "China Marines," the 4th Marine Regiment had been stationed in Shanghai since 1926 to protect American interests. As Ed related, "At the time, Shanghai, China, had the reputation of being the best liberty town in the Marine Corps, and it seemed as if every Marine wanted to spend at least part of his enlistment there, and I was no exception." Ed had to actively lobby for this assignment, but he eventually won it. Once at Shanghai, he was assigned to B Company, 1st Battalion of the 4th Marine Regiment with the duty of "manning one of the dozen or so guard posts throughout the American sector, each of which were manned 24 hours a day."[64]

About this same time back in Wisconsin, one of Nova Wagner's older sisters encouraged her to go along to help build a float for an upcoming Citizenship Day parade, scheduled to be held in Fond du Lac. As Nova recalled, referring to Charles Vellema, "He was there, and he asked if he could take me home, and that was the first time that we ever did any much talking, and it just grew from there."[65] Their relationship had begun.

A few months later, after graduating from Waupun High School with the class of 1940, Alfred Bohnert was working for his uncle, Walter Paskey, at the Waupun Bottling Works bottling Star and Crescent sodas and distributing these same sodas as well as beer around the local area. Having been a regular at Boy Scout meetings, where he eventually made the rolls of the Eagle Scouts, according to his sister Doris, Al also spent time in a CCC camp, sending much of his earnings home to help the family.[66]

Like Al, Robert Van Alstine had also just graduated from high school. After first working as an acetylene welder, a job he did not like, he was hired on at the Snap On Tool Company in Kenosha, Wisconsin, south of Milwaukee, as a machinist.[67] At the same time, Vergeana "Jean" McNeil was fifteen years old and working on her family's farm in Rogersville, Wisconsin, approximately ten miles northeast of Waupun. Born on the farm in the family home on 23 April 1925, she was the youngest of three daughters of Elmer and Edith (Winkey) McNeil. She had attended the local one-room schoolhouse through the eighth grade, but, as she reported, "... that's all the further I got in school. And that was at Rogersville, a little one-room schoolhouse." Life for her, as she was to state, was

> Kinda hard. Working on a farm. And we didn't have a lot of stuff, but living on a farm, you know, you usually had some chickens or pigs or something. We had a big garden. But there was one winter I remember we ate buckwheat pancakes every day for I don't know how long for dinner.[68]

The year 1940 also saw Fred Zurbuchen, the son of Swiss immigrants Anna and Gottfried Zurbuchen, living with his parents and two siblings just north of the small town of Burnett, Wisconsin, about seven miles south of Waupun. Even at the age of fifteen, when not attending Fox Lake High School in Fox Lake, Fred, like his older brother Ewald, was driving a milk truck for his father's dairy. Like many of his contemporaries, Fred had been born in the family home—on 5 March 1925. As he recalled, his life growing up was that of a "Typical country boy" where he "Did all the things that you can imagine—hunting, fishing, and that sort of thing. But," as he sated, "it was a simple life compared to what it is today."[69]

Another truck driver, but a bit older, was Arnold Visser. At age twenty, Arnold had been working as a truck driver at Johnson Truck, a Waupun based trucking firm, since his high school days. His truck route would take him from Milwaukee (approximately sixty miles southeast of Waupun) to Berlin, Wisconsin, (approximately twenty miles to the north of Waupun), and he fondly remembered that as an eighteen-year old he drove the truck that brought all of the Schlitz and Blatz beer to town for Waupun's Centennial.[70]

One of six siblings—the second eldest son of Cornlius and Hattie Visser, and born on 28 August 1920—Arnold had graduated two years earlier from Waupun High School. His father, Cornlius, was a building contractor who would eventually build 107 homes by hand in Waupun. In describing his childhood, Arnold stated that "it was active with the neighborhood we had, and we could play on the street and sometimes use a slingshot . . . we played our football games and baseball games all by hand, and enjoyed each other right in the town." As a child he also worked for Carl Johnson on Johnson's ginseng beds when the growing of ginseng in the Waupun area was big.[71]

As Arnold recalled, the Visser house was one of only four in town at the time to have an oil furnace, an International oil burner. "[N]obody had a oil furnace. They just came out. It was a gun burner. . . . We had to put brick in the back for the wall . . . for the burner. . . " And, unlike many in the area, their house also had indoor plumbing.[72]

Although the Visser house had indoor plumbing, a good oil burning furnace, and electricity, it did not have a refrigerator; which were rare commodities at the time. As such, Arnold vividly remembered Harris' weekly horse drawn ice wagon coming down the street to deliver ice for the home's icebox. Many times the iceman would chip off a piece of ice and hand it to the children, which, at a time before popsicles and other frozen delights, was quite the treat. However, it also was not without its dangers. As Arnold recalled, one time his sister "must have grabbed a piece of ice and had it in her throat, and my mother has a hold of her, and aaagh! Well, finally it melted" before she chocked on it.[73]

In the nearby town of Beaver Dam, Wisconsin, the county seat of Dodge County, which the southern half of Waupun is situated in, by 1940, sixteen year old Morris Page did not particularly like school any more. As such, he began to skip quite a bit of it. Therefore, between attending high school classes as he felt the need, he began working at Fredrick's grocery store in Beaver Dam as well as delivering newspapers. Morris' family had moved to Beaver Dam from Milwaukee a few years before, and to Milwaukee from Campbellsville, Kentucky, in 1929, where Morris and his twin sister Marie were born in the family home on 27 August 1924 to Eugene and Bertha Morris.[74]

About the same time, Carl Manthe graduated from high school in Milwaukee and began working at the Hansen Glove Corporation as a clerk, and Howard Boyle, also having graduated from high school and as a devout Catholic, was attending college at Holy Cross College in Worcester, Massachusetts.[75] Along with Carl, Howard, and Al Bohnert, the class of 1940 also included Elva Drews, who graduated from Randolph High School at the age of sixteen. She quickly moved to Milwaukee to find a job. In those days, however, as she pointed out, "you couldn't get a work permit until you were seventeen. So I ended up taking care of kids and going to business school nights." But once she turned seventeen she was able to get a job in an office at a Milwaukee company by the name of Harnishfager.[76]

That same year, seven years old Charlotte Mehlbrech was attending school, as she recalled, "in Wisconsin Rapids, Wood County, and I went [would go] to eight grade. All classes, all in one schoolhouse, all grades in one room. There was eight grades in one room. There could be up to fifty children in there at a time with one teacher."[77] (Wisconsin Rapids is approximately sixty-five miles northwest of Waupun.)

Having been born in her grandmother's house to Elwin and Ruth Mehlbrech on 21 September 1933 in Marshfield, Wisconsin, approximately 100 miles northwest of Waupun, Charlotte was one of the couple's seven children; two girls and five boys. As she related, her parents "were full-blooded German. My dad also, and his mother's name was Fox, and that's German. And they also were all from Germany. So I am actually a full-blooded German." As she was to recall, "[T]hey [her parents] and the great grandparents and my grandmother, they always talked German when they didn't want us to know what they were talking about." She, however, never really learned the language herself.[78]

Charlotte was to remember her childhood as nice. As she stated:

> We had a very nice mother. My dad worked hard. I know when he was first married he was a sharecrop[per] on a turnip farm, and that was in Pittsville, Wisconsin. Then when they moved to town, Wisconsin Rapids, he worked for NEPCO Nursery at [the] nursery. And then he got in Edwards Paper Company. And we had a small, little farm. We had our own milk and our own meat; we made our own butter, we had chickens, like that. And he was also a musician.[79]

Relating about her life when she was growing up, Charlotte recalled that

> we didn't know that we didn't have things. We would have oatmeal for supper sometimes. Although, on a farm you were lucky enough to have a lot of things 'cause you grew your own, made your own butter and so on, had your own cream.
>
> And I went to school. I started when I was five years old. Because I was so young they had me . . . learn the alphabet and how to write my name, or print my name. And I thought my mother gave me a long name, and I used to cry about that. And the name never did fit in the blanks [on the school forms].[80]

As with Charlotte's family, the Bohnerts, the Vissers, the McNeils, the Ueckers and many of the rest, life in 1940 was still a bit of a struggle for most in Wisconsin, as it was across the whole country, but it was also peaceful. However, although not really affected by it in Wisconsin, or in the rest of United States for that matter, War in Europe, by this time, was already raging. President Roosevelt, with Germany's successful invasion of Denmark, Norway, Holland, Belgium, Luxemburg, France, and the Netherlands, and with German troops on the coast looking across the English Channel, on 19 July 1940, in anticipation for the *possibility* of war, and realizing the country's navy was woefully inadequate in size, signed the Two Ocean Navy Bill calling for the building of 201 ships. Prior to this, due in part to the 1922 Washington Treaty, which limited the size of the navies of the signatory nations, the United States' Navy had dwindled in size. On the contrary, other nations' navies had increased, including those of Japan and Germany. Although since 1933 the President had signed several bills and allocated money to again begin building up the country's naval forces, the United States Navy was still way behind, especially if the nation was to fight a two ocean war, which may indeed come.

Included in this new bill were funds allocated for the construction of forty-three submarines. Since the anticipated need for these submarines would overwhelm the Electric Boat Company at Groton, Connecticut, the only commercial source of submarines at the time, a search for alternative shipyards was conducted. Less than two months later, on 9 September 1940, the Manitowoc Shipbuilding Company in Manitowoc, Wisconsin, was contracted to build an initial ten of these submarines. Once built and tested in Lake Michigan, they were to be sailed down to Chicago, then ferried down the Illinois and Mississippi Rivers.[81]

Just seven days later, Roosevelt, on 16 September 1940, also signed the Selective Training and Service Act, effectively initiating the first peacetime draft in U.S. history. The way now was open for the United States to begin building up its wartime forces.

Having graduated from high school, and too poor to attend college, nineteen year old Jeanette Rochon was at the time working at the Aluminum Goods Manufacturing Company, which made coffee pots, among other aluminum items. The company was a small factory in Two Rivers, Wisconsin, which is just north of both Manitowoc and the Manitowoc Shipbuilding Company along the Lake Michigan coast, and approximately sixty-five miles northeast of Waupun. The Aluminum Goods Manufacturing Company's main office and factory was actually located in Manitowoc, although the plant that Jeanette worked at was in her hometown of Two Rivers. As she recalled, "I was assembling spouts and ribbons to assemble on a coffee pot. Twenty-five cents an hour, nine hours a day, five [hours] on Saturday. And then I get home and [every] two weeks my mom would take my check to buy groceries and pay the rent. I was lucky if I got ten cents to go to a movie." Her father had died, and with the depression still on it was still financially rough for the family.[82]

Having been born on 31 July 1921 in Bemidji, Minnesota, to Joseph and Eva Rochon in "a house made into a little hospital," the family had moved to Two Rivers when the lumbering business had fallen on hard times. As Jeanette recalled, her father "was a lumberjack—and that's all he ever knew how to do. He did that in Bemidji, you know, in Minnesota. But then, of course, the woods gave out. So then we moved to Two Rivers because there's some factories there, and he worked in the factories for awhile."[83]

In Two Rivers, Jeanette attended school from kindergarten to the eighth grade at St. Luke's Catholic School, then moved on to Washington High School. In recalling her childhood growing up in the depression years, she was to state:

> Well, it was a terrible depression. We had nothing, *nothing!*
> If you had two cents to rub together you were doing well.
> It was a terrible time. . . . The only store bought dress I
> ever had was when I graduated high school. I got a little
> cotton store bought dress. Otherwise my mother made
> my stuff and I always looked kind of blump. We couldn't
> afford it, that's all. That was terrible![84]

Like Jeanette, Walter Riel was working full time in 1940, and had been for several years before. But unlike Jeanette, Walter had not completed school. Even when he was only eleven years old he was made to work for the neighboring farmers during the summers. "Fifty cents a week," he recalled. "Dad took the fifty cents to help buy groceries, but I got my meals with it, . . . I was leading the horse on a hay fork, and clean the horse barn, clean the cow barn, feed the chickens, stuff like that for my neighbors. But it give me something to do." In continuing, he reported that, "the big wages at that time were $25 a month." About his education Walter recalled, "I didn't even finish the eighth grade of school. At that time my dad hired me to a farmer and says, 'Get to work.' That's the way it was in that era."[85]

Once he reached the age of seventeen, Walter stopped working on farms and took a job in Waupun at the Ideal Shoe Factory, which was located next to the National Rivet and Manufacturing Company. This job lasted for only about nine months, when he then began working at the rivet factory.[86]

Born on 8 June 1923, he, his parents, and nine siblings had lived in the country outside of the village of Brandon until he was in the sixth grade. At that time the family moved into Brandon proper. As Walter recalled his life back then:

> [I]t was kind of tough. We lived in the country most of the time, no electric, no telephone, no newspapers. It was during the Depression, and things was rough. But we always had enough to eat. My mother was great at preserving things in those days. That's when the big crock pots came about, you know. Preserving and canning. She'd can everything she could get a hold of. So we always had something to eat along the way.[87]

Like the Riel's home, many of the homes in the area, especially those in the rural areas, still did not have electricity or telephones in 1940. The electric and telephone companies were co-ops owned by local residents, and many of these in the 1930's and even the 1940's did not yet connect to farms. For example, as late as 1930 only one in every six Wisconsin farm houses were connected to electrical power lines, while another ten percent had costly generators with connecting storage batteries that proved costly to both obtain and run.[88] Things were not much different ten years later, due to the Depression.

By this time Walter had been dating Catherine Vanderwoody, a girl from nearby Randolph. He also owned a car. One of the farmers he had worked for had, in 1939, purchased and given him a 1931 Ford Model A. The purchase price of the eight year old car was $75.00. As Walter recalled, that "was three month's wages, you know. I said, 'Dad wouldn't let me have one.' 'Well,' [the farmer says] 'do you like it?' I said, 'Yeah.' 'Well,' he says, 'I'll buy it for you.' He gave it to me. That was pretty nice of him."[89]

October of that year saw eighteen year old Tillie Dykstra return to her parents' farm near Cambria from a year stay in California where she had worked on a dairy farm. Her father, Jense, was ill and the family was going to move, so Tillie returned to help them. Once back home she got employment on a fox farm near Markesan, Wisconsin, about twenty miles northwest of Waupun.

Towards the end of 1940, eighteen year old Irving Henry Meyer, having just graduated from high school, began his job for the Milwaukee Railroad as a telegrapher. He had spent the past seven or eight months after graduation "just laying at home. My folks got sick of that," as he recalled. "They said I was gonna go to school; Chillicothe, Missouri. But like on Friday—I was gonna leave Monday [for college]—Friday he called, the chief dispatcher, told me he had a job [for me] to go to. In fact, the first job was [in Waupun]." It was actually during those months of "just laying at home" that Irving had taught himself Morse Code, which was used by railroad telegraphers.[90]

Irving had been born in Richland, Wisconsin, situated approximately thirty-five miles southeast of Waupun—most likely in the family home, although Irving could not state for sure—on 9 May 1922 to Charles and Ann (Menz) Meyer. Irving was somewhat of a rarity for the times, being an only child. He had attended Woodland Grade School in Woodland, Wisconsin, about seventeen miles southeast of Waupun, and both Mayville, Wisconsin, and Berlin, Wisconsin, high schools, eventually graduating from the Berlin High School. Mayville is approximately thirteen miles southeast of Waupun, and Berlin is about twenty-seven miles north of the town. He recalled Woodland being a small town where there were only three children his own age, including himself. In remembering the Depression, Irving related that he

> didn't notice so much. Of course, I was on the more or less the tail end of it, I guess. . . . I know my dad had to have an operation at the time; appendicitis. And one in a million you live, and he lived. But then the little bit of savings I had put away we had to use for the operation. That was before we had insurance. About 1930.[91]

Irving's job as a telegrapher, besides receiving and sending telegraph messages for the trains and Western Union, was to take care of the express and keep the books and orders for the trains, as well as issuing and collect boarding tickets at the ticket window. As he stated, "See, those days didn't have computers. It was all . . . most of it was all handled by telegraph."[92]

The end of 1940 would see young Bessie Douma turn five years old.

Born in the family farm house off State Highway 73 in the rural township of East Friesland, Wisconsin, to Duey and Martha (Aslum) Douma on 20 December 1935, Bessie was the seventh of nine children in the family. East Friesland is about a mile east of Friesland and approximately fifteen miles west of Waupun. Like many farms of the area, the Douma farm at first did not have electricity, nor did it have running water. Although electricity and a telephone would be installed while Bessie lived in the home, running water would not.[93]

While things back in Wisconsin were going on rather normally, in the Far East U.S. Marine Ed Babler's time as a part of the 4th Marine Regiment during 1940 and the early part of 1941 was a mixture of fun, excitement, and growing concern. The city of Shanghai contained many foreign nationals. Several of these maintained their own settlements throughout the city, including the United States, England, France, Russia, Italy, and Japan. Due to the turmoil that existed throughout war-torn China, all of these nations maintained armed troops in the city to protect not only their citizens, but also their countries' interests. Although Ed had became somewhat of a boxing celebrity among the differing nations in Shanghai, who would put on bouts between their best boxers for local titles, and Ed's other experiences in the city were pretty much what he expected when he originally lobbied to go there, the situation in the city by early 1941 was becoming nearly untenable between the Japanese and the Europeans. According to Ed:

> During the later months of 1940 and early 1941 we
> began experiencing trouble with people infiltrating
> into the American sector and starting riots. It was,
> incidentally, the Japanese who were creating many of
> these disturbances, including the starting of strikes and
> setting of fires. As a result, having to give up our once
> all-night liberty, we were placed on twenty-four-hour
> standby. In case of trouble we were ready to board our
> truck at a moment's notice and could be rolling down
> the street in a matter of minutes, dressed and equipped
> for any emergency.... In the early spring months of 1941
> the fires, rioting, robberies, and murders began occurring
> more frequently.[94]

Across the globe in Europe, on 22 June 1941, German Dictator Adolf Hitler, with his ongoing seemingly unstoppable attempt to conquer all of Europe, boldly and quite unannounced launched *Operation Barbarossa*, the German invasion of Russia. In Germany, as a ten year old girl, AnnaMarie Kretzer vividly remembers hearing her grandmother saying, "Oh no, that's the end, he's crazy," when they heard of the invasion. As she recalled, her parent's quickly replied, "'Shhhhh,' because you couldn't say much." In elaborating, AnnaMarie was to state, "People were scared, they couldn't talk, you know. Children would say to their peers, 'Yeah, my mom said this, my dad said that,' and then they would have taken our parents . . . my parents were mostly in fear, and I kind of took it as it was."[95]

Even with this new invasion and escalation of the war in Europe, the United States public and government were to remain adamantly neutral and isolationistic, simply watching as Hitler further enlarged his hold on Europe . . . hoping against hope to stay out of another European conflict.

Less than a month later, on 18 July, David Allen Lyon was born to Blanche Josephine (Vandeberg) and Morris George Lyon at what was the Schwartz Clinic in Waupun. Of the clinic David recalled that

> it was a twenty some bed clinic, if I recall correctly, and it was across from what is now and was then the public library [the old Carnegie library, which is now the Waupun Historical Society]. That's before they had a hospital in town. It was an interesting place because they didn't have separate rooms. They just [had] like two rooms with beds in 'em. That's where I was born.

David was to have two younger brothers; one, Dennis, would die at birth.[96]

While the Lyon family was still celebrating the birth of their first child, things were quietly heating up in Washington, D.C., and elsewhere. Throughout 1940 and 1941, the Japanese had continued their expansion into China and other Western Pacific Rim countries. In response, on 26 July 1941, after hearing that thirty thousand Japanese troops had landed at Saigon and Haiphong in Indochina, President Roosevelt signed a decree freezing all Japanese assets in the United States, denying the

Panama Canal to Japanese shipping, and placing a crippling embargo on the export of strategic raw materials to Japan. That same day, retired United States Army General Douglas MacArthur, who was currently employed as a Field Marshal of the Philippine Army, was recalled to active duty and made commander of the United States Army Forces Far East (USAFFE). With the prospect of war with Japan in the winds, operations were soon to be put into motion to reinforce and consolidate the American bases in the Pacific, including the Philippines, where MacArthur was headquartered.[97]

Three days later, on 29 July, twenty-one year old Charles Vellema, having registered for the draft back in 1938, was one of those drafted into the U.S. Army under the Selective Training and Service Act. He and three others from Waupun, Glen Towne, Ben Loomans, and Ken Kohlman, went by bus to Milwaukee for their physical examinations. But not all of them were to be accepted. As Charles recalled, "We were examined and . . . Kenny Kohlman, who was probably the one that wanted to go in the service the most, he didn't pass the physical, so he went back home to Waupun. And the rest of us went [to the Army]."[98]

However, after being inducted into the Army, the three of them were to go their separate ways. As Charles explained:

> [W]e went to Camp Grant, Illinois. They were just going to determine what branch of service you were going to go in. But I was in the Infantry, so I went to the infantry training. I think, maybe, Ben Loomans, he became a policeman when he came home, maybe he was in the police in the service too. And Glen Towne must have been a truck driver, because he was a truck driver back in civilian life. He was driving a truck.[99]

During that same month, Ed Babler saw his name on a list of Marines to be transferred from Shanghai to the Philippine Islands. Soon afterward, he, with several others of the China Marines, left Shanghai for the island of Luzon in the Philippines where he would be assigned to the 700-man 1st Separate Marine Battalion under the leadership of Lieutenant Colonel John P. Adams. Once there, Ed and his fellow Marines set up and lived in tents located in an open area adjacent to huge radio towers not far from the Cavite Navy Yard, which was along the Manila Bay southwest of Manila, the country's capital city. The 1st Separate Marine Battalion was assigned to guard both the Navy Yard and a nearby large Navy fuel depot.[100]

Back in Wisconsin, Edward Uecker, now fourteen, spent the summer working for his uncles on their farm that abutted up to Edward's family's farm, and working at the American Storage Canning Company in Fairwater, Wisconsin, just up the road from his family home near Alto. "Well, first I worked, you know, in the peas," he recalled.

> When I was fourteen years old I drove a truck. . . . And there were eighty pound boxes of peas that came out of the viner . . . I drove a truck hauling peas from the viner. The viner, you know, they didn't have self propelled [pea combines back then]. They put them in boxes, they weighed eighty pounds apiece. We'd stack 'em five high on the truck. You get muscles in a hurry, *boy*. But . . . that's what I did. Then I worked for my . . . uncles on the farm, too.

To get to work at the canning company Edward would take the bus. As he stated, "I got $3 a week, and I paid my bus fare out of that and the rest was mine. Of course, bus fare was only 80 cents a week."[101]

About his uncles and life on the farm, Edward stated that his uncles "generally didn't go out very much, you know, they stayed right on the farm. Go to church probably. But it wasn't an easy life. I think if it was now, the generations now, oh, there'd be a lot of complaining, but. I don't know, I guess it's because we weren't the only ones there [working like that], you know."[102]

Charles Vellema, part of President Roosevelt's effort to quietly prepare the country for war, spent the rest of that summer and fall in military training, first at Camp Wheeler in Macon, Georgia, where he went through basic training, then at Fort Bragg, North Carolina, where he was trained in "half-tracks, motorize infantry." About Fort Bragg itself he was to relate:

> Fort Bragg was [an] artillery training camp for World War I. It was a great enormous acres of wasteland. In this area where we were the sign said, "Motorized Animal Area." So we still had horses or mules that pulled the caissons.

So the sign said, "Motorized Animal Area." So there were still animals there in Fort Bragg when we were there.[103]

One of his first duties at Fort Bragg was to "guard the airport, and all we had was a broomstick," he stated, "we didn't have rifles yet then. That was just for training . . . you had your password and you had to use the password back and forth. That was quite a thing." He was in a rifle platoon, and, although he was initially issued a 1903 "Bolt action Springfield, like they used in World War I," he was eventually trained in the use of the M-1 Garand rifle and .45 automatic pistol. Charles recalled that "We had lots and lots of target practice . . . had a box of ammunition, you could just shoot all day long at targets. We really learned how to use a rifle."[104]

It was at Fort Bragg that Charles' unit was put into companies, regiments, and divisions. Fort Bragg was the home of the 9th Infantry Division, so he was made a part of L Company, 47th Infantry Regiment, 9th Infantry Division. As he stated, "We had lots of training because first we thought we're gonna be in half-tracks." But it wasn't just military tactics training that he experienced at For Bragg. As he recalled:

> [T]he main thing what I never realized from coming from up north, segregation was still on there, so we were in one area and the colored boys had a whole other area with the camp. When we went to town . . ., I never knew that the back of the bus was for the colored people and the front was for white people. I think one time I probably walked [indicating with his hands to the back of the bus], because there [meaning in Wisconsin] usually you had to go to the back of the bus. So when you got down there, then you had to stay in front of the bus. That was something new to me.[105]

With the year nearing an end, although times were still somewhat tough for many in the United States with the Depression still ongoing, Americans were living in peace. As a nation with strong isolationist feelings, it was a country that wanted and fully intended to remain at peace . . . and clear from any European strife. After all, it was just a few decades before that to this very end this same isolationist country had refused to ratify the Versailles Treaty, which ended World War I, or join the League of Nations that its own President Woodrow Wilson had so laboriously lobbied so hard to create. It was feared that ratifying this treaty or joining the League of Nations would once again lead to the country becoming embroiled in another European war.

However, the war in Europe was indeed raging, and had been for a good two years, and Hitler had recently expanded it by invading Russia. But it was still *not* an American war, and, as such, had little real affect on Americans. It was also known by the general public that Japan had been becoming more and more aggressive in Asia and the Pacific, but this too was of little concern for Americans. After all, the Pacific was a long way away, the United States had a very powerful navy situated between Japan and the west coast, most Americans considered Japanese as a lesser people, a people that could be easily and quickly swatted away if needed to be, and President Roosevelt had just instituted strong economic and political sanctions and pressures against them. Certainly, Japan would heed these and come to their senses . . . so the general American thought went.

As a result, the fall of 1941 saw the general American public going about their business as usual: farmers, like Edward Uecker and his uncles, toiling on their farms, factory workers, like those at the National Rivet and Manufacturing Company, producing goods, rural school teachers, such as Nova Wagner, teaching in their one-room schools, college kids, like Ges Mintzlaff, attending to their studies, and children helping their parents when needed and playing when not. In fact, there were signs that the Great Depression was even on the wane. One could say it was almost good times; at least, good times seemed to be in the offing.

But, as President Roosevelt, his cabinet, and the U.S. military leaders knew very well, the clouds of war were indeed brewing, especially in the Pacific. Marine Ed Babler also could easily see that things were heating up, and heating up around him and his fellow Marines stationed on the Island of Luzon in the Philippines, only a few hours of flight time away from the Japanese air bases on the Island of Formosa (modern day Taiwan). In addition, word had recently been received that the rest of the China Marines were now enroute from Shanghai to the Philippines as part of an American military buildup on the islands.

The Day of Infamy

S unday, 7 December 1941, for most Americans began as any average Sunday. People awoke, had breakfast, and went about their normal Sunday routines. Many, as usual, attended their regular religious services. Others relaxed while some went to their place of employment or milked cows and fed their farm animals. But at approximately 8 o'clock in the morning in Hawaii—1 p.m. Central Time (Waupun, Wisconsin, time) and 2 p.m. Eastern Standard Time (Washington, D.C., time)—Japanese carrier launched naval fighters, dive bombers, and torpedo planes were attacking United States military installations and naval ships at Pearl Harbor. This attack, as well as attacks on other Allied outposts in the Western Pacific, took the United States by storm . . . and shock.

The news of these attacks spread quickly, especially for a time before television, cell phones, and the internet, when radio, telegram, newspapers, and, when installed, telephones were the quickest means of communication. Because of this, however, although many people were to learn of the attacks the afternoon of the same day they occurred, many did not hear about them until the next day, 8 December.

"I was in the barracks," recalled Army Private Charles Vellema:

> It was on Sunday about four o'clock in the afternoon, North Carolina time. We had an old radio. . . . The plastic cover was all off [of it], we just had the tubes. And most everybody was gone on Sunday. I remember being in there, and then news came over that Pearl Harbor had been attacked . . . it was hard to believe that something like that could happen.[106]

In Wisconsin, upon hearing the news, Nova Wagner was "Scared! I just knew it would mean more young men would be called on, and I had brother-in-laws, my sisters were married." She had also been dating Charles Vellema, and she knew full well he was already in the Army.[107]

Marine Ed Babler, stationed outside of Manila in the Philippines, was right in the middle of the action. As he recalled, "On 8 December the air raid sirens began blowing. After several minutes we heard the Japs had bombed Pearl Harbor. Expecting to be hit next the Cavite Navy Yard and all the airfields in the area were immediately put on alert."[108] It should be noted that although Manila is only six hours 'ahead' of Hawaii, due to the international dateline, 8 a.m. 7 December Hawaii time, the time of the Pearl Harbor attack, relates to 2 a.m. 8 December Manila time. The initial air raid sirens that Ed is referring to did not sound until sometime after daylight at Cavite, several hours after the attack on Pearl Harbor.

Although the Japanese war plan had originally included an air attack on the Philippines to coincide with the attack on Pearl Harbor, due to a storm front over the Island of Formosa, from where the Japanese aircraft were to be launched, the initial air raids against the Philippine Islands did not take place until approximately noon of that day, nearly ten hours after the commencement of the attack on Pearl Harbor.

Due to the impending war with Japan, a build up of aircraft had begun in the Philippines, leaving General Douglas MacArthur, the commander of United States Army Forces Far East (USAFFE), with the largest concentration of B-17 bombers in the United States arsenal. At approximately 12 noon on 8 December the Japanese high altitude bombers, dive bombers, and fighters from Formosa appeared over several of the United States airbases throughout the Island of Luzon. Controversy surrounds the circumstances, but, like at Pearl Harbor, when the Japanese aircraft arrived over the Philippines many of MacArthur's aircraft were lined up on the airstrips in neat rows being fueled and loaded with ammunition and bombs, their crews walking out of the mess halls heading for the planes. Within a matter of minutes nearly all of these aircraft were destroyed either on the ground or trying to take off, along with many of their crewmembers, effectively, in one fell swoop, leaving the Japanese in nearly uncontested control of the air over the Philippine Islands.[109]

Although these initial air attacks did not directly affect Ed and his fellow Marines at the Cavite Navy Yard, their time was coming. In addition, with little or no effective Allied aircraft left in the Philippines to oppose the Japanese, not much could be done to stop any future Japanese air assaults.

Jeanette Rochon was still working at Aluminum Goods Manufacturing Company in Two Rivers, Wisconsin, when she heard the news of the attack. As she recalled, "It was on a Sunday, I know that.... Oh, everyone was just frantic, really upset ... very! It was so unexpected. Terrible!"[110]

On Sunday, 7 December, Walter Riel was on a date with his girlfriend Catherine. He didn't hear about the attack until he came home later that night and his dad told him, and even then it really didn't mean too much to him. As he explained, "All we had was a battery radio, no electric where we was at." The family also didn't receive newspapers. "So," as he continued, "I didn't know anything was going on in the world, really. Just that we knew that there was a war someplace [Europe], but just not by us, you know. So it really didn't shock me because I didn't know what it was all about." As a matter of fact, Fond du Lac, Wisconsin, about twenty miles from his home, "was the furthest I ever got before I went into the service. I never got any further than that, so it was a small world we was living in."[111]

Doris Bohnert, having quit high school after her junior year to help support her family, was working at the National Rivet and Manufacturing Company at the time in the rivet inspection department. As she remembered, "We were at work when they came in and told us [about the attack]. We thought it was terrible. We were sort of scared, you know." [112] Al, her brother, who was still working for their uncle at the Waupun Bottling Works, was to state that upon hearing of the attack "everybody figured the war was coming on. And it did."[113] Lois, their sister, and her good friend Dorothy Bal were ushered the next day into the Waupun high school gym with the rest of their fellow classmates and students. As Dorothy related, "[F]irst thing in the morning we all got in the gym and they had an assembly telling us that war have been declared."[114] As she recalled of the day before, 7 December, "It was about four o'clock in the afternoon, on a Sunday afternoon when we heard [the news]. We were at my aunt and uncle's at Beaver Dam. And it came over on the radio that Pearl Harbor had been [attacked].... We were just shocked. We couldn't believe it."[115]

Lois stated that the attack was a "Surprise. . ., you couldn't really believe anybody would do that. Then we were really against the Japanese. I remember that if any people had knick-knacks in Japanese they got rid of them."[116] Dorothy furthered that "I think we were in shock, maybe, for a day or so, because we couldn't believe that anybody would do something like that. . . . Maybe some people kinda expected that it was coming, but I don't think the majority of 'em had any idea. It just [was] like out of the blue."[117]

Joan Laandal, sixteen years old at the time, remembered standing behind the bar in her family's *Laandal's Lunch* restaurant-tavern in Waupun listening to the radio, her father sitting on a stool next to a window where he could look outside while at the same time keep an eye on the bar. She remembered that it was in the afternoon that they heard the news broadcast. As she related, "And all of a sudden it came over. Well, I had brothers that were of age to be in service. This was 1941, but unbeknownced to my mother, my brother Bob had already enlisted . . . in the Air Force. . . . I thought my mother was gonna have a heart attack, because you send your kid to war you send them to death."[118]

University of Wisconsin students Ges Mintzlaff and Leonard Schrank, by now engaged to be married, were in the Madison campus' school medical library—Ges had changed her major from home economics to X-ray technician, and Leonard was following his brother Raymond into medicine, studying to become a medical doctor—when, as Ges recalled, "someone walked into the library and said, 'Do you know that we are at war with Japan? They bombed Pearl Harbor.' It was right when it happened, it was right after lunch, maybe 1:00, 1:30 [p.m.]." "Well," as she continued, "then everybody closed their books and they ran to radios to listen."[119]

To her and Leonard's reactions, she was to recall, ". . . we both sort of had tears in the eyes . . . [and] my husband said to me, 'There goes the end of my career. I'll have to work more.' He wasn't my husband then, he was my boy friend." Leonard, however, was not drafted just then. As Ges continued, ". . . the Army insisted they wanted him to graduate as an M.D., and they could use him much better then than a pre-med," so they gave him a deferment to the draft to finish his medical training. About her personal thoughts at hearing of the attack, Ges was to state:

> [W]e were just shocked. We didn't think any nation would ever attempt to attack America. And then I kept thinking of the boy next door or my cousin in Milwaukee who was in the Navy. And he was in the boat that was in the . . . laying in the bottom of Pearl Harbor. He was only eighteen. And I thought about him.[120]

34

Vergeana McNeil, then only sixteen years old, recalled that the news was "Scary, [we] didn't know what was going to happen." She was "at a Lutheran bake meeting" when she heard about the attack, "and it came over the radio, and the dad of the girl where we were having the meeting came over and told us."[121]

When nineteen year old Tillie Dykstra heard the news she was working in a hotel in Portage, Wisconsin, thirty-five miles west of Waupun, where she had recently taken a position after leaving her job at the fox farm. "I know it was terrible," she recalled. "I just thought there's gonna be a war, you know. I had lots of brothers" who were of military age.[122] She also recalled that even back a couple of years before when she had been working in California the tensions between the Japanese and the Americans were high. As such, she related that

> when I worked in California there were a lot of Japanese around, and I was kind of afraid, you know. And I know on Sunday night I went with my brother and his wife to church, and I had to take the little one out because he was crying, and I was walking up and down the street and here were Japanese right behind me, and I was afraid.[123]

Irving Meyer was at the home of family friends when those gathered heard the news over the radio. He thought it was about noon that the news was broadcast, but he couldn't remember for sure.[124] Shirley Karmann, then eleven years old, remembers "sitting on the floor listening to our radio shows, there was an interruption, and President Roosevelt started telling us that the Japanese had bombed Pearl Harbor . . . the only thing I can remember is the worry that my Dad would have to go to War." However, John Karmann, Shirley's father, was too old to be eligible for the draft. Besides, he was also a prison guard and the Maximum Security Prison in Waupun, so Shirley's fears were never realized.[125]

The day of infamy found Gladys Jolly, now twenty-one years old, and several of her friends enjoying the day on a fishing outing. As she related, "[W]e went into a restaurant . . . and it came over the radio . . . 'War has been declared and Pearl Harbor has [been attacked].'" The young men she was with, as Gladys recalled, were all members of the 32nd Division of the Wisconsin National Guard, and "they all knew they better get back to Ripon and train. So we went with them . . . none of us were talking. We were quiet. Maybe we were crying a little bit, because we felt like we're gonna lose these boys, and that was true."[126]

Gladys also stated that "We knew that Hitler's on the move and the Japanese Emperor, whatever he was, they were on the move, but we really didn't seem to realize it. We just lived our lives being Americans, enjoying ourselves, you know. They're over there and they're having their fight, see. But I think when Pearl Harbor hit it hit us home."[127]

Elva Drews, still working in Milwaukee, remembers being at a Christmas concert at the Triple A Shrine on 33rd and Wisconsin Avenue. As she related:

> It was in the afternoon, and they interrupted the program, and the guy came on stage and said, "President Roosevelt just announced the Japs bombed Pearl Harbor." Everybody just cried! They all went to pieces. And the orchestra played . . . something like *God Bless America*. I don't remember what the tune was. But then we went home. We didn't . . ., there was no more concert, they just stopped everything. That's where I was.

She was also to state that the news of the war was "Horrible, because almost all the guys in my high school class were in the military. They took 'em all except for those on the farm."[128]

Truck driver Arnold Visser was lying in front of the family's Majestic radio as he always did on Sunday afternoons listening to the Reverend Prageler, a Christian Reformed minister from Sheboygan, Wisconsin, when the reverend's program was interrupted by the news that Pearl Harbor was attacked. As Arnold stated, "I went to the school, but I never knew where . . . Pearl Harbor was."[129] Fred Zurbuchen remembered that he was at work in his father's dairy, and that around noon his father came into the factory and reported that the Japanese had attacked. Like many others, Fred remembered that it was "a big surprise . . . the sneak attack alone was obviously a horrendous thing."[130]

Still in high school and catching rides with his dad to and from both school and his apprenticeship job at the same machine shop his father worked at in Neenah, Wisconsin, sixteen year old Theron Mickelson heard about the attack on the radio. As he recalled, "I guess my dad and I talked about it on the way home from work . . . most [people] thought that's too far away, they're not gonna get over here. And we're in the middle of the United States so, you know, they weren't going to worry too much about it."[131]

It was on Monday morning, 8 December, at about 7:00 a.m. that Edward Uecker, by now a fourteen year old freshman attending Brandon High School, heard the news just before he was about to leave for school for the day. As he recalled, "I had a radio in my room. The guy came on there and said that Pearl Harbor had been attacked, life lost, *USS West Virginia* went down. It was the first one." Next door to Edward's family's farm was his grandmother's farm. On it lived not only his grandmother but also his two uncles. One of his uncles, as the result of having contracted polio, wore leg braces. Edward's other uncle, however, was Elmer Uecker. As Edward related, Elmer was

> an ex-Marine, I mean a *Marine* . . . barrel-chested, big here [gesturing large arms], yeah. Anyway, he was . . . I don't know how many years he served, but he had served aboard the *USS West Virginia*, you know. The Marines fired the guns on those battleships. . . . Just before I left [for school] I went out to the barn and told my uncle. He said, "That's a lot of bull shit. That ship is *un-sinkable!*" He had a picture hanging on [his] wall, you know, showing all the men. . . . "No," I said, "that's what he [the man on the radio] said." "I can't hardly believe that," he [Elmer] said.
>
> So I went to school and they had it on the radio then. They put a radio in the—you know, it was all radio [then]—they put a radio in the assembly hall. And the president had spoke, you know, and they told about how the sneak attack had taken . . . all the ships that were on the line and just gave them their [order]. And anyhow, I got home that night and had supper, and I did the [chores]. "I could hardly believe that shit. That ship went down, that ship," [Uncle Elmer said]. So he [Elmer] did something that you rarely would do—I'll donate that, if you were dying or something [meaning that people rarely called long distance]—he used the telephone. And he called a fellow he had been with in [the Marines that was now living in] Ohio—and he came to see Uncle Elmer

a couple years later. But, he said, "Yeah, it's true, Elmer."
It was like somebody put a pin in him [Elmer]. "I can't
believe it," he says. "I can't believe it," he said. That's what
happened. That's when I heard about Pearl Harbor.[132]

The war was soon to become the talk around Edward's school. As he
explained:

I remember we talked about it in school, and we said,
"Yeah," the fellas said, "you know where we are gonna be
out there in a couple of years," you know . . . they were
really concerned that we would be at war. We didn't know
how to react to it. It really bothered us. . . . Some of 'em
had brothers that were [of draft age], we knew they would
start drafting immediately. And we were afraid of that, of
being at war. We just resigned ourselves that we would be
at war. And, you know, it really cut our youth. . . . We had
to work as adults from then on because labor was tight.
Oh, . . . some of those big farms that took a lot of help to
[run]. Weren't mechanized now as we were [meaning
today farms are much more mechanized than they were
back then]. But that was our thoughts about it. . . .
    I remember a bunch of us went into the boiler room,
and we sat in the boiler room and we talked about it.
I remember one was Johnny Luger. He was [would
become] a Marine. He got hit in the lung by a sniper in
the Marine Corps. He . . . lives out in Montana now. His
folks were immigrants of Austria. He was the first to [go].
They lived across the marsh. And I remember him saying,
"You know where I'll be a year from now," he said." He
enlisted in the Marine Corps, he didn't get drafted.[133]

As Edward related, the general feeling of many of the local people was
one of outrage at the attack. He remembered such sentiments as:

"That's a sneak attack!" and, "Boy, I'll tell yah, you could
never trust those Japs anyhow!" Boy, I'll tell yah, they
were down on 'em [the Japanese], you know. . . . Of

course, they were down on the Navy too, you know, bringing in all those ships in there. And when that word got out that they put in all those [ships] on a row.... And, of course, FDR [Franklin Delano Roosevelt] got raked over the coals quite a lot. But he protected the admirals, you know. . . .

A lot of sober faces in church. Of course, prayers would be said, you know. A lot of sober [faces]. Some of them women would cry. They knew what was coming, you know. It was some hell of a time in your life, you know that? *God*! Wasted![134]

Although Marshall McLean was too young at the time to remember hearing about the beginning of the war, Charlotte Mehlbrech, also quite young, remembered that she

was over to the neighbor girl's. And I couldn't have been more than, oh, I don't know if I was even ten. She had a playhouse, and she was the only child and she had things that I didn't have, and we played over there. And she had a sticker, and it said, "Remember Pearl Harbor, 1941." And . . . we had heard on the radio previously [about the war]—we listened to Gable Hater at 6 o'clock every night while we were eating supper—but I first really become aware of it when I came home and told my parents about the sticker, and they said, "Well, remember? Don't you remember? They were bombed over there." And that's when I first remember.

Charlotte also recalled her father saying, "'If it can happen there, it can happen here.' And so all I can remember is being scared, you know. And when you hear . . . see an airplane, we would get scared."[135]

Like Marshall and Charlotte, Bessie Douma was also quite young, just shy of her sixth birthday. But she does remember her father, Duey, who also, like many in the area, spoke Dutch besides English, telling the family that they all

had to be in the kitchen at 8 o'clock and we had to all be

very quite because the president was going to give a very important speech. And so we were sitting there and he [the president] gave his speech, and he [Bessie's father] said in Dutch—I suspect to protect the younger ones because we didn't all understand that [language] back then—that he said . . . "We are at war."[136]

Robert Van Alstine, now twenty years old, was in his second year as a machinist at the Snap On Tool Company in Kenosha, Wisconsin, when he heard the news. As he recalled:

I was upstairs in my bedroom, and I really didn't think too much about it. I knew it was bad, of course, but I didn't relate it to me. It should have I suppose, but I was too young to put it together . . . I think I had expected that I was gonna end up [in it] because of what was going on in Europe, Hitler, and whatever. I suppose that I put two and two together and said, "Well, this is just gonna speed it up a little bit."

As Robert also recalled, the Snap On Tool Company had already been in the business of supplying war materials, making "plastic stop-nuts on a contract base for [the] military." As he stated concerning the general feelings of the news of the Pearl Harbor attack by those around him, "I don't think it was even discussed. Yeah, in that respect I don't think I was any different than most of the other people. I don't recall any of my peer people discussing it. I don't recall it at work, but they were already doing government work."[137]

According to Josephine Aarts, then a fourteen year old Waupun school girl, "I think we were all scared, I think, or excited, you know. . . . Because we knew it was gonna be war, you know. I think the whole town was all shook up."[138]

Harriet Louise Whiting was only four years old at the time, and like Marshall McLean does not really remember hearing about the beginning of the war that she would spend her formative years during. She does, however, vividly remember her grandfather nearly constantly listening to the radio for news about the war. One of six children of Ralph Ethan and Janet Isabel (Hyslop) Whiting, Harriet was born on 1 June 1937 in the family's farmhouse a few miles outside of Waupun on County Highway X.[139] Also four years old and again too young to remember the attack was James "Jim" Charles Laird. Born on 1 March 1937, Jim was the only boy and youngest of his three older siblings to Rush Ford and Joanna "Hanna" (Loeffelholz) Laird in the family home in Dubuque, Iowa.[140]

Cora DeMunck was still attending Alton Public School in Alton, Iowa, with her best friend Pauline Hoeven. And, although, like Marshall McLean and others, she was quite young when the Japanese bombed Pearl Harbor, being only twelve at the time, Cora recalled that those around her "all noticed we were all going to have to sacrifice some things and many of the younger fellows would have to go to war. And so I guess that was what we were prepared to do."[141]

While the United States population was still reeling from the suddenness, boldness, and audacity of the attack, not to mention the shocking fact the they were now forced into a war, two days after the initial attack on Pearl Harbor, on 10 December Philippines time, Japanese bombers attacked Ed Babler and his fellow Marines for the first time. As Ed recalled:

> The 10th of December began as a clear and sunny day without even a single cloud in the sky. Being my day off I was spending time in the barracks located next to the [Cavite] Navy Yard when the air raid sirens suddenly began sounding. I quickly dashed outside and gazed up into the sky where I immediately saw an approaching flight of bombers heading directly towards the Navy Yard. . . . When they were about two miles away I lost no time in finding a low spot in the ground to slide into. . . . Within moments, I heard a rattling sound and realized the bombers had released their bombs. Several seconds later I could hear the sound of crashing buildings around me. . . . After the sound of the exploding bombs had stopped, I slowly raised my head and looked around. The Navy Yard was scattered with fire, smoke, and debris.[142]

That same day saw the first of several landings on Luzon, the main Philippine Island and the island Ed was on, by Japanese soldiers under the overall leadership of Japanese General Masaharu Homma. Over the next couple of weeks Homma would land more troops at several locations, all of which would head for the Philippine capital, Manila. General MacArthur, instead of initiating the Orange Plan, attempted to use the 60,000 mostly ill-trained, ill-equipped Philippine Army (lead by United States Army and Army Reserve officers and non-commissioned officers) to repel the Japanese from the beaches, or, once landed, beat them back into the sea, all the while holding back his American forces.

These later 19,000 well-trained, well-equipped American troops by this time also included the 4th Marine Regiment, the China Marines, which had been transferred from Shanghai and arrived at the Olongapo Navy Yard, located on the northwestern end of the Bataan Peninsula, on 30 November and 1 December onboard the *SS President Madison* and the *SS President Harrison*, respectively. Once in the Philippines, the 4th Marine Regiment was initially mainly given the mission of protecting the Olongapo Naval Station and the Mariveles Naval Section Base, the latter located on the southern most tip of Bataan.[143]

The Orange Plan, initially developed in 1926, assumed that the Japanese would attack the Philippines as a principle target. It called for the abandonment of the Philippine capital and the withdrawal of American and Filipino forces to the Bataan Peninsula.[144] Different defense plans were named after different colors. Orange was the code color for Japan with other potential enemies having other designated colors. The Orange Plan was developed under the assumption of a surprise attack by the Japanese on Luzon, the principle island of the Philippine chain. Being heavily jungled and mountainous, Bataan would provide land-side protection to the nearby fortified island of Corregidor, as well as its three other smaller sister fortress islands, each mounting large coastal guns that dominated the sea approaches to Manila Harbor.[145] With its thick jungle and rocky volcanic terrain, and with the proper amount of supplies and pre-invasion preparations, the Bataan Peninsula indeed would make for an ideal defensive position.

However, MacArthur did not want to abandon Manila. Instead, he wanted to fight the Japanese on the beaches. As a man of honor, MacArthur may have certainly found himself in what could be called an impossible position. After all, President Manuel Luis Quezon Antonio y Molino (commonly called Quezon), the Philippine President, had made MacArthur a field marshal in the Philippine Army. MacArthur had also spent much of his military career in the Philippines. His father, General

Arthur MacArthur, had even once been the U.S. Military Governor of the Philippines, and Douglas served under him as a junior army officer. As such, Douglas MacArthur felt a great loyalty to the Filipinos. In his position as both Philippine Army Field Marshal and Commander USAFFE, MacArthur may have considered himself essentially serving two presidents, President Quezon and President Roosevelt, both of these presidents having conflicting demands. Although retreating into the jungles and mountains of the Bataan Peninsula was advantageous to the United States, it would at the same time mean abandoning the Filipino people. This may certainly have been unthinkable to MacArthur, regardless of how militarily expedient the move would be.[146]

Regardless of the reason, MacArthur put the Orange Plan on hold and sent the fledgling and under trained Philippine Army to deal with the invading Japanese—with little or no air support. As such, he held back the 11,000- to 12,000-man American-trained Philippine Scouts Division (the only actual combat-ready Filipino unit), the 4th Marines, the 1st Separate Marine Battalion, the U.S. Army's 31st Infantry Regiment, and the 192nd and 194th Tank Battalions, the latter two of which consisted of an amalgamation of several United States National Guard units from throughout the United States, which were on Luzon for training.[147]

On 11 December, the day after Ed's position was bombed on Luzon and General Homma's Japanese troops began their invasion of the Philippines, although not obligated to do so under the Tripartite Pact between Germany, Japan, and Italy—which stated that *only* if one of these countries were attacked, not if one of these countries was the aggressor as Japan had been, the others would join the fight—Adolf Hitler declared war against the United States. Within a few short days, with little apparent warning, at least as far as the American public saw, the United States went from being at peace to being fully embroiled in a two-theater war.

Although now thrown into a two-ocean war, it was still only in the Pacific that U.S. forces were actually in the fight on 11 December. And while the Americans in Hawaii were still dealing with the aftermath of the attack there, in the Philippines, for the first few days after the initial 10 December air attack on the Cavite Navy Yard, Ed Babler and his fellow Marines had experienced only false air raid alerts. As he was to write:

> Two days went by without any further excitement
> except an occasional sounding of the air raid sirens;

43

two excitement-free days that we all gladly accepted. I imagine that there were planes in the air flying over the islands during these days, but all we saw or heard of them was the occasional and sporadic air raid siren.[148]

In fact, like they had been on the morning of 8 December, on the 11th the Japanese airfields on Formosa had been socked in by monsoon rains. However, on 12 and 13 December, the Japanese Air Forces returned to the Philippines, and with a vengeance, attacking targets throughout the Island of Luzon.[149]

One of their targets on the 13th was the huge radio towers at the Sangley Point Radio Station, not far from where the now, still smoldering, Cavite Navy Yard had stood. Under and around these same towers were pitched the tents of the 1st Separate Marine Battalion, Ed's battalion. As Ed recalled:

> [T]he air raid sirens began sounding steadily, and we assumed that there actually were enemy aircraft in the area. In fact, we soon heard word of enemy aircraft in route to the Manila area, which included our location at Sangley Point. We listened intently, and several minutes later we could hear the now all too familiar roar of Japanese bombers.[150]

Just like when the Japanese found Ed in the open at the Cavite Navy Yard, they again found him in the open by his tent at Sangley Point. "I realized that the radio towers that overshadowed our tents were probably the bombers' main target," he wrote. "Bombs could easily bring these towers down, crushing any man that happened to be under them." Once he realized this, he quickly began running as fast as he could to get away from the area. But, he didn't get far before the bombs began to hit. As he added, "I hit a shallow spot in the ground and quickly buried my face into the turf as the lead bombers dropped their loads. With a thunderous sound the bombs slammed into the radio towers as well as the ground all around me."[151]

Ed survived this latest bombing unscathed; however, several of his fellow Marines did not. As he remembered, "Our casualties were light . . . only losing one Marine who was hit by shrapnel, and six others requiring first aid."[152] Although Ed recalled only one Marine casualty during this air raid, according to 4th Marine Regiment historical documents relating to the bombing at the nearby Navy fuel depot, which was also being guarded by members of the 1st Separate Marine Battalion, five Marines were killed and eight were wounded in that day's bombing at Sangley Point.[153]

In addition, the low-frequency radio towers that Ed's camp was picketed under were destroyed. The loss of these was very grievous, since it meant that U.S. Navy submarines in that area of the Pacific Ocean could now only be contacted when surfaced . . . and then only at night.[154] Added to this loss were the contents of all of the 1st Separate Marine Battalion's tents, "leaving us," as Ed recalled, "with only the clothes on our backs."[155]

While Ed and his fellow Marines were scraping together provisions to replace theirs that they had just lost, cranes were needed to assist the massive salvage operations that were underway in Pearl Harbor. The Manitowoc Shipbuilding Company, back in Wisconsin, not only built ships, they also built cranes. As such, about eight days after the Pearl Harbor attack, the Navy Department sent the company an emergency order for six of the largest cranes produced at the yard to be shipped directly to Pearl Harbor to assist in the harbor cleanup. These were quickly assembled and shipped, the last one departing the yards in just over a month's time.[156]

On 20 December, Marine Lieutenant Colonel Adams received orders to move the 1st Separate Marine Battalion to the Naval Section Base at Mariveles, located at the southern tip of the Bataan Peninsula, which was across Manila Bay from Sangley Point. The move began on 21 December, with the last of the Battalion evacuating and destroying any military remnants at the Cavite area on Christmas Day.[157] As Ed Babler remembered:

> Orders had been issued for us not to smoke under any circumstances during our march. Although we traveled by night and in areas unfamiliar to us, our officers were very efficient and had a greater knowledge of the country. They also seemed to have had advance information about the movement of the Japanese troops. I believe Filipino scouts may have furnished the officers with these bits of

> information. . . . Regardless of where the Japanese troops
> were, we marched into the jungles of Mariveles [Bataan]
> and awaited word on any of their movements.[158]

It was, indeed, more than likely members of the elite Philippine Scouts Division that gave Ed's officers the information they needed.

Finally realizing that holding the Japanese at bay without using his combat-trained regiments was not working, and still refusing to commit them, on the evening of 23 December, after forty hours of setback after setback, General MacArthur finally implemented the Orange Plan.[159] However, by this time Brigadier General Charles Drake's supply corps, although desperately and heroically attempting to move tons of food, ammunition, fuel, and medical supplies to the Bataan Peninsula, was hampered by air raids, lack of vehicles, lack of personnel, and, most importantly, lack of time, even with General Jonathan Wainwright's Northern Corps—the under-trained Philippine Army—fighting a delayed retreat.[160] As a result, they were only able to relocate a portion of the much needed supplies to the peninsula. In addition, without relying upon or initially implementing the Orange Plan, the pre-invasion construction of the planned Bataan fortified defensive positions had also been neglected.

It was to this situation and these Bataan jungles that Ed and his fellow 1st Separate Marine Battalion, along with approximately 100,000 others—83,000 U.S. and Filipino soldiers and 26,000 Filipino civilian refugees[161]—were all struggling to quickly retreat to. As Ed recalled:

> We spent the next four days and nights sleepless as we
> slowly retreated backward . . . . The stillness of the nights
> seemed to create a tension and nervousness that was
> enhanced whenever the birds and animals made their
> noises, which tended to keep us awake. The tall jungle
> trees and dense under growth shielded us from the
> planes flying overhead, but it also made it easier for the
> Japanese snipers to get in closer. It boiled down to the
> fact that neither you nor your enemy wanted to reveal
> your position.[162]

Continuing his description of his retreat into the Bataan jungles, Ed wrote that:

[T]he Japanese were landing more and more troops everyday, and they started moving tanks in our direction. They also bombed the areas to our rear with incendiaries and explosives in attempts to prevent us from conducting a full retreat. . . . There wasn't a hell of a lot we could have done if we encountered the Japanese troops either, because all we had were our rifles and .30 and .50 caliber machine guns. We had no alternative but to move back.[163]

The joint defense plan for the Philippines called for the transfer of the Marines to Army operational control. Admiral Thomas Hart, USN, Commander-in-Chief, Asiatic Fleet, had initially argued against such a move. However, he was finally overruled. General Richard K. Sutherland, USA, MacArthur's chief of staff, ordered Colonel Samuel L. Howard, the commanding officer of the 4th Marine Regiment, to proceed with the 4th Marines to Corregidor as soon as possible to take over beach defenses.[164] As Ed recalled:

It had been agreed that the Marines would be transported to the island of Corregidor to provide a vital part of the island's defense. It was intended that we would establish a beach defense there, and it was to this end that we had been steadily working our way through the Mariveles [Bataan] jungles.[165]

The 1st Separate Marine Battalion crossed the channel to Corregidor on 26 December. The 2nd Battalion of the 4th Marines, along with the forward echelon of the Headquarters and Service Companies, made the trip on 27 December, with the remainder of the regiment, including the 1st Battalion, making the trip on 29 December.[166] As Ed remembered:

The last night in these jungles found us waiting for pitch darkness for our march to the beach to board the several barges that would take us across the bay to Corregidor, a trip that ultimately went smoothly. Almost everyone agreed that one day the Japanese would climb the many rocks and crevices of the Corregidor cliffs, and I believe the Army was happy to see us Marines arrive to help augment their forces on the "Rock," as the island of Corregidor was called.[167]

Once on the island, the 1st Separate Marine Battalion was integrated into the 4th Marine Regiment as the 3rd Battalion. Ed was again a member of the China Marines.

Corregidor, also known as Fort Mills, was affectionately called the "Rock" by many of those who served on her. A little over a mile wide at its widest, it was three and a quarter miles long and divided into three sections: "Bottomside," "Middleside," and "Topside." One of the most impressive structures of the island was the system of tunnels. These tunnels, begun being constructed in the early 1930's, housed, among other things, a three hundred-bed hospital, a naval communications center, fuel and ammunition storage, and, eventually, housing for General MacArthur, Philippine President Quezon, and U.S. Commissioner Francis Bowes Sayres and their staffs and families. The fort itself, as well as its sister forts of Frank, Drum, and Hughes, were designed to guard the entrance and anchorages of Manila Bay from any seaborne threat.[168]

It was just after 9 a.m. on the morning of 29 December, "just as the Marine units were being organized at our new home on Corregidor, [that] the air raid sirens began to sound," recalled Ed. "In a matter of a few minutes a flight of Japanese bombers were overhead and dropping their load of bombs directly on the main barracks Topside. . . . This was the first air raid we experienced on the Rock, and I thought it was a warning of what could be expected."[169]

Ed was assigned to a machinegun squad along the southern cliffs of Middleside overlooking the south dock, a dock used by small boats to offload supplies and personnel. Besides their .30 and .50 caliber machineguns, the Marines were equipped with "our good old-faithful 1903 [Springfield] rifles, a .45 Colt, and a supply of grenades," as he wrote.[170] Ed and his fellow Marines were effectively surrounded and, if not actually known to them at the time, abandoned to their fate. Ten year old Charlotte Mehlbrech's uncle, Stanley Sommers, in the Navy, was one of those left behind and now trapped on Bataan, also abandoned to his fate.[171]

Back in the United States, Army Private Charles Vellema had been granted a weekend leave. He took this opportunity to go back to the family farm near Waupun. While there, he proposed to Nova Wagner. Although happily engaged, with the war on neither of them knew when the wedding would be, or, for that matter, when they would see each other again.[172]

Before the end of the December arrived, according to Gladys Jolly, the 32nd Division of the National Guard, including several of her friends from the Ripon and Green Lake areas, shipped out. As she recalled, "On a Monday morning we all went up to the train. These boys came with the gear and stuff, and we said goodbye, you know, to them, never realizing I was doing [going to do] the same thing a couple months later."[173]

Seeing her friends go off to war, along with the war itself, had quite the impact on Gladys. So much so that she herself decided to join the Army. As she related:

> Well, it was on a weekend, and I went to work Monday morning; 7 o'clock we had to be there. And I guess I was out having too much fun. Dancing—I was a great gal for dancing[, and] roller skating. And I guess I was tired . . . 'cause my dad did say that when I passed him on the second floor [he was also now working at the same knitting factory], he said, "If you'd go home and get some sleep nights," you know. "Why don't you go home and go to bed," you know. I said, "Whoa, I'm gonna join the Army!" And when the screwman [foreman] came in . . . and had this pile of mittens, menders—he always knew I could do a good job fixing the menders—and he handed them to me and said, "Well, when you got time I want you to fix these." And I looked right at him—and I put them down on my table—and I looked right at him and just that quick [she snaps her fingers], I said, "I'm not fixing 'em." He stepped back and said, "What?" "You know, Herman, what you can do with your gloves!" And I said, "I am gonna join the Army."
>
> I had no anticipation. Really didn't! I packed up my stuff, my little old scissors, and—I was on the third floor— passed my dad on the second floor. He couldn't figure it out. At 9 o'clock in the morning and I'm going down the

> steps, you know. He said, "Where are you going?" I said,
> "I'm gonna join the Army." And he said, "Yeah, well,"
> you know, "you go home and get some sleep. Out tearing
> around all night long."

Having seen her National Guard friends off to war, and wanting to be more of a part of the war effort herself than simply mending gloves, just that quick, Gladys left work and went straight to the recruiter's office.[174]

In Waupun, the *Laandal's Lunch* restaurant-tavern was also to see its share of National Guard units off to war. As Joan Laandal recalled, "[A]t our restaurant our family served the National Guard when they were stationed in Waupun prior to leaving just before action." They would "come up Main Street, marched up Main Street to our restaurant, and they had three meals a day. I was in school, but at noon I had to work; help serve, clean and wash glasses, bar glasses especially."[175]

Also in Waupun, the day before the end of the year, 30 December 1941, Arnold Visser and Grace Derksen were married. The couple moved into Grace's parents' home on the Derksen farm on State Highway 151 north of Waupun. At the time, as Arnold related, the farm, like many in the area, did not have electricity or indoor plumbing, and Grace's father still farmed using horses.[176]

As the year drew to a close and the newlyweds settled in, they, along with the rest of the country, were still stunned, yet they were also beginning to mobilize for war.

1942

The first of the year saw Gladys Jolly in Milwaukee, Wisconsin, going through an army entrance exam and physical. Upon arriving in Milwaukee and departing the train, she met another young lady that was also heading to the Army, so the two of them walked together to the induction center, taking in the sights along the way. In recalling of her actual induction process, Gladys stated:

> So her and I went into this building, and they started processing us, you know. We were there all day.
> Went through physicals, went through interviews . . . you know, everything. And then they posted us around about, oh, I think it was about 4 o'clock or 5 in the afternoon, who was to be accepted. Well, naturally you are scared. Well, geez, if I don't join I have to go back home to the needle works or something. But I was accepted. And so was my girlfriend, Eddie. So we were at that time good old privates.[177]

Gladys was then shipped back home to Ripon, Wisconsin, to await her entrance date. As she stated concerning her homecoming:

> Well, I had to call dad because they were going to send us back on our trains; well, dad because the trains came into Ripon. But on the way back it came into Fond du Lac [Wisconsin]. It seemed that was the stopping place, so dad had to come over to Fond du Lac and get [me]. He wasn't too happy with me. But yet he said, "If that's what you choose out of life, then I'll except it." But he said,

"It . . . was hard to lose you and your brother." He said,
"We were proud of you.

Gladys' brother had also joined the Army; therefore, both of Arthur and Rose Jolly's children would go to war.[178]

Elva Drews wanted to do her bit for the war effort as well. Working in the office at the Milwaukee company of Harnishfager wasn't enough. So, having recently turned eighteen, she took a government civil service test. Upon passing the test she was trained as a teletype operator and placed in a four-woman office receiving and sending teletype messages shipping war materials throughout the country from the Milwaukee and Chicago areas. As she recalled, she shipped all "kinds of ordinance. Vehicles, tanks, guns, ammunition, you name it, like to ports and army depots throughout the United States."[179] Elva was actually a member of the WAACs (Women Auxiliary Army Corps), which was created by Congress on 15 March 1942. The WAACs, unlike the WACs (Women Army Corps), which would be created a little over a year later, were not officially in the military and worked in the industrial sector, but did, nonetheless, wear a form of uniform.[180] Elva was to refer to her uniform as an Army Ordinance uniform.[181] In contrast, Gladys Jolly would be amongst the first 1,500 women to be inaugurated into what would be the WACs, actually a member of the military.[182]

In the Philippines, help, promised from Washington, was not only hoped for, but expected by both the American and Filipino forces attempting to hold back the Japanese invading forces. However, senior military and government personnel knew otherwise. President Roosevelt had, as recently as June 1941, signed the secret 'European first strategy' pact with British Prime Minister Winston Churchill. This pact, which was turned into the Rainbow 5 War Plan, committed the United States forces to defeating the Axis Powers in Europe first, while fighting a defensive war in the Pacific.[183] Unbeknownst to the American and Filipino forces on Bataan and the offshore coastal garrisons of Corregidor and her sister fortress islands, as well as those on the southern island of Mindanao, including Marine Corporal Edmond Babler and sailor Stanley Sommers, Rainbow 5 War Plan doomed the defenders to annihilation, starvation, or surrender. A lucky few, including General MacArthur, Commissioner Sayers, and Philippine President Quezon would be evacuated. The others would be sacrificed.

Ed spent these early days and nights of 1942 on Corregidor manning his machinegun post along the southern cliffs of Middleside overlooking the island's south dock. As he wrote, "Every night I stayed at my gun position because it was at night that I expected the Japanese to attack. I had a hell of a time getting any of the other men to pull duty with me at my position during these nights. I had the same problem during the daytime whenever we were receiving any of our many" bombings and shellings. These bombings and shellings were soon to become nearly constant. As Ed recalled, "Every day we could either expect a flight of enemy bombers or the Japanese to shell the hell out of us with their 155s. One day alone it seemed as though the air raid sirens had sounded continuously all day long, and I counted 15 separate air-attacks."[184]

Ed also spent time during this period assisting the army gunners at one of their huge 12-inch coastal guns. These guns were designed to protect the bay from enemy attack by sea. As he was to write, "My job at the 12-inch gun itself was easy. All I had to do was help carry the powder to the gun prior to it being readied to fire." As Ed reported, this gun position was constructed of concrete. The gun itself was located in the center of a 40-foot diameter pit, and a powder room was located in one corner, sealed with a large steel door. As he recalled:

> We would dash back into this powder room and shut the steel door as soon as we delivered the powder to the gun. . . . Moments after we fired a round towards Bataan and were safely tucked away inside the powder room we would hear the roar of the incoming shell fired by the Japs in response. About two seconds later we would hear the shell land and explode inside the pit.[185]

Back in America the nation soon began gearing up in earnest to deal with the war. Throughout Wisconsin, like throughout the rest of the country, factories began re-tooling to produce war materials, and farms maintained, if not increased their productions. Bessie Douma's older sister, Dorothy, worked at Rockwell in Randolph, Wisconsin, during the war making ammunition boxes.[186] This is of interest, since it is a prime example that even very small communities contained war producing factories during World War II. Randolph, today, has a population of less than two thousand people.

By 1942, Manitowoc, Wisconsin, was literally considered the center of the world for manufacturing aluminum products. Besides the main office and factory of the Aluminum Goods Manufacturing Company, which was considered the largest aluminum parts manufacturing plant in the world, Manitowoc was also the home of the Aluminum Specialty Company, the Wisconsin Aluminum Foundry Company, and the National Tinsel Manufacturing Company. All of these quickly began retooling for the war effort.[187]

As soon as Jeanette Rochon, at the time still working at the Aluminum Goods Manufacturing Company's Two Rivers, Wisconsin, plant assembling aluminum coffee pots, heard that tests were being giving for work at the Aluminum Specialty Company making anti-aircraft shells, she went to take the test. As she recalled, it was given "at Manitowoc at the high school. And I went, and there were, I don't know, a couple hundred, and I was in the top seven—a smarty!" So she went to work in Manitowoc at the Aluminum Specialty Company "making twenty millimeter anti-aircraft shells. . . . We had gauges," she recalled, "and we would gauge that little firing pin or whatever that was. And if it didn't fit right or was bent a little bit, throw it out!"[188]

With the increase in need for naval craft, on 1 February, the Manitowoc Shipbuilding Company was approached to add to their shipbuilding for the Navy. This new contract would include the building of thirty-six Tank Landing Craft V (LCT-5) vessels. To insure the ten submarines previously ordered as well as the LCT-5's were ready on time, the company was soon to employ between 8,000 and 9,000 men and women bused in from as far away as the Wisconsin cities of Sheboygan, Appleton, and Green Bay, with the busses also picking up workers from smaller towns and even farms along the way.[189]

On 18 February, the president of the shipyard, Mr. Charles West, received a Letter of Commendation from the Secretary of the Navy, Frank Knox, for the yard's performance to date. This would be one of many such official commendations the yard would receive. On 3 April of this same year the Navy "E" for excellence would also be awarded to the shipyard. The company would eventually receive six of these coveted awards alone during the war.[190]

It was not only the Manitowoc Shipbuilding Company that was to build war ships in the mid-west. Shipyards began springing up on practically all inland waterways throughout the United States, constructing many different types of sea-going vessels. These shipyards would eventually build more than 4,000 craft ranging from small aircraft rescue boats, to landing craft, to mine sweepers, and even larger LSTs (Landing Ship Tank) and Destroyer Escorts.[191]

The National Rivet and Manufacturing Company in Waupun, Wisconsin, was also going strong. Walter Riel, along with two of his brothers was working there. His oldest brother had been "drafted right away in the beginning when the draft started. But then he got 4-F for some reason or other," Walter was to recall.[192] He was then to continue at the factory. Another one of Walter's brothers, Don, received a deferment to the draft because he too was working at the rivet factory, which was considered vital work towards the war effort. Neither of these two brothers of Walter were to serve in the war; but, at the age of nineteen, Walter knew that his own draft number would also soon come up.[193]

The term 4-F was a classification for the draft. It signified individuals who were not draft eligible. It is reported that thirty percent of those of draft age during the war were considered 4-F. This category included people with bone malformations, muscular disorders, mental diseases and ailments, sexually transmitted diseases, and circulatory and hearing deficiencies. Even a hernia was a cause to be classified as 4-F.[194]

Also working at the National Rivet and Manufacturing Company making rivets was eighteen year old Emil Hopp, and, in March, Tillie Dykstra "was called to National Rivet," and began working in the inspection room. When she received word of her new job at the rivet factory, Tillie left her position at the hotel in Portage and moved to Waupun where she and one of her sisters rented an apartment on East Franklin Street. Both Tillie's sister and her father also worked at the factory along with Tillie. Like the Manitowoc Shipbuilding Company, the National Rivet and Manufacturing Company was also to receive a coveted Navy "E" for excellence award from the government—the rivets produced at the factory would be vital to the nation's aircraft industry.[195]

Unlike many of the others, Doris Bohnert had to give up her job at the plant by this time. Constantly inspecting the small rivets began to have its toll on her eyes. As she recalled, "My eyes were getting bad and the doctor said I couldn't work in the rivets anymore. Then I would go blind. So then I quit." Through a childhood friend, Audrey Lammers, Doris was able to find work at the Wisconsin State Child Center in Sparta, Wisconsin. The Child Center, as it was commonly referred to, was a type of state-run orphanage. So she packed up and moved the 110 miles across the state to Sparta, where she would take care of one- and two-year old children. "Nobody wanted the small ones because they had to change diapers," Doris recalled. "And I didn't care, I liked the small ones. So I had the smaller ones."[196]

When Doris began working at the Child Center, she met twenty year old Robert Arthur Daniels, who was already working at the center as a truck driver. According to Doris, "[H]e had to take stuff down to the other institutions and delivered the food and stuff." Born on 19 December 1921 in North Dakota, Robert had already attempted to join the military, but was classified as 4-F due to having had Polio as a child and had been refused entry. Most of the other men still working at the Child Center were older, so they too were either deferred or actually too old to serve.[197]

At age sixteen, Theron Mickelson was still attending high school in Neenah, Wisconsin, while working after school in an apprenticeship at a Neenah machine shop. He wanted, though, to quit high school and join the Navy, since his father had served in the Navy during the First World War as an airplane mechanic, rising to the rank of chief petty officer. His father, however, refused to allow Theron to join the military until Theron had successfully graduated from high school.[198] Friends Lois Bohnert and Dorothy Bal were also to spent the year in high school, in their hometown of Waupun.

It was about this time that nationwide blackouts began becoming more and more encouraged, even mandated, by the federal government, and Waupun was no different from the rest of the country. According to Lois Bohnert, "They had wardens for each block," whose job it was to enforce the blackout drills.[199] These air raid wardens were everyday local citizens. One of Waupun's was Dorothy Bal's father. As she recalled concerning her father's air raid warden duties, "I remember my dad had Fond du Lac Street from the end on to the Powder Puff," the Powder Puff being a gas station. As she continued:

> [H]e'd drive all around every so often, and all the lights would be turned off.... [H]e stopped a guy one time after everybody was in the dark and this guy was coming in the car with the lights on, and I wish I could remember what excuse he gave my dad why he was out on the street, but it

was something crazy. I can't remember if he told my dad he wanted to get home before it started or what, but . . . there he was with all his car lights on.[200]

In nearby South Byron, Wisconsin, Marshall McLean was also experiencing black out drills. As he remembered, "[W]e did practice blackouts. Occasionally we had such and certain time we couldn't have any lights on, and had to have your shades pulled."[201] Ges Mintzlaff recalled that "When they said lights out, we went lights out. I mean, we didn't try to do anything the government didn't want us to do. And I think we felt relatively safe way back here in the Middle-West. I think had I lived on the East Coast I'd been a little concerned."[202]

Concerning the blackout drills, Elva Drews recalled that as a teletype operator in Milwaukee for the government she was the first to know when Milwaukee was to have an air raid drill, "a mock air raid," she was to call it. As she stated, "It came out of Chicago. Everybody had to clear out [of her office]. I was bonded. Everybody had to clear out, and I took the message. And then took it to the head guy. So I was the first one that knew Milwaukee was going to have a mock air-raid."[203]

Charlotte Mehlbrech remembered that

> we had blackouts that you would have to have your windows covered with black. And black was all sold out so you'd have to have . . . take green or blue, dark blue [cloth]—you couldn't even buy that—and you covered your windows, and they would have practices of this. And they would have a warden, he was the only one that was allowed on the road. And he would go up and down the road, and then if he thought he could see too much light or anything out of your windows, he would come up to your house.[204]

Charlotte also stated that in talking to a woman years after the war, the woman had told her that they "couldn't even get any colored dark [cloth back then], so we tried newspapers and would tape it over the windows." "And this," as Charlotte continued, "was with the idea that if we were actually to be under attack . . . all the lights would be out. There wouldn't be any lights anywhere. And for the practice time just the warden could have his light[s on] with his car when he went all around to check. And this was in the country."[205]

As Charlotte related to, it was not just in the cities that black out drills were conducted. They were conducted in the countryside as well. Harriet Whiting's father, a farmer, for example, was an air raid warden in one of the rural areas surrounding Waupun. And, as she explained, like her father, the wardens had to go through training:

> [H]e would have to drive up and down the road—and he must have had to do it with the lights out in the car, we were not allowed to go with him—to make sure you couldn't see lights from anybody's windows. And he also had to attend first aid classes. And he said he always volunteered to be the patient because then he could lie on the floor and sleep.[206]

Even DiAnna Reif, just an infant at the time, being born in the middle of the war in the family home in Waupun on 22 September 1943 to Charles (called Chuck) and LaRone Reif, remembered the blackout drills. As she recalled, "I can so vividly remember the blackouts and how my parents . . . would switch off all the lights. And they would usually take us kids to the basement."[207] Young five year old Jim Laird, having moved with his family from Dubuque, Iowa, to Cuba City, Wisconsin, in the far southwestern part of the state, about 120 miles southwest of Waupun, was proud to do his part for his family during the blackout drills. As he explained, "I said, 'Oh, mom, mom, I have an idea!' We had a big board with fuses on it and then one of these toggle switches that would break the circuit. And I said, 'I'll just run over and pull that and all the lights will go out.' And, of course, mom let me do that and I felt like such a big man."[208]

Blackouts and blackout drills along the East and West Coasts of the country made very good military sense to lessen the likelihood of enemy aircraft and ships from sighting targets at night. After all, along the East Coast German submarines were using the night skyline, illuminated from the glow of the city lights, to locate Allied ships leaving port or travelling along the coast, sinking hundreds of these within sight of the U.S. shoreline. In addition, the West Coast was within the range of Japanese aircraft carrier planes. But why conduct blackout drills in areas as far inland as Wisconsin, literally over a thousand miles from either coast line? In looking back at the situation, Jim Laird quite aptly stated, "[W]hen you think about it, the government must had done some of these things to make the people feel partially the danger and partially involved, because, you know, the reality of the chances of planes getting all the way over Wisconsin and bombing us was pretty far out."[209]

Across the ocean in Germany, AnnaMarie Kretzer not only had to worry about air raids, which in Germany by this time were real threats, like her fellow German youth of Arian race, she was also *expected* to join the Hitler Youth, whether she wanted to or not. As she was to state:

> [O]f course, we had to become Hitler Youth. Age ten it was a must. And you know, when you are ten years old, gee, it was fun at first. But then it got boring. It was always . . ., everything centered around Hitler and the big parades we had, and not only during the week, but on Sundays. But you *had* to join.[210]

Her father, however, tried to get her out of it as much as he could. As AnnaMarie related, he would write "an excuse that I had to work out in the vegetable garden or pick bugs from the potatoes. Then one time the leader said 'Another excuse? Well, you better be working out there, we may come and check.' So you were always under fear."[211]

She also recalled that not everyone in Germany was a Nazi, but it was difficult for those who refused to join the Party. For instance, "My father refused to join the [Nazi] party, he couldn't find employment as he indicated on the application the [sic] he was not a member of the party. He did odd jobs, until finally some small business man hired him without questioning his party affiliation."[212]

The family was also plagued in other ways out of fear of the Nazis. For example, the Nazi swastika flag not only had to be flown on special occasions, but it had to be a certain size in correlation to the dimensions of the home it flew on. As AnnaMarie reported, on one occasion

> My grandmother bought some little flags and stuck them in holders in the old bay window, and the brown shirted guys, the SR [SA, *Sturm Abteilung*], came by to check, and they said, "They were not big enough. For a two story house, no way, and you better see to it that it gets changed.

We'll be back." And my uncle bought the biggest one he could find and hung it from the upper balcony; so they were satisfied. So you see, we were always in fear.[213]

In the United States people of German descent were taking stock as well. Nearly all were as patriotic towards the United States as anyone else from any other heritage. Charlotte Mehlbrech's family was no different, her grandparents having come directly from Germany. In having come from Germany, her grandmother, however, still had items in their home from her mother country. For instance, as Charlotte related:

> [T]hey had beautiful pillows with the swastika on. And that, I was told, meant *good luck*. And she had them on this couch—and I was there when they decided to do it—they had those beautiful pillows and they were afraid someone would come and see them. And my great grandma, she talked real broken [English], and she says, "Well, we could just turn them around." But, "No, somebody might turn it around." So while I was there . . . they burnt them in the furnace. And they had other things also with this emblem. . . . I was told it was a good luck emblem. But then Germany took it for their flag.[214]

By April, without the promised relief force having arrived, and it now being quite evident that it would not, the situation in the Philippines had become desperate. So much so that with estimates varying, due to dwindling supplies on the Bataan Peninsula, on 9 April General Edward King was forced to surrender nearly 70,000 to 80,000 American and Filipino military personnel to Japanese General Homma's forces.[215] Many of these were sick or wounded; all were near the starvation level due to the severe shortage of rations. These prisoners were marched into captivity on what became known as the infamous 'Bataan Death March.' Again, estimates vary, however, many thousands of Americans and Filipinos died on this march due to the Japanese open brutality towards their captives—one historian lists over 7,000,[216] while another lists 25,000.[217] Many of the prisoners who were already nearly emaciated by the time they surrendered died of sickness and fatigue along the way; others succumbed from wounds received during the battle of Bataan. Still others were beaten to death or outright executed by bayoneting, shooting, or beheading by the Japanese. One of these prisoners on this death march was Charlotte Mehlbrech's uncle, Stanley Sommers, who would be one of the lucky ones to survive the horrendous march into captivity.[218]

While Stanley and the other American and their fellow Filipino soldiers and sailors from Bataan were suffering on the Death March, Ed Babler and his fellow Marines, soldiers, and sailors on Corregidor and the other three smaller island fortresses in the Manila Bay still held out. Still others were holding out on the large southern island of Mindanao. As a result, the bombings and shellings would now become more intense against these forces, especially those on the Rock with Ed. General Douglas MacArthur, however, and Philippine President Quezon and their families, along with many of those on their staffs, had been earlier whisked away from Corregidor on 12 March, and three days later flown out of Mindanao to the safety of Australia. Around the same time, Commissioner Sayre, his family, and staff had been evacuated by submarine.[219]

After subjecting the American and Filipino forces to more and more bombings and shellings, on the evening of 5 May, the Japanese began their long anticipated invasion of Corregidor. As Ed recalled:

> Early that evening . . . the Japs started shelling the Rock, releasing a monstrous attack with their 155s and 240-millimeter siege guns. The shelling continued without letup, and we were losing men. After it became pitch dark, the skies became filled with thousands of Japanese flares. It looked like hundreds of 4th of July fireworks all being displayed at one same time and was actually a beautiful sight with the flares lighting up the sky for what seemed like miles.[220]

The Americans would fight hard for their island. Of the 2,400 Japanese troops in the first attacking wave, less than 800 would make it ashore, and 60 percent of their landing craft and supporting gunboats would be destroyed. As Ed eulogized:

> The Americans fought hard, with many individual hand to hand fights taking place. No one writes about those

brave men who fought because they were expected to do so and died only because they were outnumbered. The real heroes are the men who died on the battlefield of Corregidor.[221]

Ed, along with his 3rd Battalion, was on the opposite side of the island from the invasion, so he did not actually get into the fight with the invading forces. His position was, however, attacked from the air. As he related, "I then saw three dive-bombers swoop down and fire at several of the gun positions in my area, including mine. The dive-bombers made at least half a dozen dives on these gun positions with bullets hitting mine by the hundreds, or at least so it seemed." On one of these passes a bomb hit near enough to Ed's dugout that his machinegun was disabled and Ed was temporarily buried under debris.[222]

The next morning, on 6 May, after sustaining shelling for twenty-seven straight days and feverishly attempting to fend off an invasion, the forces on Corregidor, under General Jonathan Wainwright, surrendered, leaving the Philippine Islands entirely in Japanese hands and adding several thousand additional American and Filipino troops to the rolls of Japanese held POWs, including Corporal Babler.[223] As Ed recalled:

> For a brief time it was quiet, then suddenly I heard the noise of three motor-launches approaching the dock below what was left of my position. I at once noticed the motor-launches were flying the Japanese Rising Sun flag. It made me mad to think that those dirty bastards had strafed the hell out of me just thirty minutes before the launches pulled up.[224]

Along with Ed, roughly 13,700 other American and Filipino troops surrendered that day on Corregidor, including 1,487 of his fellow 4th Marine Regiment, the China Marines. Of the 4th Marines, 89 had been killed or died of their wounds from attempting to repel the Japanese landings, another 167 had been wounded.[225] As Ed so poignantly put it:

> Unless it happens to you, one is unable to understand exactly how it feels to walk towards the enemy with your hands raised above your head. I can just imagine how

terrible General Wainwright felt when he was forced to
surrender all the Philippine Islands and thousands of
troops to the Japanese knowing that all the troops would
become prisoners of war.[226]

Ed's first experience as a POW in the hands of the Japanese that day
was only a prelude to things to come. As he was to write:

> Everybody stood with their hands over their head until
> one of the Japs came by and searched them. When I
> lowered my hands too early, a little Jap ran up, hollered,
> "*Kiotski*," and put his bayonet against my stomach forcing
> me to raise my hands back over my head. . . . A laugh or
> movement by an American while being searched was
> rewarded with a hit from a Japanese rifle butt.[227]

Upon being searched, the Japanese relieved their new prisoners of
anything of value, including watches and rings. Ed and his fellow POW's
were then marched to an open area along a beach, which became their
home for the next few days.[228]

While Ed was becoming a POW in the Philippines, back in Wisconsin,
Ges Mintzlaff and Leonard Schrank were still studying in college, Ges to
be an X-ray technician and Leonard to be a medical doctor, with Leonard
still being issued deferments from the draft so he could get his medical
degree. There was little time to rest, however, especially for Leonard. As
Ges recalled:

> [H]is draft board would keep deferring him because the
> Army kept saying, "Let him graduate." So instead of
> doing four years in medical school for his last residency
> on surgery, he did three years without a day of vacation
> and no time off at all. I mean, on weekends . . . just kept
> their routine. Everything kept going.[229]

Throughout the year, Nova Wagner would continue to teach school
outside of Alto, Wisconsin, just west of Waupun, and during the summer
months when school was out she took on odd jobs around the area. "I did
a lot of babysitting for people in Brandon, I worked in a restaurant," and

also "forked cans for the canning company," she recalled.[230] Nearly every town in the area around Waupun had one or more canning companies during this time period. In addition to working, Nova would keep up a steady stream of letters to her fiancé, Charles Vellema, never really knowing where he was other than he was in the Army's 47th Infantry Regiment of the 9th Infantry Division, which was normally stationed at Fort Bragg, North Carolina. However, with the war on, she knew he could be nearly anywhere, even heading for battle.

Like her neighbors and many other Americans across the country, Nova would also contribute to the war effort in any form she could, including donating "blood for blood banks when they were around."[231] David Lyon remembered that his mother also contributed to the war effort by folding bandages. As he stated:

> [A]t least once a week, my mother folded bandages. She always got material—and I don't know where it came from—but she was always folding bandages and packaging them. In retrospect, I think, possibly there were programs like that that kept the civilian population . . . in a sense in participating in the war and the victory. I don't really think they used a lot of that stuff. I think it was almost make do work. But I think it was almost like propaganda to keep the civilian population, you know, give them a sense of participation and keep them excited about the war and what was going on.[232]

David continued recalling his mother folding bandages in stating:

> [S]he'd make like slings for broken arms and that. And then she'd package them up in paper. And where she sent them I have no idea. But there was always somebody who picked them up or she gave them to somebody after she had them all folded. And I remember they'd bring like sheet material, cotton material, over to the house that they would rip up and make into different kinds of bandages. And they would be told, you know, what was wanted.[233]

Bessie Douma, six years old at the time, remembered collecting milkweed pods for the war effort. As she recalled, she had to walk the two miles from her family's farmhouse to and from a two-room schoolhouse in East Friesland, Wisconsin. After the walk home in the afternoons, her mother would give Bessie and her siblings "a little lunch, and then we were all handed a gunny bag and we had to go and pick milkweed pods. And that was always 'Hurry, get out there, get it done before it gets dark.' And so that's what I recall doing after school . . . and we did pick a lot of them."[234]

The milkweed plants grew, and still do to this day, wild in the ditches alongside the country roads in the area. As Bessie stated, "[I]f you open a milkweed pod there's that silky stuff inside, and that's what they made the parachutes with for the war. That's why we were asked to pick those milkweed pods. And then my father brought 'em somewhere with a truck." Portage, Wisconsin, according to Bessie, is where the pods were collected, but as she stated, "I'm sure he didn't bring 'em that far, but there was a point where he had to bring those" to. Bessie continued by stating that the work "was all volunteer work," we did not get paid for it, and "we were proud to do so, that we could help with that."[235]

Although Bessie remembered milkweed pods being used by the military for parachute material, it was actually used to replace kapok in the making of lifejackets.[236] Kapok, from the kapok tree, became difficult to obtain during the war since much of it was grown in the South Pacific, which was now in Japanese hands.

Marshall Mclean, attending grade school in South Byron at the time, also picked milkweed pods for the war effort. As he recalled, "We would . . . walk down the railroad tracks and fields to pick milkweed pods for the Military for life preservers."[237] As a young five year old school girl, Harriet Whiting was also to pick the pods alongside the roads while walking to and from her one-room country school, the "Waupun District Number Eleven Mapledale School, not far from Waupun." Besides collecting milkweed pods, Harriet also recalled bringing in used toothpaste tubes for recycling as part of the war effort. As she stated, "You would bring the stuff in to the school and then somebody would collect it from there."[238]

Jim Laird, who was in his first year of grade school at the time, not only remembered picking milkweed pods, but also recalled that since metal was hard to come by because of the war effort, tinsel was also not available, so his teacher used cattail fur to decorate the school's Christmas tree. He also remembers separating the aluminum wrappers on chewing gum from the paper wrappers for recycling as well as collecting other metals. "I got into a movie free," he recalled. "I thought it was the greatest thing in the world. I got into a movie free because I took my wagon load of metal, scrap, and things that had accumulated around the house over the years upon years, and that went to the war effort."[239] For this, the young five year old received a free movie ticket.

Paper was saved and re-cycled as well, and items such as band-aids were scarce. As Charlotte Mehlbrech was to remember, "[W]e saved our paper in school. We used both sides, and you didn't [discard it] . . . they threw it in a basket, but you weren't to crumble it up. You were to save it like we save paper now for recycling. We had to save our paper." She also recalled that, "You couldn't even have band-aids at school. They were rationed out. I mean, if you got hurt [you] had to be . . . scraped bad enough or you wouldn't get the band-aid, because there's only one box for the whole school.[240]

It was not just in the United States that items were collected for the war effort. In Germany items were collected as well. But under the Nazi regime, according to AnnaMarie Kretzer, this sort of thing was more than a patriotic act to support the war effort. It was an actual duty assigned to the students at her school. "War duties at school!!!!" she was to write. "Gather mulberry leaves to feed the silk worms, collect papers, bones etc [*sic*] for recycling. AND gather herbs and dry them during the summer weeks and turn X-amount of pounds in at the end of summer vacation."[241]

Back in the United States, with the massive increase of military production, consumer goods began to take a back seat to military needs, with many normal staples of life being siphoned off for the military's use. As a result, the United States Office of Price Administration (OPA), in May of 1942, began freezing prices on sugar and coffee. Soon other items as well would be included: tires, cars, bicycles, gasoline, fuel oil and kerosene, solid fuels, stoves, rubber footwear, shoes, processed foods, meats, canned fish, cheese, canned milk, fats, and even typewriters and chicken wire.[242]

To help assure these items were available for the military, and to ensure American civilians would get their fair share of what was left over of the items, a nation-wide, government run rationing program was begun under the auspices of the OPA during the spring of 1942.[243] All

Americans were expected to support and enforce these efforts, and most if not all eagerly stepped up to the challenge and did their part. There was, however, some adjustments the public would have to get used to. As Nova Wagner remembered, "[T]here were so many items you couldn't purchase that you were used to . . ., clothing," for instance.[244]

Rationing came with the issuance of rationing cards. Regardless of having the money available to purchase an item that was on the ration list, and regardless of the amount of these items available at any given time, one had to have a ration coupon for the item to purchase it. These small coupons, or "cards" or "stamps" as many would also call them, were about the size of a postage stamp and came in booklet form. Ges Mintzlaff remembered that these consisted of "a little book, maybe six by three [inches]. And you had cards in there for your flour, your sugar, your shoes. I can't remember about clothes because we made do with what we had. We didn't spend a lot of money during those years," since without the cards, many things could not be purchased.[245]

Concerning the rationing books and rationing, Charlotte Mehlbrech, only about ten years old as the time, remembered that

> [E]veryone in the family got one . . . every child, every person. . . . But it was for shoes, for gas, and anything . . . I often thought it must have been butter, also. And I know it was sugar because I went to a church camp and I had to have five pounds of sugar. And my mother was very upset because I had to have money [also], of course, for the camp. And it was camp Winmore is the name of it. And I had to take that five pounds of sugar.
>
> And ladies had to can without sugar, they would can without sugar because they thought they could maybe have enough stamps for to buy and put the sugar in later when we took it from the sealer, you know. But it was very hard on the people.[246]

As an eight year old at the time, Bessie Douma also remembered that everyone, even children, were issued ration cards. Interestingly, she still had a ration booklet when interviewed, which she brought along. It had been issued to her when she was eight years old. On the front cover it contained her name, height, and weight, along with the Rural Route 2,

Randolph, Wisconsin, address where she lived at the time. As she stated, "I was eight years old when I was given this book, and I was four feet and three inches tall and weighed fifty pounds." She then read a statement contained on the back cover of the ration card:

> This book is the property of the United States Government. It is unlawful to sell it to any other person or to us it or permit anyone else to use it, except to obtain rationed goods in accordance with regulations to the Office of Price Administration. Any person who finds a lost war ration book must return it to the War Price and Rationing Board which issued it. Persons who violate rationing regulations are subject to $10,000 fine or imprisonment or both.

When finished reading from the booklet, Bessie stated, "Did they not mean business, huh?" relating to the $10,000 fine.[247]

The families were expected to manage these booklets and their corresponding stamps. Since Bessie's family had nine children, and each received their own set of ration cards, this could be a challenge. "[C]an you imagine having eleven books and you were suppose to keep track of how much sugar each one used?", she stated. Although she could not recall what each book was for, Bessie did remember that each book had different looking coupons. "There is a platoon boat stamp, and there is a tank stamp . . . and this one I think is . . . a cannon," she continued.[248] According to Dorothy Bal, the rationing booklets and cards had expiration dates on them. "I know they were only good for . . . so long," she stated, "and then they weren't any good. And then the new one would come up."[249]

Besides rationing cards, "change" in the form of small coins were issued. As Marshall McLean, only about nine years old at the time, recalled, "I remember the little blue and red, kinda like nickel like things you used for grocery stores and groceries. And I think my mother had a book, kinda like food stamps like."[250] Harriet Whiting also remembered, as she stated, "little coins things. They weren't made of metal, of course. They were some sort of pressed fiber or something." As she recalled:

> They were change. Yeah, you might need three stamps for sugar . . . or maybe it was like two and a half stamps

for so much sugar. Well, then you would get these things like change. And they were different colors. I know there were blue ones and red ones, and I can't remember if there were green ones and yellow ones. I almost think there were, but I do remember red and blue. And they were different values.[251]

Like sugar, gasoline was one of the many items rationed. "I can remember my folks getting stamps for certain things. Like for gasoline mostly, gasoline was rationed," recalled Josephine Aarts, who was fifteen years old at the time.[252] "Well," remembered Elva Drews, "I rode streetcars in Milwaukee. You couldn't even get a taxi cab ticket. Well, they didn't have the gas. You had to ride the streetcars or the buses. Or [you] walked."[253] According to Marshall McLean, each vehicle had a sticker affixed to the windshield indicating how much gas the vehicle was to be allotted. "I remember every car had a windshield sticker with an A and B, C, D, or F, whatever," he recalled. "If you just used your car for pleasure you didn't get as much as if it was [used for] business purposes."[254]

Just as Marshall had recalled, by the end of 1942, after voluntary gasoline rationing was not working as planned, the OPA began issuing both gas rationing cards and stickers to automobile and other vehicle owners. To receive these, one had to certify to a local board the need for the gas use and, with the rubber shortage, that one did not have more than five serviceable tires. Once this certification was validated, a sticker would be issued along with reoccurring monthly gas ration books. These stickers, as Marshall had related, would be placed on the vehicle's windshield and would consist of alphabetical figures relating to the vehicle's use. A black sticker containing a white A was issued for nonessential use, with the owner allowed to draw only three or four gallons of gas per week. A green B sticker represented someone whose driving was deemed essential for the war effort, including industrial workers, allowing the purchase of eight gallons of gas per week. A red C sticker signified a minister, railroad worker, physician, or mail carrier, while an X sticker was reserved for members of Congress and other important government officials, both stickers of which allowed for more gas than the basic white A and green B stickers. Truck drivers supplying the country with food stuffs and other commodities and supplies were issued a T sticker, which granted them unlimited amounts of gas. In addition, to help conserve rubber, not so much gas, a national Victory Speed limit was soon set at 35 miles per hour and the Idle Tire Purchase Plan was established by the OPA denying gas rationing to anyone owning one or more passenger car tires not being used.[255]

Even with hard times and rationing, and regardless of the legalities involved, many people would help others who were in greater need. As Nova Wagner recalled, "[O]ur home didn't have a mother doing the usual cooking and baking, we girls managed everything. But we didn't blend much with sugar, so I turned some of my rations over to his [Charles'] mother"—Charles Vellema, Nova's fiancé.[256]

Both Dorothy Bal and Lois Bohnert stated that people became "a little closer together" during the war because so many of their sons and daughters were serving in the war. As such, they would help each other out when needed, including sharing ration cards. "I remember my dad used to get extra gas," Dorothy related, because some of the farmers would bring their unused gas ration cards to the filling station manager "telling him to give it to somebody that could use it."[257]

Like Dorothy, Josephine Aarts also remembered farmers giving away gas stamps. As she recalled, "[T]he farmers would get too many sometimes. And he [her father] would get some from his good friends, farmers, so he had a few extra" for the family's Ford Model-T.[258] Likewise, Lois Bohnert also remembered her uncle giving her youngest brother Ralph gas stamps for his use when Ralph came home on furlough from the Army. Lois was also to relate that although her and her friends did not have a car, for some entertainment they "used to chip in money [and their gasoline ration cards], each of us, and we'd go ride around for a little bit."[259]

Charlotte Mehlbrech also remembered trading ration coupons. "I know we traded the stamps . . . through the family. But I don't know if that was legal or what, or nobody ever seemed to question it," she stated.[260] Harriet Whiting recalled that from time to time the grocer would call her parents and ask for stamps for others in need. He would say:

> "Well, now, I let some people take sugar even though they didn't have stamps for it. Do you have extra?" And we always had sugar stamps and, of course, meat stamps and things like that. And we would used to give them to the guy in the grocery store. . . . Because I know that

they would send inspectors around to check and see. "Now, you sold so many pounds of sugar. Do you have the stamps to account for that?" and so on.[261]

DiAnna Reif as well was to remember the trading of rationing cards. As she recalled:

> I can remember the rationing . . . with the gasoline and the sugar and that kind of stuff. I remember that because it was always a big topic of conversation when . . . we were getting ready to go to Oshkosh [Wisconsin] or getting ready to leave. But because grandpa [who lived near Oshkosh] didn't have a tractor . . . he still got the rationing stamps [for it]. But in case, you know, we didn't have enough gas stamps to be able to make it to Oshkosh, he used to send us gas stamps. And likewise with sugar.
>
> I can remember mom and grandma . . . coordinating their sugar ration stamps to make sure there was always enough. But, of course, I can remember that going on in the neighborhood as well. You know, neighbors just . . ., if somebody was short of sugar, flower, whatever, you know, they just shared. I can remember that quite well.[262]

Charlotte Mehlbrech also related that when ration coupons were hard to come by for shoes, some parents would actually modify their young children's shoes to get longer use out of them. As she stated concerning these ration coupons:

> We have to take them for the younger ones, they'd outgrow their shoes. And . . . parents would even try to repair their own [children's] shoes. They'd cut off an end of the shoes of the little children at home so the toes could be out. You see, you outgrew your shoes and you didn't have a stamp, maybe.[263]

With silk in demand for parachutes, and being a time before stockings were made of nylon—although many of the ladies interviewed would refer to them as nylons—silk stockings were another hot but hard to find commodity during the war. So much so that women would go out of their way to purchase a pair, and, when new stockings were not available, spend tedious hours mending old pairs. As Josephine Arts remembered, "Us girls was standing in line waiting for a pair of nylons. When we got almost there—that happened to me—when we were almost there they were all gone.... They needed the nylon, I guess, for the parachutes."[264]

One of Charlotte Mehlbrech's vivid childhood memories is that of her mother and stockings. As she recalled:

> [M]y mother, like everyone else, needed a pair of nylons ... and we went to Penney's store and you stood in the line. And each person got one pair to buy. And my mother could see what was going on, so—I was also maybe ten years old—and she said, "Here, you're going to buy a pair of nylons." And people were grumbling. They said, "She don't wear nylons." And my mother said, "Well, she does when she dresses up." And my mother did not lie. She hated liars worse than anything. But that was really a fib because I did not wear nylons. And so she was able to buy two pair that day.[265]

Ges Mintzlaff was to recall that

> if you got a run on your nylon stockings you mended it. You had a little gadget and you mended it stitch by stitch with a magnifying glass.... The instrument [used] had like a little hook latch, and it was real tiny, and you'd mend that run. It might take you five hours to do a run about six inches long, but, I mean, your nylons are so precious.[266]

Ges also remembered that many women, when silk stockings were not available, would actually draw a line on their leg to look like a stocking seam. Unlike today's nylon stockings, silk stockings had a seam. As she recalled:

> In those days it usually ran up the back of your leg, and you do that to pretend you had nylons on, you didn't have any. And we had ... well, I could get lyle, they called it lyle, it

was cotton or something, but you hated to wear them. But when it was cold in the winter you wear them. You know, because they were heavy, thick, and your clothes stuck to 'em. You try to walk and your stocking would hold you back [concerning the stockings made of lyle].[267]

DiAnna Reif also remembered the shortages of silk stockings, as well as the habit of women both mending holed stockings and drawing fake hem lines on their legs for the look of wearing stockings:

I can remember my mother and aunts . . . boy, if they could get those silk stockings they were just in seventh heaven. And if something happened to 'em they would sit for a long time and carefully mend those stockings. And then, of course, those were the days when . . . you needed 'em and you didn't have 'em, so then they used to use like mascara or eye brow pencil to draw lines on the back of their legs.[268]

It was not just the general public that was affected by the rationing. As Joan Laandal, then sixteen years old and attending Waupun High School, remembered about her family's downtown Waupun restaurant, "It was—especially in the restaurant business—it was difficult, you know, especially difficult. . . . We didn't serve any real elaborate things because you couldn't get certain meats, you know." As she continued, "Well, there were some things that were prohibited, you know, because the guy across the street in his home couldn't get something didn't mean we did get it, you know." She also remembered that oils and even coffee were either rationed or just hard to come by.[269]

Joan also recalled other hardships. "No shoes, you know, difficult to get shoes, and rubber, elastics, underwear, or pajamas . . ., you had buttons," she was to state relating that one had to use buttons instead of the normal rubber for elastic bands. "I'm sure it was hard for the mothers to try to figure out how to make food with no sugar or no fat, you know, that kind of thing," she continued. "But . . . [the] whole total effect was to try to help the war effort. It was nationwide. It was unbelievable. I've never experienced anything since them, that feeling and wanting to do our best and help at home."[270]

Concerning rationing, Harriet Whiting recalled that it was seemingly not as much of a problem for farmers than for people in town, "because we had our own meat and eggs, and of course . . . we had a big garden."[271] Jim Laird remembered much the same, that it was a bit easier for those in the small towns than those in the bigger cities. As he stated:

> I remember the adults, you know, talking about cousin so and so in the city needs [ration] stamps. Because, again, in a small town a lot of the things were available—we'd drive out in the country and get a chicken. But people in the city really had to rely upon the rationing thing more, and [many] would send stamps off to their city relatives in order to help them through the hard times. And I don't know, the government must have known. And I guess that they just felt that there was X number of things out there and let 'em do what they want with it. Because . . . people were doing it all over the place.[272]

By early 1942, like many other factories, most, if not all of the nation's auto factories converted over to making war materials, including jeeps, trucks, tanks, and other military vehicles. This caused the cease in new car manufacturing, even the cease in making spare parts for the cars that were already in the hands of the public. Thus, people had to make due with the vehicles they already had, regardless of what money was available, and if cars broke down they sometimes lay idle for months on end until parts could be procured or, in some instances, fabricated from what was laying around. As the owner of an auto garage in Alton, Iowa, Cora DeMunck's father's business was picking up. As she stated, "[Y]ou couldn't buy new cars, so my father was kept busy repairing cars."[273] New tires were also not available. "*Tires*," as Josephine Aarts recalled, "tires were one thing you had to wait for. *Tires.* I remember they would put patch on top of patch. Yeah. If it leaked you'd put a patch on there."[274]

Many of these patches were manufactured by the same factory that was producing the rivets that went into the making of virtually all American produced war planes during the war, Shaler's National Rivet and Manufacturing Company in downtown Waupun. Invented by Clarence A. Shaler, they were called Hot Patches because the rubber patch material was actually heated inside the Hot Patch package, then the heated patch would be applied over the hole in the inner tube. Once the patch cooled, the hole would be repaired.

After first working in the rivet inspection room at the factory, Tillie Dykstra moved on to the hot patch department. As she recalled, the patches consisted of

> a piece of steel, and they were crimped up, and inside that steel there was . . ., it looked like cardboard . . . and then it had some red stripes on it. And . . . the patches were put on that steel, and then inside was the cardboard. And . . . when they lit that, then that would heat the patch and [then it would be placed] on the tire.[275]

Harriet Whiting's family car was one of many that needed tires during the war, but replacement tires were not available in the size the car required, so her father had to improvise. As she related:

> We had an old car, and it had very narrow and not real big diameter wheels. And dad couldn't get tires, so he went to the repair shop and they welded some lugs onto the rim that made them, made the wheel a bigger diameter that he could get tires for. But, you know, you couldn't get much gasoline so we didn't go far. But there were times when he needed to get into town to get things and so on.[276]

To young five year old Jim Laird, the war shortages meant that he could not get the Christmas present he had been asking for. "I didn't get a flashlight," he said, "because I wanted a flashlight and I wanted it bad. And every Christmas I begged for it. But I never got one because batteries were so hard to come by."[277]

At the same time in Germany, eleven-year old AnnaMarie Kretzer and her family were also dealing with rationing. "Of course," she stated:

> we were way more rationed than a little bit of sugar and gas here [comparing Germany's rationing to that in the United States at the time]. Very little meat, and we had little ration cards. Butter—hardly any. But I remember, though, we were not starving as much as those in the city

because we did grow our own vegetables. We had a big cherry orchard, and my mother would say we should be grateful for what we have. And we grew our own potatoes, so we didn't have to count one potato per person, we had a little more. But everything was used, even the cherries that fell from the trees. We picked them off of the ground, they were just bruised. You could cook them up.[278]

Unlike in the United States, however, in Germany, the Nazi government, under Adolf Hitler, was even going as far as confiscating food-stuff. But AnnaMarie's family at times were able to thwart some of this. As she related, "[E]ven though the government estimated the amount in Kilo that we would harvest and had to turn in, there was always more [cherries] than they had guessed, even enough for relatives and friends . . . a few pounds here and there."[279]

AnnaMarie also remembered eating horse meat. As she reported:

We were rationed so much, but every so often if we heard on the radio or saw in the paper the horse butcher in the next town had meat available. That was government checked, I mean, government approved—and it wasn't ground up into dog food. But the store opened at 8:00 [a.m.]. And we were there by 6 o'clock in the morning. My cousin and I would ride the bike [bicycle]—it was the only transportation—ride the bike and we were maybe fifth, sixth in line. If you got there by 8 o'clock, forget it; the line was so long. And if we were there early we got double the meat. Instead of two pounds, you could get four pounds. Mostly roasts. My mother would make sauerbraten with it. It's good, it tastes good.[280]

While both the American and German civilians were getting used to dealing with shortages and rationing, Marine Ed Babler was attempting to get used to being a Japanese held POW in the Philippines. After spending the first six days of his captivity living on a Corregidor beach, working during the days carrying supplies out of the large Malinta Tunnel and huddled together at night attempting to share blankets in the open without shelter, all under the watchful eyes of their Japanese captors,

Ed and his fellow POWs were placed onboard barges for the trek across Manila Bay to Manila. As Ed recalled, "We were not given anything to eat during this period. I imagine the Japs thought that if we couldn't steal enough to eat while we were going in and out of the tunnel carrying the food to the transport, then we could just starve. It was basically every man for himself." So Ed would smuggle out "sugar, raisins, chocolate, or cookies" whenever he could find them for him and his buddies. And smuggle was the word for it. As he wrote, "[I]f a buddy didn't get anything because he was afraid of getting caught and punished by getting the hell beat out of him, we usually insured that he had some food." If someone did get caught smuggling out food, they would indeed get "the hell beat out of him" by the Japanese soldiers.[281]

On that sixth day, Ed and his fellow POWs were placed on barges and towed over to Manila. Once there, they were made to wade ashore in water "a dozen feet deep." As he recalled, "[M]any of the injured men had to be helped ashore. Everyone was soaked by the time we finally got there." Once ashore, the entire group of POWs, injured included, were made to march through the streets of Manila. Although this march was not as long by far as that of the Bataan Death March, in many ways it was just as brutal. The American and Filipinos were hot, thirsty, and exhausted, many not having eaten much in the past few days. Anyone who fell out, attempted to escape, or even showed signs of disrespect towards their captures was quickly beaten, if they were lucky, or summarily shot or bayoneted. As Ed poignantly wrote:

> Each time an American fell to the street, the Japanese guards would yell their familiar *koodo, koodo*, this time meaning get up, get up. If the American didn't rise immediately he was repeatedly clubbed with the butt of a rifle, or worse. Several times during the march I heard the crack of rifle fire and knew another American had been shot and lie dead in the street. I hoped some Filipino would pick up the body and bury it in a marked grave.[282]

Ed recalled that the march lasted about four hours. The Japanese intended it as a demonstration to the Filipino people, and had forcibly herded the Philippine civilians into the streets to witness the great Japanese triumph over the western powers. This, however, backfired.

The Japanese had just invaded the Philippines and killed many of the Philippine people. Therefore, many of the Filipino civilians witnessing this march would risk their own safety in attempts to aid both the Americans and the Filipino soldiers. Although it would prove nearly always deadly for an American to make a run for freedom during this march, many of the Filipino soldiers were able to quickly blend into the crowd with the help of the civilians. Other civilians, regardless of the danger, successfully managed to give water and some food to the passing Americans, some of these citizens being caught and beaten by the Japanese for attempting to do so. According to Ed, "Some of the Filipino civilians jeered us, but more cheered and at times even tried to help us, even though every time one of them tried to give us water they were hit with a rifle butt." As Ed continued in his description of the march:

> Quite a number of men fainted due to the heat, and if a Filipino civilian were near they would douse the man with water. If the man recovered quickly the guard might allow him to continue the march. If the man didn't recover fast enough, he was either bayoneted or shot. The choice of this action or non-action towards the prisoner solely depended upon the guard at hand. Many of the guards were sadistic and enjoyed watching an American beg to live, while others would not kill as quickly.[283]

Eventually the POWs were marched into Bilibid Prison, a civilian prison in Manila now turned into a POW camp. Ed would stay the night there. It was also there that he would be fed by the Japanese for the first time. As such, it would be his first introduction to *Lugao*, a very watery concoction of rice, which would be his mainstay for the remainder of his days of captivity. As Ed related, "*Lugao* was almost like water in that you could drink it." The next day he and others were marched again through the streets of Manila, but this time directly to the outskirts of the city to a train station where they were loaded into cattle cars. As he recalled, "About 2,000 of us were all jammed into the three cattle cars. It really was crowded as hell, so crowded that we had to stand up until we reached the end of the line."[284]

At the small town of Panginay the train stopped and the POWs were offloaded. They were formed up four abreast and marched towards their final destination, the infamous prison camps at Cabanatuan. They marched the remainder of that day, slept along side the road in puddles of water at night, and reached Cabanatuan the next day after another long march. Other than the stop at night, during the march they stopped only to eat a very small portion of *Lugao*. Water was also very scarce. Ed summed up the experience during this trip in writing:

> An individual's performance during peacetime cannot reveal how that person will react when the enemy is in control. Being forced to march until we dropped, beaten with clubs, fists, rifles, or a sheathed bayonet while all the time being provided with only a starvation diet caused loss of weight and strength, all of which made us want to strike back. It was only our better judgment telling us to have patience that kept us from doing so.[285]

The conditions at the Cabanatuan POW camp were horrendous. Diseases caused from lack of nutrition reigned. Dysentery, among others, was prevalent. Ed would experience these very same horrors at the camp, as would Charlotte Mehlbrech's uncle Stanley Sommers who had survived the savagery of the Bataan Death March and was also to spend time in the camps at Cabanatuan. As Ed recalled, "I had never experienced dysentery before and it proved very rough to watch my buddies bend over with the agonizing pain it caused. It was a horrible sight to behold: men unwashed, unshaven, and in pain, crawling towards the latrine but not having enough energy to reach it."[286] The death rate at the camp was one hundred per day—5,000 Americans would die the first six month in Japanese captivity.[287]

At the same time back in Wisconsin, Edward Uecker would spend 1942 in Brandon High School as a freshmen and later a sophomore. During the summer months he continued to work at the canning company driving a truck delivering peas, as well as working for his uncles at their farm not far from Alto. At first, his parents did not want Edward to attend high school but simply work on the family farm. However, one of his aunts had been a teacher for years and was currently a school principle in the county seat of Fond du Lac. As such, she insisted that, as Edward recalled, I go "to high school, and I'm glad. She was a very smart woman, she was."[288]

Edward also recalled that to the kids from the town—Brandon—"we weren't exactly the most welcomed people in high school, you know; farm boys. A little town, you know, some of the town kids thought they were really good, you know, they were hot stuff." But, he noted, when it came to sports, it was a different matter, with the country boys being better at the various games—football, baseball, basketball, etc.—than those living in town. So things sort of evened out.[289]

Edward also related a story about one of his teachers who Edward and his classmates fully believed was shirking his patriotic duty. As he related:

> We had a teacher—here I go, but—we had a teacher; he
> and his brother were twins, and they were [from/attended]
> Whitewater State Teacher's College [in Whitewater,
> Wisconsin] . . . and they weren't flashy. But he was full
> blooded Italian. He didn't want to go to the war. He was
> a good athlete. And if we got to stay home, you know,
> to help with the farm, you know, the farm boys—and
> he [the teacher] used to date the senior girls and all like
> that—but he'd say, "Where were yah, Uecker, yesterday?
> Pitching cow shit?" "Yeah," I said. Finally, you know, we
> [students] got together, got our heads together—oh, a
> whole lot of farm boys—and [we said], "You know when
> he tells us that, you know what we aught to say?" "Pitching
> cow shit sure beats draft dodging." He got red as a beat.
> Oh, that guy was so mad at us, you know. Boy, he was so
> mad at us. A draft dodger, that's what he was.[290]

In 1942, Elmer Rigg was still teaching school in Vandalia, Illinois. As he was to relate, he was, at thirty-six years old, "released from going into service because I was teaching as a teacher." However, some of the younger teachers he taught with were not so lucky with regard to the deferment from the draft. As Elmer reported:

> [W]hen the war broke out . . . we had a teacher in there that
> had been in the tank corps. He got a letter one morning
> asking him if he'd be interested in going back into the
> tank corps. He wrote them or called them or something
> about he was teaching now and wasn't interested in the

tank corps. He got a telegram back the next day [saying],
"Whether you are interested or not, you report to Fort
Knox on such and such a date."[291]

Another teacher, according to Elmer, "came in one morning. He said,
'Well,' he said, 'this will probably be the last time I ever see you.' He said,
'I got to go into the service.'" This later teacher, as Elmer related, was to
be killed on D-Day.[292]

On 6 June, the Navy Department let a second contract with the
Manitowoc Shipbuilding Company for an additional twenty submarines.
The first four of these were to be built the same as the previous ten, the
remaining sixteen would be a new class with a heavier hull and capable of
diving to a deeper depth.[293] Three days earlier, seventeen year old Morris
Page, tired of high school, which he was skipping more and more of
anyway, decided to join the Marine Corps. So on 3 June his father drove
him to the Marine Corps recruiting office. But to Morris's dismay, the
Marines would not take him. As he stated, "I was too light and too small,
and they didn't take me." Although disappointed, he wasn't dismayed.
Next door was the Navy recruiter's office, so in he and his father went. At
age seventeen, the Navy, as did the other services at the time, required
the signature of a parent or guardian. Morris' father agreed and signed
for his son to join, and five days later, on 8 June, Morris went off to navy
boot camp at Naval Station Great Lakes, located on the shores of Lake
Michigan just north of Chicago.[294]

The next month, on 2 July, Arnold Visser received his draft notice.
Within a few days, saying good-by to Grace, his wife of just over six
months, and leaving his truck driving job at Johnson Truck in Waupun
behind, he was off to the Army. By 20 July he was a member of the 95th
Infantry Division at Camp Swift in Texas.[295]

A few days later, on 31 July, Alfred Bohnert and his friend Gerald
Roger Hall went to Milwaukee and enlisted in the Marine Corps. As Al
recalled, "We both passed, so we decided, 'Well that's good.' So they gave
us, what was it?, thirty days to report back. From there we went to San
Diego [California]—*post haste.*"[296]

Alfred's younger brother, Ralph, only seventeen years old in 1942, lied
about his age and joined the Army. Lois, their youngest sister, recalled
that Ralph wanted to go because Al "was going in the Marines, and so
Ralph said, 'I'm going in the Army.' So he went down and enlisted and lied

about his age." Ralph's lying about his age would eventually come back to haunt him when he applied for his Social Security benefits years later upon his retirement. It was to cause some confusion about his correct age.[297]

Lois also recalled that she had a laugh a few weeks after Alfred went into the Marines because "we got a card in the mail that he was supposed to report for or to the Army, you know, or whatever. He was already long gone in the service."[298] In addition to serving their country in time of need, the two boys' going into the service also helped the family. According to Doris, their oldest sister, once the two brothers joined the military they began sending "a good portion of their service pay home, and the family, then, for the first time in many years, began to see the light at the end of the tunnel."[299]

On the same day that Al Bohnert and Gerald Hall were in Milwaukee enlisting in the Marine Corps, Robert Van Alstine was also there being sworn into the Army, and very likely in the same group as Al and Gerald. The twenty-one year old had just recently been drafted from his job at the Snap On Tool Company in Kenosha, Wisconsin. As he stated when asked the question of when he decided to enlist, "I didn't—the government did. I turned twenty-one in ah, let's see, on 5th of July, on the 31st of July they swore me in up in Milwaukee." At the end of the physical he was given a choice of entering the Navy or the Army, but it was a quick choice that he wasn't expecting and had little time to react to. As he recalled:

> [A]ll of a sudden they had—and they had a lot of people there—they said, in this group that I was in—and there probably were forty to fifty naked guys standing there— and they said, "Everybody that wants to be in the Navy take one step forward." Up to that point nothing had been ever mentioned about Army, Navy, or going in or anything. And you had about fifteen, twenty seconds to think. Nobody said if you don't take the step forward what's gonna happen. All that said was, "If you want the Navy . . ."[300]

His father had volunteered for the infantry in the First World War and had fought with the Rainbow Division in France, eventually gaining a field commission to second lieutenant. So, as Robert aptly put it, "Because my dad was in the Army—I am not going out on ships anyway—I stood still, so I ended up in the Army. There was no choice for the Air Force at that time."[301]

Young six year old Bessie Douma, besides harvesting milkweed pods for the use in making kapok lifejackets for the navy, spent her time that summer on the family farm, like many of her fellow neighborhood children, working in the fields. And, since like many farmers of the period, the Douma family did not own a tractor, much of the work was done either by hand or with the help of horses. Therefore, at age six, Bessie would "drive the horses on the farm while my older brothers and sisters picked the corn and threw that on the wagon, because all was done by hand back then," she recalled. "And then at the end of the summer we got paid. My dad would take us to town and he gave us all an ice cream cone, and that was our pay for the summer."[302]

Although of age, Bessie's two oldest brothers were not to serve in the military. As she related, "My oldest brother did not go in the Army. I expect because he had to help on the farm because there was like eleven of us [nine siblings plus her parents] living off the land." She recalled that her mother wrote a letter asking that he could stay at home. It evidently worked. Another of Bessie's brothers was disqualified as 4-F. As Bessie stated:

> There were some hurt feelings during the war because quite often they left the men on the farm. They left them on the farm and they took people from the cities. So there was hard feelings between the two, between the city dwellers and the rural area. And . . . I thought it was because that was their livelihood and so much had to be done by hand back then. But then someone said to me they thought it was done because there had to be enough food sent to the troops, also.[303]

In August, after three months at the Cabanatuan POW camp, Ed Babler was ready for a change. As he recalled, "[J]ust sitting around the camp and, being hungry all the time, thinking of food and water, I soon became bored. I never did like the onion soup and rice they served us either, not that they served us much of it." So when a notice was posted by the Japanese guards promising "good food, good living conditions, and excellent working conditions" for volunteering to go to an airfield to work, Ed took the chance. He and approximately three hundred others were trucked out of Cabanatuan to the piers in Manila, where they were loaded aboard "an old, rusty looking transport." Once onboard, they were crowded into and sealed inside the hot, pitch-dark hold for a trip to the Philippine island of Palawan. But once at sea, the hold door was opened and the POWs were able to access the deck and were treated relatively kindly during their trip to the island.[304]

Once at Palawan, however, conditions soon worsened. Not only were the guards savage to the POWs, but the *promised* good food, good living conditions, and excellent working conditions proved to be more than false. Again they were to live in appalling conditions, eating, as Ed would recall, only *"lugao"* and "soup similar to . . . millet soup but with a different type of weed; a weed too coarse to enjoy," and precious little of either. In addition, the work was grueling. All the work on the airfield had to be done by hand, and this included clearing a forest of trees. As Ed described it:

> Each coconut tree had about a million roots, and the only way to get them out was to dig a trench about six feet away from the trunk to expose them. We would dig this trench about fifteen inches deep all around the entire tree and then chop off most of these exposed roots. The whole process took my partner and me about five days to finish one tree . . . .. The next step was to carry away the rocks and fill in the holes and low spots on the airfield. We had the use of wheelbarrows to help with this.

Ed aptly summed up the progress they made on the airstrip in writing, "I had only been in Palawan several days when I realized that it wasn't hard to comprehend that the Japs were not going to win this war by building airfields with picks and shovels."[305]

The treatment at the camp was the same as that experienced during Ed's stay at Cabanatuan and his marches through Manila and to Cabanatuan. As he recalled:

> The Japanese guards assigned to the work details at Palawan were very tough, especially after several

escapes. Throughout our imprisonment in the Japanese POW camps we were always in threat of being beaten, sometimes for little or no reason at all. In Palawan many of these beatings were administered because a man, hungry, was caught stealing some limes or coconuts.... The usual punishment for stealing limes was a gun butt to the forearms.[306]

Back in the States, in late August, nineteen year old Carl Manthe's uncle wanted him to join the Army. Carl, however, had his sights on the Navy. So, on 27 August he enlisted in the Navy and went off to boot camp at Naval Station Great Lakes, the same location that Morris Page had just completed his navy boot camp earlier that same month.[307] On 1 September, Gladys Jolly, after first enlisting at the first of the year, officially entered the Army. As such, she would be one of the first 1,500 women to join the Army during the war in what would eventually become known as the Women Army Corps (WAC), which would officially replace the WAAC's on 1 July of 1943.[308]

It was also in September that Marine Recruits Alfred Bohnert and Gerald Hull were experiencing Marine Corps basic training at Camp Elliot near San Diego, California. Reality had struck as Al laughingly recalled that "We were both wishing we hadn't gotten into boot camp."[309] Both of them were to be assigned to the 3rd Marine Division. But, as Al related, they were not to serve together in the same units of the Division. "[D]uring boot camp," he explained, "I got blood poisoning in my left elbow. So they sent me to the sickbay for, I don't know, a couple of weeks, I guess, to get rid of it. When I came back out of there everybody that I went through boot camp with was long gone. They were on their way already."[310] Basic training in those days was no picnic for those going through it. According to Lois, Al's sister, he received his injury in boot camp when "a Marine kicked him, you know, when he was rifle shooting, or whatever."[311]

After several unsuccessful attempts to enlist in the Army due to having had Polio as a child, twenty year old Robert Daniels was finally accepted on 19 October and left his job at the Wisconsin State Child Center for the Army. When he left the Child Center, he was informed by the Center, as most employers informed their employees who were to go off to the war, that his job would be waiting for him when he returned.[312]

Also in October, very soon after his nineteen-year old brother, Ewald, was drafted into the Army, seventeen-year old Fred Zurbuchen joined the Army Air Corps. As he recalled his thoughts at the time, "I'm not going to let him [Ewald] fight the war alone, so I'm going to give him a hand on it." However, at age seventeen, he had to have signatures from his parents, who, at first, weren't too happy about doing so. Nonetheless, as he stated, "[A]fter seeing my brother going in, why, I guess they submitted to it."[313]

Enlistment, vice being drafted, had its perks. As Fred recalled, "By enlisting, I had a choice of the branch of service," so he was able to get into the branch of service that he wanted to, the Army Air Corps. He would spend the rest of the year at Jefferson Barracks in Missouri in basic training.[314]

Navy Seaman Second Class Morris Page, upon completion of boot camp, was assigned to the *USS Harry Lee* (APA-10), an attack personnel transport ship. Morris would eventually be promoted to Seaman First Class.[315] Seaman First Class is today equal to a Seaman, Private First Class, Airman First Class, or Lance Corporal, depending upon the branch of service, which is an E-3 and is just below the ranks of a non-commissioned officer. Many Seamen were non-rates, which meant that they did not have a specific military specialty. Morris was of this kind, and, therefore, he would be used by the Navy as they saw fit.

About this same time, Robert Van Alstine found himself at Fort Bragg, North Carolina, going through Army boot camp, and then, as he stated, after "the basic training was over, then they decided that they wanted to send me out to Fort Sill, Oklahoma, for specialized training as a gun mechanic. And I went through that out there for about thirteen weeks." There he would be trained to maintain everything "from pistols to 155 mm Long Toms," a large field gun. This was not all to Robert's liking, however. As he remarked, "I am not a hunter; I don't like guns— never owned a gun. And . . . the field artillery was a scary place to be for me."[316]

Besides many of the American men and some women joining or being drafted into the military, it was not only the humans that were going to war. According to David Lyon, Waupun

> even had a dog participate in World War II. You know, there was a guy named Jockey Guth that used to run Jockey's Bar, which was across [the street] from which is

now the National Bank, which was then the old hotel. And one of his dogs, a dog named Duke, he donated to the war effort. Duke became a Marine Corp Devil Dog in the Pacific. . . . And I remember after the war we used to go down to Jockey's—my mom and dad would go down there because it was a nice family type bar—and I can remember the pictures on the wall. Jockey was really proud that Duke had been able to participate in the war effort.[317]

According to Joan Laandal, the upstairs of the building next to Jockey's Bar housed what she called the armory, where soldiers lived. "They didn't do too much training up there," she said. "[B]ut they slept up there and ate at our place [the *Laandal's Lunch* restaurant-tavern]. I don't know what else they did. Where they were billeted I have no idea.[318] These could certainly have been national guardsmen awaiting deployment, or possibly military liaison personnel for the several manufacturing plants in the area, or even POW camp guards in the later parts of the war.

On the morning of 8 November, across the Atlantic Ocean, *Operation Torch*, the invasion of North Africa by a combined Allied army consisting of American, English, and Free French forces, got under way. Destined to be the first real offensive test for the Americans in the war, this invasion consisted of three task forces: the Western—designated to land in French Morocco; the Center—to land in Oran; and the Eastern—landing in Algiers. General Dwight D. Eisenhower, in his first combat command, was in overall command of the operation.[319]

Prior to this time, Charles Vellema and the 47th Infantry Regiment had been training at Fort Bragg, North Carolina. First, they trained in infantry and half-track tactics, since they were originally to go into battle riding in half-tracks. Then they switched to training for amphibious landings in landing craft, including conducting mock landings off the Chesapeake Bay in the Virginia Beach, Virginia, area. With their training complete, by the end of October, Charles and his regiment were members of a convoy heading for North Africa. According to Charles, the trip took twenty-one days. As he recalled:

I think it was some two hundred ships that was on this flotilla. And this was right in thick of the German submarine warfare that was going on. And . . . like all day long we'd be going into the sun; get up the next morning, then all day long we'd go with the sun behind us. They just did that, they said we zigzagged for twenty-one days so the enemy never was sure where we were gonna end up.

And every now and then they had to shut everything off because they had detected [a] submarine in amongst [us]. . . . We had little ships there smaller than a destroyer. . . . They'd go zigzagging through there, and then everything would stop and they would drop depth charges. Then we would take off again.[320]

Charles' company was part of the invasion's Western Task Force's Southern Attack Group, which came ashore south of Casablanca at Safi in French Morocco. Upon establishing a beachhead and securing Safi, the Southern Attack Group was to push north towards Casablanca. The initial landings occurred in the early morning hours of 8 November.[321]

Safi was a seaport with long piers protected by breakwaters and submarine nets. According to Charles, Navy frogmen were able to clear the nets prior to the actual invasion, then two U.S. destroyers, one containing Charles' L Company and the other containing their sister company, K Company, "went all the way in behind this breakwater. And they [the destroyers] just ran, speeded up and ran us right into the sandy shore. [Then w]e jumped off in front of the destroyer." As Charles continued relating, they were up against the "French Foreign Legion, because France was under German rule at that time, so our enemy was the French Foreign Legion, partly." He added that "we were really fortunate; the Germans had just had maneuvers in that area and they left about a day or so before we got there."[322]

Charles' mission for the assault was to protect the local power plant. As he was to state, "[I]t was kind of dark when we got there. And I don't know how many men I had with me, but that was our mission, was so they wouldn't destroy power."[323] Upon arrival on the beachhead, Charles and his company came upon a tent containing eight or ten Arabs. As he explained:

Well, they didn't know us and we didn't know them. All we had on [for identification] was a U.S. flag sewed onto our clothes, so they knew what that was for. I didn't know whether to shoot 'em or what to do with them. We just sort of went in there, and they mumbled and we mumbled; we just kept them from doing any harm. Then we got them all outside.... [W]e didn't have to fire a shot.[324]

Although Charles and his group of soldiers didn't have to fire at all in the landing, as he related:

[T]here were some fighting further away—we could hear them—where the French Foreign Legion was. But they said what happened; the officers of the French Foreign Legion knew that there was going to be a landing, and they had a big party the night before so most of the soldiers were so drunk they didn't know what was going on that morning.[325]

Since the task force assigned to the Safi landings had only one small escort aircraft carrier assigned to it—the *USS Santee* (CVE 29), capable of carrying only between twenty-five and thirty-two aircraft[326]—and since this aircraft carrier would be designed more for fleet defense than land support, the aircraft carried onboard would have been designated to protect the ships of the landing force more than the landing forces themselves. Therefore, as Charles reported, his commanders told then that "if you hear an airplane, it is not ours because we don't have any, not at that particular time."[327]

It was, and still is today, normal procedures for soldiers to dig fox holes or protective trenches whenever they stop for the night or any extended period of time for cover in case of an attack. However, Charles and his companions did not bother to dig any at Safi since the Arabs had already dug some. But, as Charles related, "the Arabs used that as their restroom or whatever you wanna call it." Nonetheless, trenches, whatever they happened to contain, were present, so Charles and his group did not believe they needed to dig new ones. Therefore, the next morning after the initial assault on Safi when an aircraft did indeed arrive over the battlefield, an Italian bomber, as Charles laughingly related, "We all dove in this. Yeah, what a mess!"[328]

As with most everything in war, not everything went as planned or was as humorous as having to jump into piles of human waste. As Charles continued to explain:

> [T]he plane went right over us. I could see the plane just as clear as it could be. And they dropped the bomb, and my best buddy was killed. He was further back. He was our first sergeant. He was from Fond du Lac. He kind of watched over me before we ever got over there. But then he was killed that day. The shell fragment hit him; and the bombs went off pretty close to us, but close enough that all the shell fragments flew away [from us].[329]

A month later, on 7 December, one year day for day after the attack on Pearl Harbor, nineteen year old Walter Riel and a friend, both realizing they would shortly be called up for the draft, went to Milwaukee and enlisted in the Army Air Corps.[330] During the Second World War, the United States Air Force was still a part of the Army and was known as the Army Air Corps, or, at times, the Army Air Forces. It wasn't until 1947 that the United States Air Force was created as a separate branch of the military.

As Walter recalled, "[W]e decided, well, maybe we'd like to join the Air Force and, 'Yeah, that sure sounds good to me.' So that's when we decided to go. So we went to Milwaukee and enlisted in the Air Force on December 7th and was inducted on the 9th of December." Like one of his brothers, as an employee at the National Rivet and Manufacturing Company, Walter too could have been deferred from the draft, but as he related, "I didn't want to, [I wanted to] fulfill my duty to go."[331]

Early that same month, shortly after the successful landing in Safi, Charles Vellema was picked for a team of trainers. His group, consisting of himself and six other sergeants, were to go to the different American outfits in the area and deliver and instruct the use of the newly developed bazooka. As Charles explained:

> [T]hey said they needed six sergeants. They picked up from [my] regiment, and I happened to be one of them lucky ones. So they loaded six of us with a ton of rocket ammunition and a rocket launcher [the bazooka and its ammunition] in a DC-3 plane . . . we had to demonstrate

how to use the bazooka. They flew us and we stayed overnight. . . . [We l]anded one night on somewhere in the desert. . . . And the next day they landed a little closer [to the front lines], but they never shut the engines off on the plane. We got out and as quick as we could get to the ground the plane was gone.[332]

As Charles recalled, these flights were hazardous due to German fighter aircraft in the area:

When we were flying on the DC-3s we flew through the mountains and valleys between the mountains because they [the Germans] had fighter planes around then, and it was so crooked that a fighter plane couldn't fly straight through there, so we flew below the mountain peaks with the DC-3.[333]

Charles was to spend most of the rest of December delivering bazookas and their ammunition, and instructing the soldiers how to use them. Once this training was completed, an officer said to Charles and the five other sergeants with him, "You got to get on this train. It's an old forty and eight. . . . You stay in this car and eventually it will get you back to your unit."[334]

The condition on the train was quite primitive. As Charles explained, "We didn't have . . . much food. A few K-rations or whatever, and straw in the bottom of the thing. I don't know [recall] what we used for a restroom because it was just a railcar, unless they had one corner or somewheres or something." In continuing, he stated, "I don't know how many days it took us on the train. And it was cold, too. It was in December, and no heat."[335]

The "forty and eight" the officer referred to was to become a mainstay at many American Legion posts. As Charles related, "It means eight mules and [or] forty men can ride in this little box car. Forty and eight [Forty & Eight]. You see that, I think, [now days] when you have some [American] Legion things [going on]."[336]

Christmas night, on the way back from the front to his own outfit, found Charles sleeping on the marble floor of a makeshift Red Cross building in Algiers, Algeria. The next day, upon rejoining his unit, he discovered that they were marching to the front, right back over the same ground that he had just passed. [337]

As the year came to and end, Private First Class Gladys Jolly, again, one of the first 1,500 females to join the U.S. Army during the war, returned home after basic training on a ten-day leave. Of her basic training she was to recall:

> [W]hatever they threw to the boys, they threw it to us. Sometimes we didn't quite make the what-cha-ma-call-it course they put us through. Fell in a puddle a couple of times, fell in the hole a couple of times if you wasn't watching what you were doing. We were trained and trained hard. I think it was trying to . . . what?, separate the sheep from the . . ., I don't know. It's just, you know, we were trained hard. Everything, even on the rifle ranges with the big M-1's [Garand rifle]. The first time I ever had one of those, because they weighed heavy, and I was laying on my stomach, or I don't remember what position, and knocked me flat on my . . . you see, when I pulled the trigger. . . .
>
> We were trained hard because they had to do that because we were in the first fifteen hundred, so they wanted to find out, you know, are they gonna be able to handle and do the job?[338]

About coming home that first time, Gladys stated, "I got off that train at Fond du Lac, I had my uniform [on]. You lived in that uniform. . . . And dad was very proud of me.[339]

1943

The beginning of 1943 saw nineteen year old Walter Riel begin his military training. "My basic training was [in] Atlantic City [New Jersey]," he recalled. "That was an Air Force training camp. Then they sent me to Camp Crowder, Missouri. That was a Signal Corps [school]."[340] It was at Camp Crowder where Walter realized that he was no longer in the Army Air Corps. As he explained, "That's where I said, 'What am I doing here?' Because I enlisted in the Air Force to be a mechanic. They says, 'Quit your bitchin',' and handed me a wrench and a telephone poll. But that's the way it happened at that time, see."[341] Although he tried to get back into the Air Corps, he would have difficulty doing so.

Also entering the military, having recently turned nineteen and receiving his draft notice, was Emil Hopp. After saying goodbye to his job at Shaler's National Rivet and Manufacturing Company, he entered the Army on 27 January. Like the State of Wisconsin had done for Robert Daniels, Shaler's also made the promise to hold Emil's job for him until his return. Emil would then spend the next several months at Camp Howze in Texas in training, after which he was assigned as a medic to A Company, 311 Medical Battalion, which was attached to the 86th Infantry Division.[342]

Gladys Jolly returned to the Army from her leave and would spend the next couple of month in Ames, Iowa, attending transportation training to be a mechanic and a truck driver. As she related about her training:

> I was the second highest in my class of one 115 girls in mechanics. I was a driver. And I knew more about mechanics than I did about pushing a baby buggy around. Like my mother said, "Don't put any good clothes on her. Throw on a dress and send her up by her dad." But my dad was a kind of a guy that taught us. And I loved

mechanics, and I still do to this day. It's really odd. I can fix everything, you know. It's just a natural, see.[343]

In January and February, the 3rd Marine Division moved from San Diego to Auckland, New Zealand. Marine Alfred Bohnert was among those who made the move as a member of the Division's C Battery, 1st Battalion, 12th Regiment, which consisted of 75 mm pack howitzers. As he recalled, it took his transport ship seventeen days to reach New Zealand. Once there his unit underwent additional physical training, including thirty-mile hikes in eight hours while wearing full combat gear.[344]

Concerning the howitzers, Al laughingly stated that "When we first got in there they had wooden wheels. They finally had to take them off and put on the rubber tire ones. Geez, that was a mess."[345] As he was to describe, the pack howitzers "had the pellet, or the bolt, or whatever it was [meaning the shell]. And then we had . . . four powder bags that you could use to propel the pellet, depending on how far you wanted it to go." The further the range to the target, the more powder bags would be used up to a maximum of four per shot.[346]

Even though he was a member of a howitzer company, Al would not normally man the guns. Instead, although he did not attend a school to be one, he ended up being a cook. "[I] didn't need to [go to school]," he explained. "I could cook better than what they had in there. I finally made it up to what they called a field cook, like a sergeant." As he continued:

> When we first went over there, nobody had any idea what was going on then. And some of the guys said, "Geez, I wish I could get some bread. Anybody know how to bake?" At the time, we had a corporal in charge of the kitchen. The sergeant in charge of it—he didn't get shipped the same time we did—he came three, four weeks later. And so the corporal said, "Gees, anybody know how to make bread?" I said, "Yeah, I do, why." He said, "Oh, what do you gotta have?" So I told him. Pretty soon we had some bread made . . . mixed by hand. It was something else.[347]

On 18 February the *USS Peto*, the first of twenty-eight submarines to be built at the Manitowoc Shipbuilding Company, having been towed down the Illinois and Mississippi Rivers to New Orleans, Louisiana, and then proceeding on her own power through the Gulf of Mexico and passing through the Panama Canal, left on her first war-time patrol.[348] February also saw, now a sergeant, Arnold Visser transferred to the 97th Infantry Division at Camp Swift in Texas. As a member of the 97th, Arnold would spend the rest of the year in training, including four months of it in the swamps of Louisiana.[349]

That same month the Battle of Kasserine Pass was fought in the Dorsal Mountains of Tunisia in North Africa. It was to be one of the focal points of the North African Campaign. It also proved to be a disaster for the Allies. Although many of the British involved were seasoned fighters, it was the first major battle for the Americans, and in the case of the Battle of Kasserine Pass, unlike that at Safi, the Allies were up against Rommel's hardened Afrika Korps led by none other than the legendary German Field Marshal Erwin Johannes Eugen Rommel himself. In addition, not only had few of the Americans ever seen any actual combat prior to this battle, many of them were green with little formal training. Added to this, the tanks used by the Americans were greatly inferior to those used by the Germans, both in armor and in the size of the guns they mounted. The German tanks could not only outshoot the Allies' tanks, but the Allied shells could not even pierce the armor of the German tanks. The Allies also had little if any air support compared to the Luftwaffe, the German Air Force, which quickly proved to have nearly total air superiority over the battlefield. Worst of all, many of the green, inexperienced Americans were to flee in near panic in the face of the enemy. If it was not for the British scavenging up a make-shift task force on the flank of the pass giving the Americans time to disengage and regroup at the rear, the disaster would have been even greater. This turned out to be quite the embarrassment for the Americans, which both the British and French would allude to for many months to follow.[350]

Charles Vellema was to see action near this battle site. As he recalled, "We lost one whole battalion to the Germans, must have been just like a mountain pass and then to let them walk into there, and that's the last they ever saw of that bunch of men."[351] Although the celebrated battle itself lasted only from 14 to 17 February, the fighting around the pass was maintained for several weeks afterward. It was during this period that Charles' company manned a position at the pass on what he described as a chalk mountain. "[I]t wasn't stone, it was chalk," he stated.

We tried to dig in that, and finally we did get about deep enough we could lay in. And we were on that for weeks. We could always hear these tanks in the distance. And we had, like wadis we called them, like washouts, only they're quite deep, thirty feet deep, sometimes maybe twenty feet. We saw a lot of American tanks—this was in the Kasserine Pass—where they had fought, and [destroyed] U.S. tanks were down in there.[352]

Charles' unit was plagued by mortar shelling on its chalk mountain position. "[E]very day about four [o'clock] in the afternoon . . . they start dropping mortar shells," he related. "And every day somebody would end up with a mortar shell in beside them. Once in a while a mortar shell wouldn't go off and he'd wake up with a . . . shell lying there beside them."[353]

Charles was also to win the Bronze Star Medal for his valor during this fighting. His unit was assigned to make a sweep around the hill to see if they could get through. "We no more than started to this first wadi, and they just dropped shells galore," he recalled. "And that's when a lot of 'em were killed. . . . And I went back from where we were pinned down, all the way back to where the rest of the company was . . . and reported to the company commander what had happened. That's where I got this Bronze Star was that I went back [through the open area]."[354]

As Charles went on to explain, when he arrived back to were his company commander was, the company personnel were all so hunkered down in their fox holes that no one even saw him coming. "[T]here wasn't a soul stirring," Charles stated, "I could have walked in there and shot the whole works, they were all down tight."[355]

Although Charles was to eventually receive the Bronze Star Medal for his action that day, it wasn't until years later that he would actually receive it. As he reported, "[T]he officer that told me, he says, 'I'm putting you in for a Bronze Star;' well, he was killed that night. So that's why I thought I'd never get the Bronze Star. But then he must have somehow had it written down somewhere, so I got the Bronze Star. So I was pretty lucky."[356]

Robert Daniels was also in North Africa at this time with the Army as an MP (Military Police). Included among his duties was the guarding of German and Italian POWs. As such, he was to make several trips on naval transport ships transporting these POWs from North Africa to the

United States. He would recount that during these trips his guard force consisted of only fifteen to twenty-five MPs, while the POW contingent would be a couple of thousand.[357]

On 20 February, Army Private First Class Robert Van Alstine reported to Camp Gordon, Georgia, for duty as a gun mechanic on tanks in the 654th Tank Destroyer Battalion. However, the guns in the tanks were three inch naval guns equipped with an electric breech, which, since the Army normally did not use such electric breech guns, Robert had not been trained to maintain them and consequently had no idea what to do with them. After looking at the gun and reporting back to his captain, as Robert recalled, the captain said:

> "What do you think?" And I said, "I don't even know what I am looking at." This was after I was out of the [gun mechanic] school about a week, you know. And he [the captain] says, "Well, we can use you anyway." They had asked for a gun mechanic, and I don't know what they expected to get. But . . . [the] Army was so confused at the time that that's how it all worked out.[358]

Since he could not work on the gun in the tank, the unit did not know what to do with him. So for the next eight months Robert was moved around within the battalion. "I was in a tank," he recalled. "I was an anti-aircraft gunner—although we didn't have an anti-aircraft gun—you know, that type of thing." Finally, he was assigned to drive the jeep for his captain.[359]

Earlier in the year, because of the war and the need for service members, the governor of Wisconsin had begun allowing the granting of high school diplomas early to selected high school seniors. As Theron Mickelson recalled:

> [I]n about January of '43 the governor of the State of Wisconsin said that any person that has passing grades would automatically get his diploma—a passing grade at the end of the first semester would automatically get his diploma. Well, I happened to be one of those. So even though I would have graduated in June, I was gone in March.[360]

Having wanted to join the Navy, Theron, now officially a high school graduate, once again approached his father for permission to join. This time Theron's father consented. On 24 March 1943, as a seventeen year old high school graduate, and with his father's approval, Theron entered the Navy. He traveled down to Naval Station Great Lakes for his sixteen-week boot camp as a member of Company 404.[361]

Nova Wagner, like the year before, again would spend 1943 teaching at a rural, one-room schoolhouse outside Alto, Wisconsin; however, in a different schoolhouse. Her new school, unlike her first one not far away, had a telephone, and at this school Nova taught more students than at her first school. "[A]round eighteen," she recalled. "All boys but one. I had one girl." [362] Jeanette Rochon would continue her work in Manitowoc, Wisconsin, at Manitowoc Specialty making twenty millimeter anti-aircraft shells. Still living in Two Rivers, Wisconsin, she and four or five others would take a bus each way for the short two- or three-mile trip south to the factory in Manitowoc.[363]

Upon turning sixteen, Josephine Aarts—she had finished attending the 8th grade, her highest grade she would attend, at Waupun's South Ward School a couple of years before—was able to get a job in Waupun at the Huth and James Shoe Factory. Besides the prison, the Central State Hospital, and the rivet factory, Waupun had two canning companies as well as several small shoe factories, of which Huth and James Shoe Factory, like the Ideal Shoe Factory, was one of. After growing up poor, recalled Josephine, we "thought we was earning big time money now. Enough to go to the theater and go to the big ice cream shop," the later being the Super Big Ice Cream Shop that was a Waupun staple for years.[364]

Charlotte Mehlbrech, now eleven years old and a member of 4-H, would spent time helping collect items for the war effort. As she related, "[P]eople brought old pots and pans, and they'd be pretty old because people hung onto things. . . . But we just had everybody brought [bring] all this metal and rubber and old tires . . . but there wasn't too much of that because people didn't give up hardly anything like that."[365] Joan Laandal, in Waupun's high school at the time, also remembered that they would round up scrap metal for the war effort. As she recalled:

> Well, Herby Northrop, God bless his soul—who lived across the street from the high school, and he was a good looking kid, and he used to sit in the row by the

window in Mr. what's-his-name's history class—and one day out of the blue, Herby stands up and he says, "There goes another load of bullets." And everyone who could see looked out through the upper window. It was a big truckload of scrap metal. And Mr. . . ., *Calhoun*, Mr. Calhoun says, "Good," and then we continued right through the class, you know. . . . Herby just stood bold upright and said, "There goes another load of bullets."

Well, speaking of that, we did go and collect scrap metal. And we used the truck from Kohl's Feed Mill, because Orland Kohl was in my class, and he drove the truck and the rest of the kids were . . ., a bunch of us were in the back. And then we'd go down the street and everybody would yell, "Scrap metal, scrap metal!" And you go house to house and pick up old dish pans or old pots and pans. And that all went on the truck for wherever it went to be made into bullets.[366]

Edward Uecker related a similar tale, but with a somewhat different twist about collecting scrap metal for the war effort *before* the U.S. actually became involved in the war. As he stated:

You know they got started before the war started, then they made a big giant scrap metal drive. We, instead of having school, we'd go and look for the farmers to bring scrap metal. We'd go in gravel pits where they dumped from the canning factory. It smelt like, oh, God!, you know. But scrap metal, scrap metal. We never got a penny for it. We thought it was for the war effort. Then they showed pictures of it that the boys out east had sold car loads and car loads of scrap metal designated for Japan. And that's how we got our scrap metal back. We just couldn't believe it when we seen that. That was all sold to Japan. You know how they brought it back?! . . . [Y]eah, before the war started. We thought it was gonna go, you know, for the Americans because they were gearing up for war then, you know. Then Pearl Harbor; I mean we . . . oh, God, we went and got even more scrap metal [after

Pear Harbor]—old hay rakes. Oh, God, old tractors, old machinery. But that's what we did to start with.[367]

When asked if these items were donated, Joan Laandal quickly replied, "All donated. No, no [meaning yes]. All donated."[368] Although most everything was donated, at times some of the rural schools might receive articles for their assistance. As Harriet Whiting, then six years old, remembered, "It almost seems to me that the rural schools would get baseballs for turning in the milkweed stuff."[369] And, as earlier reported, young Jim Laird had received a free movie ticket for his small wagon load of scrap metal.

Sometime during this period, the *USS Harry Lee* (APA-10), the attack personnel transport ship that Morris Page was stationed onboard, as Morris related, "broke down, and I got put ashore in Virginia Beach [Virginia]. We slept in a tent there, and did odds and ends."[370] It was Camp Bradford which Morris was put ashore and worked at. Camp Bradford is now what is called the Little Creek Amphibious Base, located on the southern shores of the mouth of the Chesapeake Bay in Virginia Beach, Virginia. Originally named after a Confederate Army officer, during World War II Camp Bradford constituted an area approximately half the size of the present day amphibious base and began as a Seabee Training Base. However, on 16 March 1943, it changed its designation to an Amphibious Training Base. As such, over 100,000 troops were trained there between May 1943 and January 1944 in amphibious landings. Attached to this base was also a degaussing facility, which de-magnetized steel ships, making them less prone to attracting and detonating magnetic mines.[371] It was this same base that Charles Vellema had trained at for beach landings the year before.

It was here at Camp Bradford that Morris formally became part of what he called the "Amphibious Force." While there, he assisted in the degaussing of ships and trained on various amphibious landing craft, including and especially the Higgins boats.[372] The Higgins boat was designated a Landing Craft, Vehicle, Personnel (LCVP), and named after its designer Andrew Higgins. As such, it was a small, wooden, flat bowed boat—the bow would drop and be used as a ramp for the disembarking of troops and light vehicles. The Higgins boat was commonly and extensively used throughout the war by the Allies both in the Atlantic and on the many island hopping campaigns of the Pacific Theater to carry combat troops ashore during amphibious landings. According to Morris, "They used to have airplane engines in them. And then they set up for Gray marine diesel, because that was too dangerous, the gasoline ones."[373]

Morris also related that the Higgins boats, although made of wood, "had quarter inch steel on the plates on the side for protection" and two .30 caliber machineguns. The larger landing craft, what Morris referred to as "tank landers," were mounted, as he recalled, with the larger .50 caliber machineguns. The Higgins boats that Morris served on were manned by four crewmembers. As he was to state, "You had four guys on them. You had two machine gunners, the guy that run the ramp, and the guy that steered it." Each of these four crewmembers were also expected to know the others' jobs, because, according to Morris, "You had to do any of 'em. Anyone they called on, why, you did it."[374]

The early part of 1943 also found Marine Ed Babler still suffering through long days clearing trees on the Philippine island of Palawan in upwards of 108 degree weather as a Japanese held POW. By this time, after a full year in captivity, his shoes had given out, so he was working barefoot in the thistle and sharp rock covered jungles. "Darn near every day my feet bled from the sharp and craggy rocks I was constantly stepping on; the guards only laughed and muttered to themselves at my predicament," he wrote. "The underbrush was very thick . . . and in it was plenty of thistle-type weeds." Each time Ed would sit down to pick the thistle heads out of his feet, the guards would yell at him to get back to work. When asked about replacement shoes, according to Ed, the Japanese would only state, "'We get you shoes very soon.'"[375]

The horrid conditions, including the beatings, still continued. The food was still the same watery *lugao* and millet-type soup, and little of either, which forced the prisoners to steal food. "The punishment for stealing coconuts was different [than from stealing limes]," as Ed related. "One of the punishments was being tied to a flagpole in the morning and left in the hot sun until after it went down. . . . [R]egardless of their condition, [they] still had to go back to work on the airfield the next day after their punishment."[376]

After several months of this, Ed came down with Pleurisy, an inflammation of the membranous pleura sacs which line the thoracic cavity, eventually enveloping the lungs. The American military doctor at the POW camp was unable to grant him a non-work pass, so Ed had to still struggle on the airfield project while sick. As a result, one night he almost died, but was uncharacteristically saved by a Japanese doctor that gave him two pills and a can of condensed milk. Then, just as uncharacteristically, the Japanese doctor took Ed off the work detail, assigning him instead to the POW camp to, as Ed was to write, "stand the nightly prisoner-guard duty watching the camp for fires and escaping Americans." This, however, would place Ed in a sort of Catch-22 situation. As he recorded, "Watching for fires I would do, but I wasn't about to prevent any Americans from going over the fence if they thought they could make it through the jungles to freedom." As such, he was called on the carpet by the camp's commanding officer when eight men did make an escape attempt on Ed's watch.[377]

As a result, Ed was taken to the commanding officer's office where he was grilled by the Japanese lieutenant in charge of the camp. As Ed recalled, "[J]ust when it appeared as though I would be shot, the interpreter said, 'Ok, you may go.'" The eight escaped POWs, however, were not so lucky. They were quickly rounded up, brought back to the camp, "and shot . . . in the sight of the rest of us so all could witness the incident," Ed would write. "The camp commander . . . then said the Japanese would not tolerate any escape attempts and that this was to serve as an example of what would happen to any other men who attempted to escape." In addition, soon after this escape attempt, a new regulation was posted in the camp stating that for any one escape, ten other POWs would be immediately executed. As Ed summed it up, "I was very happy that there weren't any more escape attempts during the remaining part of my four-month prisoner-guard duty."[378]

Back in the United States, upon completion of navy boot camp followed by signalman school, Carl Manthe became a signalman onboard a minesweeper stationed in New York Harbor.[379] Likewise, after finishing his Army Signal Corps training, Walter Riel was transferred to the 930th Signal Corps, stationed in Gainesville, Florida. And as he had previously tried, here too he once again attempted to get back into the Army Air Corps. But "Tough!" they said, as Walter was to recall. However, as he related, when his unit went on maneuvers in Eugene, Oregon, "[A] buddy of mine in headquarters says, 'Well,' he says, 'an Army regulation came out that all men that are miss-assigned can be reassigned by request.' So I put in my application and about three weeks later I was transferred to the Air Force. . . . So I was satisfied with all that."[380]

Fred Zurbuchen had better luck with the Army Air Corps. He would spend the year in training to be a member of a flight crew. His first set of courses were at Jefferson Barracks in Missouri where he finished his basic training and took a battery of tests. These tests ensured he would indeed be accepted into the Air Corps [as a member of a flight crew], as well as what specialty he would pursue—aircraft armorer and gunner. As he recalled, "[Y]ou have to recall that at that period the requirements to get into the Air Corps [as a flight crew member] was a minimum of two years college, which I didn't have. But I passed the equivalent test to get into the Air Corps and proceeded from there on." From there he attended the Air Corps Cadet School at Wright Patterson Field outside of Dayton, Ohio, and then transferred to the armament school at Lowery Field near Denver, Colorado. After completing his armament training, he attended gunnery school not far from Las Vegas, Nevada.[381]

On 31 March, upon Leonard Schrank's graduation from college, Ges Mintzlaff and Leonard were married. As Ges remembered about Leonard's accelerated medical training, "They got three, four years of work done in three years." Soon after their marriage the newlyweds moved to Akron, Ohio, where Leonard had been accepted at the Akron City Hospital for his medical internship, the same hospital at which his brother Raymond had served his internship several years earlier. While in his internship, Leonard would continue to receive deferments from the draft. The military still wanted him as a fully qualified MD.[382]

During the year Doris Bohnert continued her work at the Child Center in Sparta, Wisconsin. She lived in the same house that her eight young charges lived in. As she stated, "[W]e got the kids up at 6:30 in the morning, and got 'em dressed and got 'em their breakfast. Then we had to take care of them all day long." Located outside of Sparta was Camp McCoy, an army base. The Sparta City Hall housed a USO for the troops' benefit. For entertainment as well as support for the war effort, Doris and her co-workers would work at this USO and bake cookies for the troops.[383] Ges (Mintzlaff) Schrank also did her part for the war effort. As she stated, "I think everybody did what they could. I knitted scarves for soldiers, I knitted mittens . . . rolled bandages for the Red Cross, and I volunteered as much as I could."[384]

Throughout the United States, Victory Gardens quickly became one of the patriotic things to do to help out with the war effort. The food that was grown in these family gardens was food that would not be required to be grown on farms, therefore, more food could be provided from the farms to feed those fighting the war. The vast majority of Americans were to take pride in growing Victory Gardens, even to the point of placing signs in their yards and gardens stating "Victory Garden." Those in the Waupun, Wisconsin, area were no different. As Charlotte Mehlbrech recalled:

> Everybody was expected to have a garden. Of course, we did anyway. We grew everything that we could, and my mother would can it. We had giant gardens. My dad spaded them by hand, and even though he worked, he'd come home and he'd spade his rows. And we'd have big areas of potatoes, and . . . when we'd dig them we'd have a lot of fun. . . . We would see who would get their sack full first.
>
> You were expected to have a Victory Garden. It was very unusual if you didn't have some kind of a garden.[385]

As Doris Bohnert recalled, even at the Child Center they planted a Victory Garden. "Us girls that worked there went together and had the garden there," she stated. "There was plenty of room, so we had a Victory Garden there." Both the Bohnert and Bal families in Waupun were to maintain Victory Gardens also, although planting gardens for both of these families had always been a way of life. "We just planted everything that you could plant. Canned it all. My mother canned everything," recalled Dorothy Bal. Lois Bohnert echoed this in her statement, "We always had a big garden."[386]

Although the Bohnerts and Bals had Victory Gardens, Joan Laandal's family did not. "No we didn't," Joan related. "'Cause, see, we were in the restaurant business. And I think our Victory Garden came by whoever was selling vegetables pulled by a horse-cart on the street."[387]

By this time, due to the war effort, Shaler's rivet factory had constructed a wire fence around the plant, had guards manning a guard house, and required the employees to wear identification badges for security. When asked if the guards were armed, Lois Bohnert, who had recently graduated from Waupun High School and was now working at the plant in the rivet inspection department, could not recall. As she stated, "You know, I couldn't tell you that. Isn't that funny, I remember the man but I don't remember if he had a gun or not." Josephine Aarts remembered that "anybody who worked [at Shaler's] had their own name tag." She also recalled that "it [the factory] was guarded too, because they were afraid of spies coming in. They had a fence around that plant. There was a little booth like outside, I remember that, where you had to show them your card and . . . that you worked there, that you weren't trying to pull something." Tillie Dykstra also remembered the fence, the guards, and the security badges that all workers had to wear. She also remembered that Jefferson Street, which still runs between buildings of the factory, was also fenced off to keep traffic out of the area.[388]

Joan Laandal, also a recent graduate from Waupun High School, like her classmate Lois Bohnert, had as well found work at the factory. But, unlike Lois, Joan would work in the factory's office where she and others "took orders, rivet orders. And eventually," as she was to state, "I don't know how long it was, but then I was promoted. I think I got 2 cents an hour more from 51 cents to 53 cents. And then I helped on the switchboard and learned the switchboard. And then I was the relief operator there." As Lois was to recall about her job at the factory, first "I started out in the rivets. And then I got into . . ., I didn't like the rivets, working in rivets. I got into hot patches." Their high school classmate, Dorothy Bal, would also find a job soon after graduating, but across the street from Shaler's at the Ideal Shoe Company.[389]

According to Joan, the guards at Shaler's were civilian, one of whom was Frank Trilling, Sr., although she too could also not remember if he was armed. Joan did remember, however, like Josephine, that Frank was "firm about letting you in, though, because that was his duty." As she recalled one day having to "punch in" late, she stated that "I lived a couple of blocks from there and forgot my badge with my picture on it. I knew the guy [Frank Trilling] from kid on—I had to go home and get that badge. I could not get beyond that gate!"[390]

As an office worker in the factory whose original job it was to take orders, when asked if the rivets were shipped by truck or rail—the factory sat adjacent to the local train tracks and just down from the train station—Joan replied, "I have no idea. There was a train access, you know. I have no idea. I'm sure it was all done though. You know, we were all concerned with spies and that sort of thing because it was drilled into you, 'loose lips sink ships,' you know, that kind of thing. And so you didn't talk about any of that, *ever*!"[391]

The National Rivet and Manufacturing Company was a major supplier of rivets for the war effort. As such, as Tillie Dykstra recalled, during periods of the war the factory was run nearly constantly to keep up with the demand. The workers worked in two shifts "every day, seven days a week," she stated. "And I believe then for a while . . . we worked like five days and had the sixth day off and then come back again." She estimated that there were as many as three hundred workers at the plant, and well over one hundred of these were females.[392]

When asked if most of the workers lived in the Waupun area, Tillie replied, "they were from all over, like Kekoskee [Wisconsin, approximately 15 miles east of Waupun] and all over they would come . . . Beaver Dam, Fox Lake, Randolph and all over." The factory ran a brown bus. "[W]e called it the wiener bus," she stated. It was sort of "just like a car but it was long, you know, and it came from Beaver Dam, brought people from there."[393]

Tillie also recalled that the factory employed what were called floor ladies, who would walk "around and just kind of looked to see if anyone was working and so on. If someone spent too much time in the washroom she would get them out. And if we had a problem with a rivet, a question, she would take it and she would go to the foreman and ask him. That's what she'd do." Tillie went on to explain that the men and women would work at separate locations in the factory, with the exception of some men coming and going in the inspection room to deliver batches of rivets for the inspections. She also related that it was the men who actually ran the machines that made both the rivets and the hot patches, with the women mostly working in the inspection and packaging departments.[394]

Like at Shaler's rivet factory, many factories hired women to replace the large volume of young men that had gone off to war. Pabst Brewery in Milwaukee was one of these. However, as Joan Laandal related—who worked for Pabst for a while after the war in the purchasing office and learned of this later—Pabst would not hire any married women, at least not knowingly. "I don't know why," she stated, "Pabst was so insistent on that because there weren't many men to fill any jobs." However, as Joan continued, "I knew a couple of girls that worked for Pabst, and Pabst never knew they were married." Many of these "at the end of the war when their husbands came home, they just quit their jobs because they know [knew] the guys were coming back."[395]

June of that year found Howard Boyle a newly commissioned ensign in the United States Navy. Having already graduated from Holy Cross College, once the war began Howard applied for, was accepted, and attended navy midshipmen school. He graduated in June from the ninth company of the twelfth class of the United States Naval Reserve Midshipmen's School at Columbia University in New York City. From midshipmen school, Ensign Boyle was sent to Melville, Rhode Island, to attend PT boat school.[396]

Around this same timeframe, Ed Babler, along with twenty-one other POWs, was shipped back from the Island of Palawan to Bilibid Prison in the Philippine capital of Manila. As he stated, "On the list of men that were shipped back with me were five with dysentery, four with malaria, eight with broken or injured bones caused by on the job mishaps, and five with broken or injured bones resulting from beatings."[397] Ed was also lucky to be in that group leaving Palawan. A year and a half later, on 14 December 1944, the Japanese were to herd all of the remaining POWs working at the airfield, all of which were Marines, into air raid tunnels, pour gasoline into the tunnels, and light them on fire. Any Marine that tried to escape was bayoneted or shot down by rifle and machinegun fire. Of the 150 Marines in the air raid tunnels, only eleven managed to escape and make their way back to the Allies.[398]

June would also find Army Private First Class Gladys Jolly, after several months of training to become a mechanic and truck driver, assigned to Fort Leonard Wood in Missouri as a truck driver. As she recalled of her experience there:

> [T]hat was the melting pot for the trucks to come in, be repaired, and then be shipped back to another fort. Well, they sent us girls along as drivers. We would take the truck or the vehicle, we called them vehicles, down, leave 'em, and then they'd ship us back by another vehicle that needed to be taken care of. So, actually, we worked both ways.[399]

About the same time, after completing his navy boot camp at Naval Station Great Lakes that summer, Theron Mickelson went straight to the fleet without any additional formal training. As he stated, "Schools? The schools of hard knocks. . . . Well, I was a machinist apprentice before I went in, so, therefore, it gave me an MOMM rating, which was a motor machinist mate." With time of the essence as it was during the war, the Navy simply placed Theron into the rating he had already had training and experience in, and sent him on his way. Like Morris Page before him, Theron was on his way to the Norfolk, Virginia, area, which is literally next door to Virginia Beach where Morris had been. As Theron recalled:

> I left Great Lakes . . . there were, I don't know, about ten or twelve of us that left together to go to Norfolk, Virginia. Well, on the going to Norfolk, Virginia, I think it took us either seven days or nine days to get there. Now, every time a passenger train would meet an oncoming freight train they [the passenger train] had to get off on a side road because at that time that [freight] was more important than these new people coming in.[400]

Once Theron and the rest of his fellow sailors finally arrived in Norfolk after their long train ride, he soon came down with the mumps, which laid him up in the hospital for "five, six days," as he recalled. He also mentioned encountering somewhat of a culture shock in that in Norfolk blacks "were on one side of the street then and white boys were on the other side of the street."[401]

By the time Theron was released from the hospital, all of his buddies he had ridden to Norfolk with on the train from the naval station at Great Lakes had already been shipped out to the numerous ships in port. Like them, however, he also found himself soon assigned to a ship, the *USS Barnegat* (AVP-10), a seaplane tender currently stationed off the east coast of South America. To get there, he was shipped out on a cruise ship converted into a troop transport, the *USS George Washington*. He rode the *George Washington* down to the island of Trinidad in the Caribbean where he and ten others waited for a flight out. After about two weeks all eleven flew on a "PBY-2, I think it was," he stated. "[We] flew from there to . . . a town north of Brazil" for a night's stay.[402] PBY stands for Patrol Bomber (the Y is for Consolidated Aircraft Corporation), and was commonly called a Catalina Flying Boat. As Theron recalled of his short time in this town:

> The captain gave each of us 50 cents so we could get around and eat or drink whatever we wanted to. Then we could take a shower there also. And the thing there was the shower was a room about this big [indicating with his

hands a room approximately fifteen feet square] with half a dozen shower heads on it; no in between. So it was either men or women that were showering.... [H]e [the captain] took us out to eat that night. And in the meantime, somebody from the Shore Patrol come over and wanted to put us up some other place. He [the captain] said, "Hey, these kids are under my command. They're going to do and stay and eat where I tell 'em." Which we did.[403]

The next day they all flew onto Recife, Brazil, where the *Barnegat* was home ported, and waited there for about a month until it arrived back in port. It had taken him about two months since leaving Norfolk to finally arrive onboard his ship. As he recalled, "From there we went all different places" while on the ship in the two and a half or so years he was to be onboard her.[404]

By the middle of 1943 the entire country was on an all out war footing. Personal inconvenience, sacrifice, and hardship were never too extreme for the American people during the war. This included nearly everyone. The United States military alone had risen from less than 500,000 prior to 7 December 1941 to nearly 4.3 million, and this figure would almost double in another half of year.[405] For example, Lois Bohnert stated that a lot of her high school classmates joined the service even before they graduated.[406] But it wasn't just the every day farm boys and small town youths that were joining. Famous baseball stars had joined, to the extent that an all-women's league was begun. Stars like Ted Williams, Joe DiMaggio, Eddie Yost, and Yogi Berra, along with a host of others changed from their baseball uniforms to those of the military.[407] And many of these were not just to sit behind desks in the rear areas, but would fight in the thick of it with the farm and city boys.

Hollywood stars also played their parts. Current big screen names like Eddie Albert, Glen Ford, Robert Montgomery, Ronald Reagan, and Jimmy Stewart, as well as many others that would become stars in the future—Jack Lemmon, Walter Matthau, Tony Curtis, and Lee Marvin, to only name a few—put their careers on hold to join.[408] It was a time when all Americans went to war, and Americans were certainly in the very midst of it.

For instance, July 10th witnessed the beginning of *Operation Husky*, the Allied invasion of Sicily. At 2:30 a.m., Allied airborne units began assaulting several areas of the island. Charles Vellema, having left Bizerte, Tunisia, in a U.S. naval ship, was to spend the night he arrived in the harbor of Palermo, Sicily, onboard the ship. As he related:

> [T]hat night at Palermo we got bombed all night long. I don't know how they missed ... our boat. There was ships burning. Then they had little ..., I can't think of the name of them little ships that laid smoke screens, they tried to keep the fire from showing from up above."

It was most likely destroyer escorts that Charles was recalling. Nonetheless, miraculously, Charles' ship was not hit and he and his unit "went fighting in Sicily."[409]

Navy Seaman First Class Morris Page, now stationed onboard the *USS Thomas Jefferson* (APA-30), an attack personnel transport ship, was assigned to the ship's amphibious forces, specifically the landing craft crew. The *Thomas Jefferson*, like the ship Charles Vellema was on, was also off the coast of Sicily that morning, but on the other side of the island from Charles. After two full weeks of exercises in amphibious landings off the beaches of North Africa, Morris and his fellow Higgins boat crews ferried Allied invasion troops into the city of Scogliotti, on the southern coast of Sicily, during the dark, early hours; Morris piloting his Higgins boat. During this landing, which was to be the first of five major amphibious landings that Morris was to participate in, like the ship that Charles was on, Morris' *Thomas Jefferson* was also attacked by Axis aircraft. In this engagement, two of these planes—an Italian Savoia-Marchetti SM 79 bomber and a German Messerschmitt Bf 110 heavy fighter—were shot down by the ship's 40 mm gun batteries.[410]

Concerning his life onboard the *Thomas Jefferson*, Morris was to laughingly relate:

> [W]e slept in hammocks, but only one guy in [each] hammock. . . . And they had them so close together and they tipped so easy that you'd reach over to grab to stop you and tip guys down just like dominos. Then when you woke up at morning half of them was laying on the floor sleeping.

Morris didn't remember any of his fellow sailors being sea sick on their voyages, but, as he recalled, "A lot of the army guys when we was hauling them, they were sick."[411]

On the other side of the world, once back on Luzon in the Philippines, Japanese held POW Marine Corporal Ed Babler was to spend only a month in Bilibid Prison, which was now, if in name only, a hospital for POWs. He was then sent to McKinley Airfield and to conditions that he would later describe to his wife as reminding him "of a train wreck back in the States where a hundred people had been injured and everything was in an uproar. Our sleeping quarters at the field were in an old barn where hogs, chickens, and horses had been housed prior to us, and the mess from these animals had not been cleaned up." Among other duties at the airfield, Ed was assigned to build bomb shelters for the Japanese, which troubled him. As he related, "It hurt my pride to have to build bomb shelters for the Japs, and I tried not to cooperate too well—but I really had no choice. I can tell you this, though; the bomb shelters weren't constructed to withstand any bombs." [412]

While at McKinley Field, Ed also worked on details offloading cargo ships at the Manila piers. There, he and the other prisoners were able at times to steal scraps of food stuffs from the various cargos. This, however, like at Palawan, was risky. If caught they would be beaten. As Ed retells the story, he was caught more than once and received several beatings. But as an experienced ex-prize fighter prior to the war, these beatings did not have too much of an effect on him. He was to write:

> The fact that three or four guards would take turns slugging me during my many beatings didn't bother me too much. They seemed to get a kick out of taking turns hitting me with their fists and watching me fall in pain. But, in reality, I just rolled with the punches and faked being hurt. I enjoyed watching them laugh thinking they had hurt me.[413]

As Ed struggled in the POW camp and others fought the war, back in Wisconsin farming would go on as normal, much of it to provide food stuffs to those serving in the military. Harriet Whiting's family farm was quite typical of these. As such, she would spend the summer if 1943, as always, helping around the farm outside of Waupun. Unlike many of the local farms, however, the Whiting farm had both electricity and a telephone. As she recalled, it was "the old box on the wall with the hand crank" type of phone. In addition, like many of the telephone customers of the age the Whitings shared their telephone line with as many as eight other families on what was known as a party line. At one time, according to Harriet, they actually had a twelve-family party line. "[E]very ring was coded," she recalled, "so you were suppose to pick up when your ring came. But lots of times if you were snoopy you picked up when other people's ring came. But ours was two long and two short" rings.[414]

Listening in on other people's phone conversations was commonly referred to as "rubbering," as Jim Laird explained. But as Harriet stated, "sometimes that was good, because if you heard a ring come and it sounded, you know, kinda jangled and like someone was really in a hurry, you know there might be trouble. And you could pick up and listen and find out that someone had a fire or someone needed help, and people would gather.[415]

At the time, farming on the Whiting farm was not yet mechanized. Like many of their neighbors, they still used horses to draw their equipment, including their Saukie plow, which, pulled by a four-horse team, contained a seat for the driver and would plow two furrows at a time. They also used "three [horses] on the grain drill, [and] four on the drag," Harriet remembered. These horses were in demand by other farmers as well, even those with tractors. As Harriet related, her father "had many chances to sell his horses, but he needed them for farm work. But there were other people who maybe had a tractor but couldn't get gas for it, couldn't get tires for it, and so they wanted to buy the horses."[416]

Like on all farms in the area, Harriet and her siblings were expected to help out with the chores. "[W]e used to do things like get the cows," she explained.

> My sister and I, being the oldest, got to help first. But as the boys got older and could do more, then we were expected to do more stuff in the house. But we fed the calves, and my sister and I drove the horses during hay time. My sister drove horses on the wagon loading the hay and then I drove the horses on the hay fork unloading the hay.[417]

The Whiting farm was a dairy farm where they grew oats, hay, and corn to feed and bed the cows. The cows would be milked by hand twice a day, and the large milk cans, weighing as much as eighty pounds apiece when filled, in the warm summer months would be placed in the concrete water tank that that cows drank out of to keep the milk cool until the daily milk truck arrived. Not being mechanized as farms are today, although normally the planting and weeding was done by the individual farmer and his family, the surrounding farmers would assist each other during harvest time. As Harriet recalled:

> Each one would bring a team of horses and a wagon. For the grain, the farmer himself would have used his horses and his grain binder and cut the grain and then shocked it up, and then all the farmers would come. And the thrashing machine was usually owned by a group of farmers together. And they were powered by great big old tractors that were very powerful but extremely slow, so they weren't used for harvesting crops, they were just used for power to drive the belt that drove the machine....
>
> And so then . . . each farmer would bring his horses and wagon and they'd go to the fields and pitch the bundles of grain onto the wagon, take them up to the threshing machine and pitch them off into the machine. And then someone would have to man the chute that the grain came out of, and they'd put it in bags and tie the bags up, and then those would go into another wagon to be hauled to the grain bins. And the straw would sometimes be blown into the upper level of the barn or sometimes blown into a big stack out in the farm yard. And that was used to feed [the] cows and horses and so on in the winter, and for the animals to sleep on.[418]

During these harvest meets the wives of the farmers would prepare and supply the workers with food and nourishment throughout the day. As Harriet explained:

> [W]hen it got to be about noon, as a man had his wagon

empty he would tie his horses to the back of his wagon and give them a little grain and some water, and then he would come in the house and—usually they had a bucket outside where they could wash up—and they'd come in and sit down and eat. And as he finished he would get up, go back out, and take his team back out to the field. And so there was always guys coming and going.

Now, my mother usually didn't have to do it all alone because, of course, part of the time not only my grandfather lived with us but my grandmother did. And then one of my aunts, who was on a farm about two miles down the road, would come over and she would help. But they would have all kinds of food besides the meat and the potatoes and vegetables: pies, and cakes, and lots of cookies. And the guys would usually get a lunch mid-morning about 10:00 [o'clock] or so of one of these big granite jars of coffee, and if it was really hot usually a big jar of lemonade. As the guys came up they would get their lunch. And then mid-afternoon they would get sandwiches and cookies.[419]

Besides milk cows and the crops grown to feed and bed them, the family also raised other crops for cash from time to time. During the war, one of these cash crops was hemp. A few miles west of Waupun on State Highway 49 stood a hemp factory. With Philippine Jute, the fiber used to make rope, unavailable due to the Japanese having control of the Philippine Islands, manufacturers soon began to use the fiber from the hemp plant as a substitute. Hemp, being the marijuana plant, was strictly regulated. But farmers could and did receive a federal license to grow the plant, which became a rather lucrative money crop for many of the local farmers, including the Whitings. As Harriet recalled:

You could clear a hundred dollars an acre with hemp, which was big money. And not only that, but there was something about the hemp that killed off the thistles. And I don't know whether if it was because the plants were tall that they shaded the thistles out and they died off or if there was actually some kind of a chemical in the plant itself, but a farmer would grow hemp on a field and then the next year that's where he'd plant his grain, and there would be very few thistles there.[420]

Jim Laird, growing up on the other side of the state, also remembered hemp being produced for the war effort. His grandmother worked in a factory outside of his hometown of Cuba City that processed hemp. As he recalled attending one field trip for school:

> [T]hey took we students out there to see what they were doing in the hemp factory. And there was my grandmother working in that hemp plant. And she would take the hemp, you know, long strands of it, and they had all the things sticking up like nails [large comb like objects], and [he makes a 'swhooff' sound] and pull it across . . . to break up the fibers of the hemp."[421]

Also during this summer, fourteen year old Cora DeMunck traveled to Washington, D.C., on an invitation of Congressman Charles Hoeven to visit his daughter, Cora's best friend, Pauline Hoeven. Cora remembered that "the train was filled with servicemen." She was to stay in Washington for a few weeks before returning home with the Hoeven family to Alton, Iowa.[422] During this same period, rural Wisconsin grade school teacher Nova Wagner, after the school year ended, took a job making army shell casings at the Speed Queen washing machine company in nearby Ripon, Wisconsin, that had, like many other factories throughout the country, converted over to producing war material during the war.[423]

Halfway across the Pacific Ocean, by August, Al Bohnert and the 3rd Marine Division had moved to Guadalcanal where they began intensive training for the planned invasion of Bougainville. As Al related, for the most part, his stay there was quiet and uneventful, since "The organized resistance was over" by the time he arrived. However, "At night," as he was to write, "we had airplane raids, but the night frigate P-38 took care of them. There was one airplane raid [though] where they dropped a bomb about one hundred yards away. Everyone was quickly digging themselves a fox hole" after that.[424]

Across the world in the European Theater, by 17 August the Germans had successfully evacuated not only their troops, but the vast majority of their tanks and vehicles from Sicily and the invading Allies on the island. Having secured Sicily, the next move for the Allies would be the invasion of Italy. Charles Vellema and his unit were assigned as reserves for this next invasion. According to Charles, "We were waiting in Sicily. We were right on the airport in case [we] were needed in Italy. We were right there and everything was ready in an instant, we could get on a plane and fly into Italy." But his services were not to be needed in the Italian campaign, and Charles and his unit were transferred to England to await the anticipated invasion of France.[425]

Morris Page and his Higgins landing craft, however, were needed, and on the morning of 9 September, launching from the *USS Thomas Jefferson*, Morris and his crew of four made several trips to and from the hotly-contested Salerno, Italy, beachhead unloading their cargoes of Allied invasion troops. "Sometimes you went alone," Morris would recall of his various landings, meaning one Higgins boat would go ashore at a time. "We went alone a lot of times. But if you was making [an] invasion you generally circled and went in with a group. But after you got that first invasion, that first landing made, then you went in individually."[426]

In the second week of October, Robert Van Alstine was at home on a short furlough when he received a telegram form his captain telling him to report back immediately to the 654th Tank Destroyer Battalion stationed at Camp Gordon, Georgia. Although he arrived back on a Sunday to find that the outfit was shipping out, he also was informed that he and two others were being transferred to a different unit. However, with the 654th in an almost frantic state trying to pack up to ship out, Robert had difficulty in getting his transfer papers. As a private first class—being very low on the totem pole—his transfer was not very important to the unit's staff at the time. But Robert was not happy in the battalion and wanted out, so using a little fast talking and quick thinking he finally was able to get his and the other two members' transfer papers and get the three of them over to the 45th EVAC (evacuation) Hospital, also located at Camp Gordon. The other two individuals did not know what was going on and were somewhat upset when they found out what Robert had done. As he recalled, once they got over to the EVAC hospital:

> I says, "The 45th doesn't know we are coming, and the tank destroyer unit we were in doesn't know we left. I've got all our papers, so technically I don't think we're in the

Army. I've got everything we need." And, of course, they were pretty disgusted with me. "You idiot!" you know, "What did you do that stuff for?"[427]

Things turned out alright for the three, though. All three had to be interviewed by the EVAC hospital's commanding officer. If he liked them, they stayed; if not, they went back to the tank destroyer battalion. As Robert reported, "Fortunately he wanted all three of us."[428]

The 45th EVAC Hospital in which Robert was to spend the rest of the war in was a 400-bed semi-mobile hospital made up of tents. According to Robert, it consisted of 220 men, including twenty officers and several female nurses. Approximately ninety trucks were required to move the hospital and its staff from one location to another, and it would work in conjunction with two other EVAC hospitals in a leap-frog type of operation with the front line. Two hospitals would be in operation, while the third would be held in reserve. As Robert recalled, most of the personnel in the 45th were from New York and New Jersey, and had known each other before the war.[429]

Robert's job, not being trained in medical procedures or duties, would be as a registrar. While the other four enlisted men and two officers that worked in the unit's registrar office would rotate shifts every couple of weeks—the entire staff, including Robert, all worked twelve-hour shifts—Robert, as the odd man out, did not have anyone to rotate with, so he ended up working only the day shift throughout the war. One of his main duties was to collect and care for the patients' valuables. As Robert stated:

> When they [the patients] came in they used to strip 'em, and then they gave 'em [the soldiers' weapons and valuables] to me because I was one of the few guys in the Army that had any training with a weapon in their unit, you know, they were all medics. And so I took care of collecting the valuables—watches, wallets, whatever— and seeing that they get them back again.[430]

While Robert was finagling his way into the 45th EVAC Hospital, PT Squadron 29 was being commissioned. The squadron, based in Calvi, Corsica, and Legorn, Italy, consisted of PT boats 522 through 563. *PT*

555 of the squadron, commissioned on 26 October, just four days after the squadron itself was commissioned, was an eighty foot Elco class motor torpedo boat build by Electric Launch Company, Ltd. (Elco), at Bayonne, New Jersey. At the time of its commissioning, its armament consisted of four 21" XIII torpedoes in 2 tubes, and one 20 mm and two twin .50 caliber machineguns. It was capable of speeds of up to forty-one knots, and carried a crew of seventeen. *PT 555's* commanding officer was Ensign Howard Boyle, newly graduated from PT boat school in Melville, Rhode Island.[431]

Back in Wisconsin, while the war had been raging these past couple of years, twenty-one year old railroad telegrapher Irving Meyer had been receiving deferments from the draft since his job on the railroad was considered crucial to both the nation and the war effort. However, as a young, fit male he would be nearly constantly asked why he wasn't in the military, especially by mothers who had sons in the war. As he stated, "I also took tickets, you know, at the counter for the train. And . . . I got sick of mothers . . . coming and asking me, 'Aren't you old enough to go into the service.' So after a hundred thousand of those, finally, like a darned fool, [I] volunteered." It was on 30 October that Irving enlisted. He was to go into the Navy. When asked if he had chosen the Navy, he stated, "Well, they more or less chose it for me. Yeah, yeah [laughing]. They go through my records: working on the railroad and telegraphy." So six days after enlisting, Irving was off to navy boot camp and radioman school.[432]

A few days before and a world away, at 6:45 a.m. on 1 November, *Operation Cherryblossom*, the invasion of Bougainville in the Pacific Ocean, began. Leading the way in the initial landings at Empress Augusta Bay was the 3rd Marine Division. Because of the stiff initial resistance by the 40,000 Japanese troops defending the island, after three full days of fighting the perimeter from the beachhead was only an average of 1,500 yards. However, after this initial resistance the advance would become nearly unopposed until the night of 6 November when the Japanese attempted an abortive counter attack against the beachhead. Three other main battles were to ensue—the Piva Trail attack, the Battle of Piva Forks, and the engagement at Hellzapoppin Ridge—before the Marines were relieved by army units.[433]

The Marines in Al Bohnert's 75 mm pack howitzers of C Battery, 1st Battalion, 12th Regiment of the Division saw their share of battles during this campaign. As Al wrote:

Our job was to guard the airfield which was being made
for the planes to land. We were only supposed to be there
for a couple of weeks but nobody came to relieve us. . . .
There was a small island off shore and the Japanese had
long range rifles so we turned the howitzers on them and
shelled the island. Then the infantry went over to the
island and mopped up.[434]

Al added that "The landing on this island was rough. We lost 3 higgins
[*sic*] boats due to big waves." And, although they "didn't have too far
to get to the shore . . . another fellow and I had to carry a trunk filled
with dynamite." As to the amount of enemy troops they encountered, he
wrote, "They thought there weren't very many Japanese on this island but
there were a lot more than they figured."[435]

Although Al was a cook and not a front line soldier, he did see some
action on the island. As he was to write, "At night all the cooks had to
stand out [at guard] post. You had to keep your rifle under your poncho to
keep it dry as it was always raining." In addition, during one of the nightly
air raids a friend of Al's manned a .50 caliber machinegun while Al ran
the pump, which kept the gun cool. "They dropped bombs that started
things on fire," he related, "but we could put it out with sand."[436]

In addition, like his fellow Marines, it wasn't just the Japanese Al
had to battle against on Bougainville. As he explained, "While we were
there we were shaken awake one night by an earthquake. It didn't last
long." Al also stated that "anybody else that's been in a jungle knows the
mosquitoes, and it's wet and miserable." In addition, as he continued,
there were

> Land crabs. They aren't very big, but they sure make some
> funny noises. One day we were laying on the ground and I
> made me a little bed of something and laid on top of that.
> And all of a sudden a land crab came along and got a hold
> of my nose, and I whipped out my knife and pride his
> prongs out of there and throwed him in the next foxhole.

After awhile, as Al would write, "The Army finaly [*sic*] came to relieve us
and we were sent [back] to Guadal Canal [*sic*] for some rest."[437]

That same month, Motor Machinist Mate Theron Mickelson was

getting used to duty on board the seaplane tender *USS Barnegat,* sailing from port to port off the eastern coast of South America, where the crew spent their time tending PBY's and even chasing submarines. Theron reported that the ship at first had a large winch on its stern that was used to lift the planes out of the water for maintenance and repair. But this was soon replaced with a "quad .40 . . ." because the ship was also expected to hunt submarines when not repairing and servicing the PBY's.[438]

The *USS Barnegat* [AVP-10] was the first ship in its class of small seaplane tenders. She was built in 1941 at the Puget Sound Navy Yard in Bremerton, Washington. After serving in Iceland tending seaplanes from May 1942 to June 1943, including spending the November timeframe of 1942 participating in the North African invasion— *Operation Torch,* the same operation that Charles Vellema had participated in at Safi in French Morocco—she was detailed to serve out of the Brazil area.[439]

On 6 November, Robert Daniels' mother was to pass away. Still riding naval transports between the North African and the European Theaters and the Unites States as an Army MP guarding German and sometimes Italian POWs, he was able to obtain a short leave of absence to attend her funeral.[440] In the middle of November, within a month of his reporting to the 45th EVAC Hospital, Robert Van Alstine and the hospital unit were shipped out to England. Once there, according to Robert, they literally took over the small town of Wooten Underedge in the Cotswold. The village of approximately 2,500 people had little space for such a large contingent of troops, so some of the Americans, as Robert was to relate, "lived here and some there and some over the loft in the library, you know, that type of thing. There would be two here and one here and ten here."[441]

The unit also took over a large barrack type of building inside the town, which they used for a mess hall. As Robert recalled, with everyone scattered about the village, there was little way of contacting everyone, so the word was just put out that "'If you want to eat be down at this mess hall building and we'll feed you,' you know. So, it was up to you, get up and go down to this mess hall." The Army also ended up taking over the local theater, barber shop, and bakery, giving the local population free access to these, as well as free bread and baked goods in return. As Robert continued in his explanation, ". . . we took over everything in the town. It was our town. The guys had the girls . . . everything in the town was run by the GI's."[442]

Back in the Pacific, nineteen days after *Operation Cherryblossom* commenced and only a few days of rest on the Island of Guadalcanal for Al Bohnert and his fellow Marines of the 3rd Marine Division, on 20 November the invasion of the Island of Betio, commonly known as the Battle of Tarawa, began. Al Bohnert and most of the 3rd Marine Division sat off shore on their transports as reinforcements for the 2nd Marine Division, which made the initial landings. But as Al related, "[T]hey didn't need us." Al's good friend, Gerald Hull, however, who's father had a little over a year before driven both of them to the Milwaukee recruiting station, was one of those Marines making the landing. Gerald was also one of the 1,300 Marines who were not to survive the battle. Sitting in Al's living room in 2005, Al was to explain, "I ain't sure how he got killed. We heard lots of rumors but that don't amount to much."[443]

Towards the end of the year, Japanese held POW Ed Babler found himself once more moved to another POW camp on the Philippine island of Luzon. His new camp was at what had been the Nielsen Airfield, which was a much larger airfield than McKinley had been. But, although bigger, the Nielsen Field camp was little different from the other POW camps Ed had been in. The food, what little there was of it, was the same watery *lugao*, the work on the field was just as hard, and many of the guards were just as cruel, to the point of being sadistic. By this time, however, Ed could better understand his captures. As he related, "I could tell their temperament by the actions and expressions on their faces, and their temperament told me which ones I could trust and which ones I could not. I found that you had to use a certain amount of psychology with the Japanese guards to get along as well as possible with them because each one had a different personality." It was at this camp, according to Ed, that the POWs began nicknaming some of the guards by their personalities and mannerism: "Mickey Mouse," "The Angel," "The Killer," "*Moto* [Shorty]," "Pistol Pete," "Saki Sam," "The Devil," "The Beast," "The Fox," etc.[444]

Even with Ed's use of psychology, he and his fellow POWs still received beatings. "[E]veryone, sooner or later during our captivity, would be subjected to beatings with clubs or rifle butts. I think it was especially true at Nielsen Field," he wrote. "I was six feet tall, and when it was my turn to be beaten on, five or six of the short Japs would gang up on me and take turns slugging me. I honestly believe they felt proud because they could beat up on a big American Marine." Remembering when he was a boxer, he wrote, "I would have enjoyed taking on these smart little men about two years back when I was in my boxing shape."[445]

Back in Wisconsin, Elva Drews would take time every once in a while to visit her family and friends back home in the Fox Lake area from her job as a government teletype operator in Milwaukee. As she recalled, "[O] f course, there was gas rationing. And you couldn't go where you wanted to go. And I'd have to ride the train from Milwaukee back here. I rode behind the cattle car in the caboose just to get home, you know, to say hi to everybody." During one of these trips she fell in love with a twenty-three year old cheese maker named Arthur Voss. By the end of 1943 they had married and Elva resigned her position to help Arthur make cheese at Weber Dairy, near Brownsville, Wisconsin. Although the war was still on and gasoline was hard to come by, Elva and Arthur were able to go on a short honeymoon. As Elva related, "[W]hen Art and I got married my uncle gave us twenty gallons of gas in the half barrel, and we put that in the trunk of our car and went on a honeymoon. Really! [she smiled]. Now that was against the law too, to share gas with somebody. But he did it.[446]

Like most everything else produced in the United States during the war, much of the cheese Arthur made was rationed, with much of it going to the war effort to help feed the troops. As such, although he was called up twice for service, the first time he was deferred for producing the cheese; the second time, according to Elva, "he came home and said, 'I'm 4-F.' And he went to the doctor and then they told him to get out of the cheese making business because it was so wet and damp. . . . He had a kidney problem."[447]

As Elva recalled her first few years of marriage during the war, she was to state:

> [Y]ou couldn't buy a refrigerator or even an iron. Nothing like that you couldn't buy. Unless somebody gave you a used one, you went without. And it was hard. The hardest thing for me was learning to stretch meat because you had only really only enough [ration] stamps to buy three meals of meat. So you learned how to supplement it with macaroni, spaghetti. I remember making bread stuffing and cutting wieners apart and stuffing them with the bread stuffing just to extend it, because it wasn't enough.[448]

Times at the end of 1943, both at the war front and at the home front, were tough in their own rights. But fighting the war, on both fronts, continued, and enthusiastically. The United States citizens, both in uniform and in civilian clothes, were still firmly behind winning the war, and at all costs, regardless of the personal sacrifices that came with it.

Arnold Visser during WWII (Courtesy of Arnold Visser).

Morris Page and his mother, 1940's (Courtesy of Morris Page).

Doris Bohnert, Dorothy Bal, and Lois Bohnert, 1943 (Courtesy of Lois [Bohnert] Schleicher).

AnnaMarie Kretzer,1945 (Courtesy of AnnaMaire [Kretzer] McLean).

Joseph and Alfred Bohnert, 1942 (Courtesy of Alfred Bohnert).

Josephine Aarts, Emil Hopp, and Angeline Aarts, 1940's (Courtesy of Josephine [Aarts] Hopp).

Emil Hopp, 1940's (Courtesy of Josephine [Aarts] Hopp).

Howard Boyle with captured German Flag, 1940's (Courtesy of Dan Boyle).

War Rations Book Front Cover (Courtesy of Charlotte [Mehlbrech] Hagen).

INSTRUCTIONS

1 This book is valuable. Do not lose it.

2 Each stamp authorizes you to purchase rationed goods in the quantities and at the times designated by the Office of Price Administration. Without the stamps you will be unable to purchase those goods.

3 Detailed instructions concerning the use of the book and the stamps will be issued. Watch for those instructions so that you will know how to use your book and stamps. Your Local War Price and Rationing Board can give you full information.

4 Do not throw this book away when all of the stamps have been used, or when the time for their use has expired. You may be required to present this book when you apply for subsequent books.

Rationing is a vital part of your country's war effort. Any attempt to violate the rules is an effort to deny someone his share and will create hardship and help the enemy.

This book is your Government's assurance of your right to buy your fair share of certain goods made scarce by war. Price ceilings have also been established for your protection. Dealers must post these prices conspicuously. Don't pay more.

Give your whole support to rationing and thereby conserve our vital goods. Be guided by the rule:

"If you don't need it, DON'T BUY IT."

16—32290-1 ☆ U. S. GOVERNMENT PRINTING OFFICE : 1943

War Rations Book Back Cover (Courtesy of Charlotte [Mehlbrech] Hagen).

War Rations Coupons/Stamps (Courtesy of Charlotte [Mehlbrech] Hagen).

War Rations Coins (Author's collection).

German Bronze Medal given to mothers who had up to four children (front view) (Courtesy of AnnaMarie [Kretzer] McLean).

German Bronze Medal given to mothers who had up to four children (back view) (Courtesy of AnnaMarie [Kretzer] McLean).

*Fred Zurbuchen, 1940's
(Courtesy of Fred Zurbuchen).*

*Gladys Jolly, 1940's (Courtesy
of Gladys [Jolly] Hritsko).*

*Robert A. Daniels, 1940's
(Author's family pictures).*

*Tillie Dykstra, 1943 (Courtesy
of Tillie [Dykstra] Brotouski).*

Raymond and Leonard Schrank
(Courtesy of Ges [Mintzlaff] Schrank).

Charlie, Ges, and Robert Schrank
(Courtesy of Ges [Mintzlaff] Schrank).

Edward Uecker during his V-12 training,
1943-44 (Courtesy of Edward Uecker).

Stanley Sommers
(Courtesy of Charlotte
[Mehlbrech] Hagen).

Ed Babler, 1946 (Courtesy of Jeanette [Rochon] Babler).

Jeanette Rochon, 1942 (Courtesy of Jeanette [Rochon] Babler).

Elva Drews in a WAAC uniform (Courtesy of Elva [Drews] Mickelson).

Carl Manthe during World War II (Courtesy of Cora [DeMunck] Manthe).

1944

In January of 1944 Walter Riel came home on a rather rare but short leave, and he and Catherine Vanderwoody were married. Catherine would stay in Randolph, Wisconsin, in her father's home while Walter went back to the Army Air Corps and training, first at Will Roger's Field Air Base in Oklahoma City, Oklahoma, and then at Muskogee, Oklahoma, where he would train for a total of four months before being shipped out to New Zealand and the Pacific Theater of the war.[449]

Like the previous year, in 1944 Nova Wagner would continue to write letters to Charles Vellema, teach at one-room country schools during the school year, and work in factories for the war effort during the summer months when school was not in session. This summer she would spend working in a factory in Milwaukee, Wisconsin, making "the cores for Walkie-Talkies." As she recalled, "That's what I did, was helping make batteries for Walkie-Talkies."[450]

Things would be as tight as ever in the Waupun, Wisconsin, area during the year. Especially spare parts for cars. As Charlotte Mehlbrech remembered, even if you had enough gasoline rationing stamps to fill your car's tank, the car had to be working. Spare parts were still few and far in between. As she recalled, "I know my dad one time had to have his car fixed, and he needed it for work 'cause that was, oh, fifteen miles away, something like that. . . . And then he would have to go walk to town because his car couldn't get the part repaired."[451]

Since before the war, Elmer Rigg had been teaching chemistry and physics at a high school in Vandalia, Illinois, where, as a teacher he was granted a deferment from going into the service. But, in 1944, at age thirty-eight, he gave up his teaching position and moved to Waupun. Once there his teaching deferment came to an end and he had to go to Milwaukee to "get checked out [for the service]. And [when] I got back," as he recalled, "why I got a notice from Dr. Elliot from over at Fox Lake that he was on . . . the selection board, and he said at my age it was more important that I can food than it would be to go carry a rifle."[452] So Elmer took a job as superintendent of the Canned Food Incorporated canning company in Waupun, one of the two canning companies located in the town at the time; the other being the Waupun Canning Company.

Once at the canning company Elmer attempted to grow a Victory Garden. But as he related, it didn't go to well:

> We had a strip down along the canning factory, along the railroad track that came in there, a strip along there that wasn't used. So I had it dug up and plowed up and put a garden in there. And the day before the canning season started, I had one of our guys go out and clean all the weeds out of it. He went out even with a spatula and [when he was finished] there wasn't a weed in the garden. Well, then I couldn't get back to it for a couple of weeks, and I couldn't find the garden. The weeds were so high, I couldn't find anything. So I gave up on gardening.[453]

Elmer also recalled using rationing cards during this period. As he stated, "They were the one thing that kept the canning factory going, 'cause people had these ration cards and they'd go down and they'd want to use them before they were out [expired], you know. They'd go down and buy a can of peas and put it on the shelf someplace."[454]

Jeanette Rochon would also have a change in jobs this year. As she recalled, her job making twenty millimeter anti-aircraft shells at Manitowoc Specialty in Manitowoc, Wisconsin, ended, and she and others were sent "back to Two Rivers [Wisconsin] to work there [once again] at the Aluminum Goods" where they were now "making parts for Grumman aircraft, Navy aircraft." As she related, "[W]e inspected welding, all different kinds of parts. And there were a couple of oil tanks from those planes that were brought in to be replaced. We repaired [them] with our welding."[455]

Dorothy Bal and Lois Bohnert would continue to work also. Although Lois stayed on at the National Rivet and Manufacturing Company in Waupun, Dorothy moved on from the Ideal Shoe Factory to another shoe factory in town, the Tepo Shoe Factory. At this later plant, as Dorothy was to relate, they made army boots.[456]

Although, as Lois related, she did not attend any, a lot of the young ladies would attend dances during this time. However, as Lois stated, "[T]here was very few men around. All that were left was the ones that couldn't go [into the service]." She also recalled that "whenever someone had someone in the service, they had flags you could put in the windows," and that she, herself, wore two buttons indicating that she had brothers serving in the war; one button for her brother Ralph, who was in the Army, and one button for her brother Al, who was in the Marine Corps.[457]

Josephine Aarts was to recall that the Waupun area had already suffered losses in the war. As she explained, "Everybody was talking about the war; there was lot of war talk" and going to parades in Waupun for the mothers who lost sons in the war. "There was different ones from town that did get shot and didn't come back, you know."[458] Joan Laandal also remembered the flags and honoring those killed. As she stated:

> Everybody you knew had somebody in the service. We had ... the little flags in the window, the little flags during the service. If they were killed they were different, a gold star, I think. That's why they said, "Gold Star Mothers." They used to print in the [*Milwaukee*] *Journal* every night the list of the guys that were killed. It was tragic, just tragic.[459]

Jim Laird, who would be only seven years old in 1944, also remembered seeing flags in the windows of many of the homes in his town of Cuba City, Wisconsin, and as he stated:

> [L]ittle by little I began to understand those people had members of their family fighting. And one of them—turned out to be a relative—had a gold star. And when I got old enough [that] it meant something, I started to question. And it turned out that she had three sons that went in the military, and one of them was killed. They got word that he'd died, the next morning the father got up, went downtown, and died of a heart attack. So she lost both of them at that time.[460]

The war would eventually claim twenty-two young men from the local Waupun area.

Joan, like Lois, would also continue to work at the rivet factory. She reported that the work there "got busier because the rivet plant was going full blast and they were hiring lots of women." She also recalled, like Lois had, that "there were no guys around. Our friends were gone, you know. We still had movies on the corner at the Classic Theater, which is torn down now." Joan would remember buying war bonds while attending these movies. As she reported, "[W]hen I was in the movies it was on the screen, 'Buy bonds'.... Even if you paid ten cents you bought something for a bond." She was also to remember that the theater's owner's son, Milton, was one of her high school classmates.[461]

Besides the theater, at least for Joan, for the most part there was not much else to do other than play ball in the summer months on a woman's baseball team, and from time to time do a little shopping with friends. About this entertainment she was to state:

> Well, we had a, like a girl's baseball team that played other baseball teams. There wasn't a lot to do, you know. There just wasn't much to do. There was gas rationing. You couldn't very well go anywhere, you know. Once in a great while you got to go to Fond du Lac [Wisconsin] maybe to shop. But if you did, there would be five other people with you in the car, you know. I mean, you loaded up the cars. I don't recall that we, you know, did anything special.[462]

Shirley Karmann also remembered going to the movies in Waupun, stating, "I do remember many movies we went to that were about wars, planes, soldiers, etc., and to this day I still watch those when available." She also recalled that the town had a youth center in the city hall. "It was a nice place to meet with friends," as she was to state, "and some of the guys who volunteered for the Army would come there when on leave. Our director there was Mr. Giebink, a nice man, and his son was in my high school class of 1948, too."[463]

It was this year that, as a sophomore in Brandon High School, Edward Uecker and several of his fellow classmates were approached to join what was known as the V-12 program, a military sponsored pilot training program. "Victory for Grade 12" as Edward called it. "They had the books, you know, and you had to sign that slip. I didn't really bother, but if you looked real close underneath there it said this constitutes that you are now a member of the US Army Air Force." "Well," as Edward continued, "we thought, you know, you mean they are gonna teach us dumb farm boys how to fly?" So Edward and some of his friends joined up and started ground school along with their normal high school classes.[464]

"You know," Edward stated, "ground school is not the easiest thing. . . . Of course, the manuals were only like that [indicating about one inch thick] and now they are like that [indicating about four inches thick], you know," referring to the differences between the size of the books in 1944 and those of modern days. "[W]e'd have ground school . . . [where] we plotted a trip around the world . . . gas usage, everything else, you know. And . . . that took a lot of our time," he continued to explain. Edward and his classmates also began to actually fly, even in the Wisconsin winters, "[S]now, ice, we flew," he stated. "If it was our day to be there we were there, you know. . . . Of course, I still had work on the farm, too. Lot of work to do."[465]

In relating about his flight instructors, Edward was to state:

> Well, I don't want to use the word misfit, but they were different. Max Segunski, he used to be in Milwaukee then, see. He was a typical . . ., I shouldn't say it—I might as well just pull it—but anyway, you know, he couldn't get along with anybody. Every morning it would be a big argument. . . . And he [Segunski] was a good pilot, you'd see it. A little gung ho, but a good pilot. But he always was mad at somebody or somehow damn thing, you know. And he, Max Segunski . . . afterwards the war he ran the Fond du Lac Airport. And he got fired from there. And he went to Appleton [Wisconsin] and got fired from there [Edward laughed].
>
> Then we had Wells Olsen. One thing of Olsen, he had one arm—a propeller took his right arm off, his right hand off. He always had his hand in his pocket. But he didn't have a false hand. And he was a good pilot. He kind of led the way one year. Him and Max, they got along like cat and dog, but he kinda led the way to us, you know. And then this Wells was . . ., he was an extreme introvert. . . . but he was [Edward saluted], oh boy, cap

just so, you know. He could shave with his pants' creases. He was good, you know, but he would never [look you in the face], he always looked down. He wouldn't even allow his picture being taken. Then, let's see, the other one, I can't think of the other one now.

Oh, then we had a little short fellow. . . . You know that cartoon Yosemite Sam that these kids watch? Well, he was Yosemite Sam's twin brother, only he had a died black mustache. Yeah, this is true this is [Edward smiled]. And hair black and a big hat, yeah! And he had one beautiful double wing airplane, open cockpit, an *open* cockpit! . . . He always said, "This is my family. I don't have any family, fellows. This is my family here," you know [referring to Edward and his fellow flying cadets].

Then he did something, he was always working on a real oiled leather shoe string—and he chewed tobacco by the way [Edward gestured spitting]—and he'd go [gesturing untying and retying a shoe string]. So one day we got real brave and we asked, "What do you do that for?" "Well," he says, "I have a little head trouble, and I went to one of these shrink guys, and he says you're thinking too much about yourself. 'Here,' he says, 'take this,' he said, 'tie it and untie it, concentrate on that, get your mind off yourself'" [Edward laughed]. You couldn't help liking him, though.[466]

Although good pilots, Edward's three flight instructors also seemed to be quite unfit for military service. Nonetheless, they were able to serve their country and the war effort in their own way, regardless. Edward went on to tell about his flight training by stating:

I just got to tell you this story too. You might imagine what took place, you know, with these student pilots. Of course, my radio was always on, and you'd hear, "Number two! Number two, two! Chinese landing, Chinese Landing, *Chinese Landing*!" You know what that means, you know? Oh, you . . ., one wing low. And that wing would touch that strip and [gestures an airplane turning over] break its back.

Well, one day we was up I would say about nine hundred feet, just nine hundred feet, very cloudy. Oh, low clouds, heavy clouds. And we were cruising along. . . . All at once out of the clouds this double winger, so help me, Bob [referring to the author, who was conducting the interview], I could reach over and touch that guy, and that is no lie.

But my uncle, the ex-Marine, said, "Now remember," he said, "if you do something dumb, don't say and do something dumb again and making yourself look bad twice. Be sure you got an answer back for it," you know. If you met my uncle you'd know he meant it. God, some of the guys wet their pants and some of the guys filled their pants, 'cause that's how you could hear after a while when he did that. "Hey Hauser, bring the mop, we need a mop here," and all that, you know.

Then they'd come over and—they always called us cadet—"Cadet what would you do if I was a Jap or German?", you know. And I just could hear my uncle say, "Just don't say something or do something dumb." I thought for a second and said, "Sir, if you were a Jap or a German I'd have something on this plane I could fire back, return fire back to you, sir." And he got kinda quiet, "What a good answer, cadet," he said. But some of them, oh, God. You could imagine what a feeling it is that two airplanes are right, you know, that close [gesturing reaching out and touching another airplane], and he was that close!

We had a guy named there, one fellow, Martin Debone—he talked with a little accent. He made a career in the Air Force, by the way—he said to this Olsen, he said, "What if you were in an airplane and another airplane and you were gonna have a head on collision, and you couldn't do nothing about it?" "Well," he [Olsen] says, "there's two things that I would do. I'd go home and get my brother, he'd never seen two airplanes crash, and

I," he said, "I'd give it full throttle. If you are gonna have one, you might as well have a good one," he said. "Oh, okay," he [Debone] said [Edward laughed].[467]

In continuing telling of his experiences in the V-12 Program, Edward stated:

[O]ne time we were up above the lake, Lake Winnebago, you know, right above the lake. We were cruising along and then BOOM! "What the hell was that?", you know. "Oh," he [the trainer] said, "We just blew a head-gasket." He said, "I think we can coast this thing home." Oh, God! . . . But anyway, he said, "I'm gonna coast this thing home, fella."

We tried it and we made it—just. But it was as [it had] a fixed tail wheel, you know, and we ended up with about a hundred yards of barbed wire hanging on [the wheel] when we were done. I suppose that happens at every training [he laughed].[468]

Although Edward knew the program he was in as Victory for Grade 12, the V-12 Program was actually the V-12 Navy College Training Program. It originated in 1943 to provide college-level training and subsequent commissioning to qualified individuals as Naval and Marine Corps ensigns and second lieutenants. Once the war began, the Navy and Marine Corps quickly foresaw a shortage of college-educated officers to officer their ships, fly their planes, and lead their troops. At the same time, universities, large and small, began seeing emptying classrooms as their students left the schools for the military. To fill these gaps in the military officer ranks and to help stem the various universities' and colleges' fears of economic collapse, the V-12 program was put into effect. It required participants to carry a course load of seventeen credits as well as nine and a half hours of weekly physical fitness training at one of 131 participating college campuses throughout the country. Of the 120,000 personnel selected for this program, 60,000 completed the courses and were commissioned as either Naval or Marine Corps officers.[469]

The Army also had a similar program, called the Army Specialized Training Program (ASTP). It somewhat mirrored the Navy's V-12

Program but centered on engineering, dentistry, medicine, foreign languages, and personnel psychology. In the ASTP program, nearly anyone with a high school diploma between the ages of eighteen and twenty-one could apply as long as they had a high enough Army General Classification Test (AGCT) score. Nearly 140,000 men were enrolled in its highest point. However, less than a year after the program began, with the pending D-Day invasion approaching and the need for manpower on the front lines, on 18 February 1944, it was announced that the program would cease and most of its members would be sent to active units. Very few of its cadets were to actually receive commissions.[470] It was most likely a prelude to one of these programs, which Edward's instructors referred to as the V-12 Program, that Edward and his fellow classmates were being given flight training in high school for.

While Edward was a member of the program, Harold Hansen came back from the war on a rare furlough. As Edward related, Harold was older than Edward and his fellow V-12 cadets,

> but he always treated us . . . like we were brothers really, *really*. And he come home and I believe he had been on twenty-two missions over Germany; he was a B-17 pilot. And he came and talk[ed] to us, you know, and he found out we were on this program. And he was just what you would call one hell of a nice guy. He went back, and on the third mission back he got hit by anti-aircraft fire . . . over Strasbourg [France]. And the rest of the squad[ron] went on, you know, they did. And he went down on the border. They said four of 'em jumped out and three stayed. Harold, he would stay with the ship, he was a pilot, he [died].
>
> His parents went over to Germany after the war to see if they could bring the body back. And, you see, the plane went down on the French border. And it took them a while, but they finally found out where it was. And they [the crew] were buried in a small cemetery of a small Catholic church. The priest was a real frail old man, and he said, "Yes, your son sleeps with us," he said. They went out there and there was a white cross with the dog tags on it. And the grave site had flowers and it looked like they

had manicured it with a shears, which they had. And he [the priest] says, "You've come to take him away, haven't you?" Now, [Fred] Hansen told us this. "Well, yes," [Fred Hansen said]. [To which the priest replied], "Leave him here. Let him sleep with his, the rest of his crew. We consider him [them] sons of our church. The women of the church take care of this. Leave him here." Well, Fred and his wife said it was kind of hard, but yet, you know, they left him there.[471]

Harold Hansen wasn't the only friend Edward would lose in the war. He also lost Marvin Linke, whom he had grown up with. Among other things, they had hunted rabbits and pheasants together. Marvin had also worked for Edward's grandmother and uncles on their farm. When Marvin was drafted Edward's grandmother, as Edward recalled, "just cried and cried and cried when he finally left." As he continued explaining:

I don't guess he wasn't over there . . . he wasn't over in Europe three weeks. And there was a troop train, and they stopped just before you went through a tunnel. I read the letter that his mother got from one of the survivors. It was a massacre. They just slaughtered 'em. And the captain ordered the train to stop; he had the most brass on his collar. They stopped. And, of course, you know how the French are, they called and told the Nazis, and the Nazis called in the Luftwaffe. They came in and they just slaughtered them. They were using armor piercing bullets, this fella said. He found Marv underneath the shot up car. And, of course, he was dead.[472]

Throughout the year Harriet Whiting and Jim Laird, both seven years old, continued to attend their respective schools, Harriet at her rural Waupun District Number Eleven Mapledale School outside of Waupun, and Jim at the only school in Cuba City, located in the southwestern part of Wisconsin. Harriet's father was on the school board for her school, and during those days the board would meet at the different board members' homes, including at times around the Whitings' kitchen table. Her one-room school was already over one hundred years old at the time she was attending it, and, although having electricity, it did not have running water, so the students had to use the outside outhouses as restrooms. There were two of them, one for the boys and one for the girls. As Harriet recalled about attending her grade school, "There was one time when there was only five students. There were other times when there were probably twenty-five, twenty-eight, and one teacher responsible for all of it." She also remembered that "we drew slips every week for responsibilities like sweeping out the toilets, pumping in and carrying in the water. The first years we had a ... coal burning stove, so someone had to carry in the coal, carry out the ashes. And then later on we had an oil burner."[473]

In Cuba City Jim had it a bit different than Harriet was to experience at her rural schoolhouse. He spent his school days in a much larger building that had enough space and teachers for each grade to have its own classroom and its own teacher. In addition, with the exception of those students that were Catholic—who would spend kindergarten at Jim's school and then change to the local Catholic school, only to return to Jim's school for their high school years—Jim would go to school with the same kids from the time he was in kindergarten to the time he graduated from high school. All of these grades, Kindergarten to high school, were all in the same building. The school also had indoor plumbing and central heating, as well as electricity.[474]

Jim's home, however, although inside the town of Cuba City, did not have central heat or indoor plumbing, and one of his duties as a young boy was to maintain the home's heating. As he related:

> [W]e had three soft-coal burners to heat the house, so I basically was responsible for bringing in the coal for those and taking the ashes out after the fire sequences. And, of course, every night the fires went out, so when you got up in the morning the house was always cold and the fires had to be relit. Many is the time when I remember those stoves being red hot and the stovepipes being red. I'm surprised we didn't burn down the house.
>
> But a little bit later on we got a hard coal burner. And with a hard coal burner you put the coal in the top and it would stay lit all night. And I thought I had died and

gone to heaven.... [W]hen I got up in the morning there
would be residual heat in the house.[475]

Jim also related that the use of the outhouse was a challenge during
the cold Wisconsin winter months. They would use the old fashioned
chamber pots, which would then require emptying in the morning. He
also stated that toilet paper "was a luxury that you didn't have much of.
So it was the Sears and the Penny catalog and things that went out to use
in place of [toilet paper]. And," as he continued, "of course, many places
they actually used corncobs. They'd take the corncobs and soak them in
water . . . to soften them up. And then they would go out in the outhouse,
and that is what you'd use to clean up behind you afterward. Nothing
to wash your hands." This was common practice with many during this
timeframe.[476]

Upon completing his residency and after nearly three years of being
deferred from the draft in order to get his medical degree, Leonard
Schrank, now a full-fledged medical doctor, was finally drafted into the
Army as a doctor with the rank of first lieutenant. He was to serve for a
time in Brooke General Hospital in San Antonio, Texas, before being
shipped to the Philippines. As Ges, his wife related, the transport ship
he sailed on to the Philippines had 250 troops onboard, and "they all got
seasick. And he had his hands full, he said." As for whether Leonard also
became seasick himself, Ges lightheartedly replied, "No, he didn't. Well,
I guess he was so busy taking care of others he didn't have time to be sick
himself."[477]

Like Leonard, his older brother, Raymond, also a medical doctor, had
as well been drafted into the Army earlier this same year, also as a first
lieutenant. Raymond would serve in various army hospitals throughout
Europe and, being fluent in German, at times he would be used as an
interpreter when German POWs were interviewed. Prior to entering the
service, Raymond had practiced medicine in Waupun for three years.
Once in the Army and before being sent to Europe, he would spend time
at Carlisle Barracks, Pennsylvania, for training, and then short periods
of time at Lovell General Hospital in Fort Devens, Massachusetts, at an
army dispensary in New York City, and at Fort Dix, New Jersey.[478]

Once Leonard shipped off to the Philippines, Ges and their growing
family of two young sons moved in with her parents back in Grafton,
Wisconsin, where she

took care of my babies, helped my mother and made meals, learned how to cook and bake better than I did when I [had first] left [home]. . . . [M]y recreation was going to another town to bowl. And that was once a week. And we car pooled, and everybody was in one car. . . .

I babysat at night. When my kids were once in bed, then I would go to somebody else's house if they were [going out], . . . Like this one family, he was in the orchestra in Milwaukee, and they would leave by about 8 o'clock. He had a concert or something at 9 o'clock. We lived close to Milwaukee, we were only eighteen miles away.[479]

Ges recalled that while living with her parents in Grafton, like many Americans, they had a large Victory Garden that greatly helped the family remain in food. As she stated:

[O]ur garden was about a half acre. It was behind our house and behind the garage and then all the way to the lumber yards, the shed. And we planted potatoes, and mother had lettuce and celery, radishes, onions. Lots of onions, because, you know, we would put them in bags and hang them in the basement, and they dried. And she raised cabbage, and you could keep those heads in the cooler part of the basement where there was no heat. Carrots we buried in stone jars with sand in, and then the raw carrot was in there and you just dig 'em out as you needed them. Beets we kept. I can't remember any other.

We had Apple trees, we had pear trees, we had plum trees, we had raspberry bushes, gooseberry bushes, currant bushes, and, I mean, I.., oh, I even sold raspberries when we'd get an overload. I put them on a card table out in the front lawn because State Highway 57 went by our house. I could sell those quarts of raspberries in about an hour, you know, the surplus. And what other surplus we had mother canned. We canned pears and peaches and raspberries, cherries. We had a cherry tree, we had the red type of cherries. She would use that for sauce, and plums too we used for sauce.[480]

As Ges also recalled, while Leonard and Raymond were now serving the Army as doctors, their brothers and sisters also contributed to the war effort. But being older than the two doctors, they did their part in the home front:

> I had brother-in-laws, sister-in-laws who worked in Milwaukee in plants that made bullets and supplies for the war effort. Most of Leonard's brothers were doing something in that field, you know, helping with the war effort. And those guys were all older than he was and they were married and had sort of grown children by then, because his oldest brother was 102 years old when he died....
>
> I know that Art's wife worked in Milwaukee, and she was teased that she was Rosie the Riveter. And I'd imagine that is what she did, I don't know. But everybody that could help the war effort did.[481]

With many doctors like Leonard and Raymond serving in the military, it left a shortage of doctors in the United States. For instance, in the Waupun area, although Elmer Rigg had mentioned a Dr. Elliot in the nearby town of Fox Lake, according to Harriet Whiting, "the only doctor that was active in the [Waupun] area, he was actually a German, and he lived in Brandon," was "Dr. Lottenbauch. He had been in the U.S. for a long time. I think he probably came shortly after the First World War. And he must have had tuberculosis of the spine or something because he wore a brace. But he had the very erect military posture, and he walked very stiffly, and he was very, you know, very precise."[482] The shortage of doctors was corroborated by Edward Uecker when he related that

> we didn't have no doctors to speak of, you know, most of the doctors were gone. Yeah, thank God for some of these old registered nurses. There was very few doctors. Probably the closest doctor was [in] Fond Du Lac, you know, and that's quite a bit of drive if you didn't have gasoline or didn't have tires, you know.[483]

About the same time that Leonard Schrank entered the Army as a medical doctor, after finishing his gunnery and other schools to become an aircraft-crewman, Fred Zurbuchen was assigned to a B-17 in the 493rd Bomb Group in Lincoln, Nebraska. Once there and formed into aircrews, the squadron practiced bombing and navigation runs at Biggs Field near El Paso, Texas. Fred's job onboard his B-17 was that of the aircraft's armorer, which consisted of ensuring the aircraft's .50 caliber machineguns were cleaned and re-installed after each mission and their ammunition boxes were properly loaded, arming the aircraft's bombs after the plane was in the air, and operating the ball turret guns.[484]

His duty as the ball turret gunner on a B-17 was that of one of, it if not the most dangerous positions on the entire airplane. The ball turret was basically a Plexiglas bubble sticking out of the bottom of the plane in which the gunner climbed into. Once inside, a small hatch was shut and the turret could then traverse in nearly all directions aiming its twin .50 caliber machineguns, except straight up. However, once in the turret the gunner was, for the most part, trapped. He could only exit through the small hatch, and then only if the turret was in its prescribed resting position. Therefore, if the turret was damaged and could not return to the proper position, the gunner could not exit until the ground crew could extradite him. This situation, of course, would be most hazardous if the plane was shot down—the gunner could not bale out—or if the plane was damaged to the point where it had to make a belly landing without the use of its landing gear. Both of these scenarios were to happen many times during the war. There was also little, if any, protection for the gunner against incoming bullets and flack behind the Plexiglas.

After finishing their bombing and navigation training and practice runs, the bomber group, nicknamed "Helton's Hellcats," after the bomber group's commanding officer, Colonel Elbert Helton, became the last of the famed Eighth Air Force heavy bomber groups to become operational and flew to England by way of Banger, Main; Reykjavik, Iceland; and Valley, Wales. Once in Great Britain, with the first of the Group's planes to land on the airfield on 10 May, they were to occupy the Debach Airfield in Suffolk (designated station 152 Debach) for the rest of the European Theater of the war.[485]

Also in England, at Wooten Underedge in the Cotswold's, Robert Van Alstine and the 45th EVAC Hospital were moving out in preparation for the upcoming D-Day invasion of Europe. As Robert recalled, his superiors informed everyone in the unit not to "tell anyone we are leaving. We are going to pull out of here early in the morning. But don't tell anybody, we don't want anybody to know." However, with many of the men in the unit having girlfriends in the small village, as well as the unit having nearly literally taken over many of the businesses in town, most of the town folk were up and waiting the next morning when the hospital prepared to leave. As Robert was to state, "I don't know, it was two, three in the morning or something like that, and I'm sure everybody in town was standing on the sidewalks." In addition, many of the young women were crying out "'Oh, please don't go,' and 'Take care of your self,' and whatever, you know," he continued. Robert also stated that a few of the men would eventually return to the village after the war and marry some of these same women.[486]

Gladys Jolly, back at Fort Leonard Wood in Missouri, by now a Tech-5 in the Army, continued to drive trucks during the war.[487] At the same base were soldiers training to be army engineers. Some of them, such as Gladys' friend Frances Heavyrunner, a "full blooded Indian," as she reported, would not come back from the war. As she poignantly recalled:

> They were ready to ship. Their equipment and everything was going with them. And he went out the day before—you know, when an Indian gets full of Indian water [she laughed]. They called me out of bed around 11 o'clock at night and told me they had a wild Indian down in the day room. I knew it was Frances, and I went down with him. It was pretty rough! And he said he had a dream that he would not be back. He was killed in Normandy . . . he didn't come back. And this was hard, because we worked with him, you know.[488]

Navy Motor Machinist Mate Theron Mickelson, having made second class petty officer, in 1944 was still serving onboard the seaplane tender *USS Barnegat* off the eastern coast of South America. The ship had or would make port visits up and down the coast of Brazil, stopping in such Brazilian harbors as Belem, Natal, Recife, Fortaleza, Bahia, San Lutz, Reo De Janeiro, and Florianopolis from time to time where they would, as Theron stated, "go in for some reason or another to help them or bring something in," when not servicing their PBY's or hunting submarines themselves. On one occasion, as Theron recalled:

I was an engineman and I was throttle control. And we had two engine rooms on the ship, and I was in the after engine room. And the after engine room is where . . . when we were called to general quarters . . . the engineering officer come down to sit, because he was head of it. And we had another engine room in front of us.

Anyhow, we were traveling along and all of a sudden the captain over the PA system [the ship's Public Announcement system] says, "Submarine!" We had a port bow watch out and a starboard bow watch out. And going along the starboard bow reported, "Torpedo starboard." You should have heard the engineer officer, I thought he was going to climb right through the hole. It seemed like an hour, but about five minutes later the guy says, "Torpedo portside." It went right under us. Well, to find out later why, because they had their depth set for a tin can, or a DE [Destroyer Escort], and we drew three less feet of water. Now that's something, isn't it? Drew three less feet of water.[489]

Theron went on to say that ". . . we did U-boat patrol, we picked up . . ., sunk a couple of U-boats and we picked up U-boats, or people that other U-boats had knocked over."[490] Although it is certainly plausible and very conceivable, as well as likely, that the *Barnegat* picked up survivors of these sinkings as well as survivors of torpedoed ships sunk by the German subs, it was not the *Barnegat* itself that sank the two submarines, but two of the PBY seaplanes the ship serviced that actually sank the subs.[491]

About this same timeframe, young Lambert De Jager was living in Axis occupied Oostrum Holland with his family. His father had been in the Dutch military prior to the war but was now too old to serve. Lambert's older brother, however, was considered of military age, and not wanting to serve in or for the German Army, his brother and others would continually attempt to hide from the Germans, who were always looking for them. Although they "would hide in hay barns and sometimes in threshing machines," as Lambert's future wife would relate, they realized that the Germans could and did thrust their bayonets into the hay, so they felt safer at times to hide in a small building until the Germans moved on. Nonetheless, they were always on the lookout for roving German patrols.[492]

On the early hours of 6 June, *Operation Overlord*, more commonly known as the D-Day landings or the invasion of Europe by the Allied Armies, began. It was this same day that Fred Zurbuchen's 493rd Bomb Group flew its first of 158 bombing missions.[493] At 6:30 a.m., with the USS *Thomas Jefferson* lying in the Bay of Seine off the Normandy Coast, Morris Page and the other crewmembers of the ship's landing craft began transporting their cargoes of invasion troops to the beaches of Normandy. Fortunately, during this operation the ship's landing craft were gratefully to receive little damage with no loss of naval personnel.[494] Morris could not recall exactly which beachhead he piloted his Higgins boat onto, but as he recalled, he steered towards a colored flag that was planted on the beach. "[Y]ou just had a color to go by," he stated, "green beach or red beach or whatever, that had a flag that was flying." He also recalled that unlike his previous two landings in Sicily and Salerno, which were conducted in the dark of early morning, the landings on Normandy were in full daylight. As he related:

> [T]he first two [landings] I was in . . . were made when it was dark. You loaded up those landing craft, and when they got loaded you went out in a circle, and when they had so many boats there, why, we went ashore. All in pitch black. The only thing you could see was . . . [the] Phosphorous [in the water] . . . that was kicked up. . . . Normandy . . . [and] southern France after Normandy . . . Those were in the daylight.[495]

A few days after the initial Normandy landings, the 45th EVAC Hospital went ashore at Omaha Beach in landing craft. As Robert Van Alstine recalled, "They were still shooting, still shelling. They [the Germans] were up about a mile inland. Of course, that's nothing when you are talking big guns, you know." As he also stated when recalling the enormous landing fleet, "You wouldn't believe the number of ships . . . and aircraft and stuff . . . it just blew your mind."[496]

Even with the shelling, Robert's thoughts were elsewhere. "[T]he first thing that I did, stupidly, is I scraped a thing off the windshield of a jeep that had been bombed out before I had even got there for a souvenir—I had to have a souvenir," he was to state. He then made his way up a hill with the rest of his unit to wait the offloading of the hospital equipment. "[O]f course," he recalled, "there were bad storms out in the channel in those days, and the stuff wouldn't get off the ship right away. But you lay around in your sack and twiddle your thumbs waiting for it." Once it arrived, however, they set up shop and began the work of a field hospital. The 45th would eventually move, according to Robert, "somewhere in the neighborhood of about eight or ten times across France," eventually ending up next to the Buchenwald Concentration Camp in Germany.[497]

Sergeant Charles Vellema's 47th Infantry Regiment of the 9th Infantry also participated in the D-Day landings—not the initial landings, but as reserve units. Charles, however, was laid up in England with the mumps and did not take part in the actual landings. Once recuperated, he was flown with several others to St. Lo, France. Soon after arriving in St. Lo, and while waiting for his unit to return from a sortie to Cherbourg, France, Charles was to experience the too often wartime phenomenon of friendly fire. As he related:

> [O]ur planes were bombing the Germans. And they didn't have the means we do today—they'd put markers out. Airplanes would fly in and drop smoke bombs where the bombers should drop the bombs.
>
> Well, that day we had a good strong wind coming in inland, and where they landed me the smoke was going over us and went all the way back to our supply regiment. And they were, our planes were bombing our own men and even getting our headquarters. So I got a good reception.[498]

Once he hooked up again with his own company, they were under the command of General George Patton. As Charles recalled, "There we loaded on tanks, we road on the outside of tanks. And he [Patton] just said, 'With your blood and my guts,' he said, 'we can do anything.' So we did. We went through France. They said we had more German soldiers behind us that we had in front of us. We just cut a swath right through there."[499]

The 17th of June, back in the United States, saw Irving Meyer graduating from his navy radioman school at Farragut, Idaho, where he had learned both the use of radios and the International Code, which, as he stated, was "a bit different than the Morse" Code which he had been previously proficient at while working as a telegrapher with the Milwaukee Railroad back in Wisconsin. Normally he would have been given some leave upon graduating from his school, but with the pressures of the war he and some of his fellow classmates were immediately shipped off to Treasure Island, California, where they would spent the next three months receiving bills of ladings.[500]

At the same time, back in Wisconsin, Edward Uecker, although working hard at becoming a pilot and soon to be both seventeen years old and a senior at Brandon High School, was one of the V-12 and ASTP members that would never receive his commission. With the war in Europe being in full swing, and consequently more and more young men being needed at the front, the Army, as Edward stated, was "taking seventeen year olds then."[501] However, Edward's German descent would come into play. He had already taken his military physical when, as he recalled:

[O]ne night one of the members of the draft board came to our house. See, we stayed at home during this V-12 thing. We went to school just like it was part of civilian government or some name they had. And he [the draft board member] said, "Say, you know," he said, "all the rest, the majority of them on that V-12 Program there are going to have to report," he says. "[General George] Patton wants some bodies. But," he said, "we are trying to keep this a low tone not to meet a lot of rejection, but we expect at least three hundred of Erwin Rommel's Afrika Korps at Lawsonia as a prisoner of war camp. Now," he said, "you can speak German, you were born and raised to speak German, you know the Fairwater [Wisconsin] area, the farmers. That's what you'll be doing, hauling peas and working in the corn."

He said, "Why don't you take that?" [I said,] "Well, okay." Well, that sounded kind of interesting, you know, so I did. And that's what I did for two years. The first bunch [of prisoners] were about 500 of Erwin Rommel's Afrika Korps. They were tankers and they were support

units for tanks. They were the cream of the crop, boy, I'll
tell yah, they . . ., they were soldiers' soldiers.[502]

So, no longer a member of the V-12 Program, Edward found himself
working at the Lawsonia POW camp. Lawsonia was a large private
estate located just west of the town of Green Lake, Wisconsin, which is
approximately eight miles northwest of Fairwater, the later close to where
Edward lived on his family's farm.[503] It is the same compound that Gladys
Jolly was born on and that her parents had been employed at. Today
Lawsonia houses the Green Lake Baptist Assembly.

Although Edward remembered around 500 German POWs in the
first batch at the camp, the first group actually consisted of 250, arriving
on 19 June 1944 by train to work in the local canning factory processing
peas. Once the pea season was over, these same 250 POW's boarded
another special North Western Railroad train for their trip to Michigan.
A couple of months later the camp was enlarged to hold 600 POWs,
who stayed until early October to work the sweet corn. The camp was
permanently closed upon their departure in October.[504]

July would find Charles Vellema crossing the Meuse River after
fighting his way through France and Belgium. As he remembered:

> We had lots of skirmishes there . . . when we'd go through
> these towns they had an American flag and a German
> flag, so when the Germans were in town or went through
> town they're all waving [the German flags], then the
> Americans come through they were all out waving the
> Americans flags.[505]

Charles would be wounded soon after crossing the Meuse River. "We
crossed the river in a boat," he stated, "and then up to some higher ground,
and there was some trees. Whether the shell hit the trees or it was time set
to go off in the air or what, I don't know." Charles and four or five others
had just finished digging fox holes and were sitting down resting when the
shell hit. "[T]hey were all killed except me," he related. "My best buddy
died there."[506]

According to Charles, the shell was fi red from the Siegfried Line,
whose "Big shells . . . could reach us then."[507] Built on Hitler's orders

during the 1930's opposite the French Maginot Line, the Siegfried Line, also known as the West Wall, like its more famous opposite, was a stationary fortress that contained more than 18,000 bunkers, tank traps, and tunnels, and stretched nearly 400 miles between Germany and France.[508]

Although wounded by bomb shrapnel in his ankle and side, Charles assisted two others back across the Meuse River to an aid station, one under each of his arms. After being operated on, he recalled spending "two or three weeks, I guess, in the hospital" until being shipped back to England for recuperation.[509]

About the middle of 1944, after two and a half years as a POW and with the work on Nielsen Field in the Philippines complete to where heavy equipment was needed, Marine Ed Babler was again transferred to a new Japanese POW camp on the island of Luzon at yet another ex-military airfield, Zablan Field. It was at this field that Ed would be injured, falling and cutting his leg. The camp's American doctor had to operate on Ed's infected leg no less than three times, all with only, as Ed recalled, "a scalpel, gauze, tape, cotton, and some disinfectant," and without anything to relieve the pain, either during or after each operation. As he was to write, "The third operation went just like the first two—hurting like hell! The men again did a hell of a job holding me down." This third time, however, the doctor was able to get all of the infection out, and in a couple of weeks, Ed was up and walking around again.[510]

Like at the other camps, life was hard for the POWs at the Zablan Field camp—little and under nourishing food, sadistic guards, little if any medicine for those suffering from dysentery and other ailments. As Ed related, "The men were losing weight at a rapid rate due to the unbalanced and insufficient diet. Everyone walked around the camp looking like skeletons. Damn near every man had ulcers on his legs and abrasions on his skin that became ugly, festered sores; there were no medicines to help."[511]

Around the same time, in the United States at Fort Leonard Wood, Missouri, Army Sergeant Arnold Visser was approached and offered the opportunity to attend Officer Candidate School (OCS). He started OCS at Fort Benning, Georgia, on 6 July. Up to this time, Grace, his wife, had been able to accompany him to his various posts throughout his training, since he was normally able to leave the bases most nights to be with her. For instance, while at Camp Swift near Austin, Texas, even as a private, he would nearly always be given time off in the evenings, since, having a 1940 convertible—any type of car being a rarity on a military installation at the time—the officers always wanted to ride with him to Austin rather than having to take one of the base busses.[512] July was also to see Robert Daniels transferring from the MPs to the Army Medical Corps, and, like Emil Hopp before him, train to become a medic.[513]

Back in the European Theater, on his way to England to recuperate from his shrapnel wounds, Sergeant Charles Vellema and a few other wounded American soldiers would find themselves mistaken as German wounded. As Charles lightheartedly retold the story:

> When we got to Fabroche Hospital outside of Paris, France, there was hundreds of ambulances on this airport waiting. They were all in different lines, and we were all stretcher cases in this particular ambulance that I was in. We saw that ambulances on one side of us were moving and we saw them [moving] on the other side. We didn't have a driver in ours so we were just sitting there. And after a while somebody opens up the back of the ambulance and says, "*Sprechen sie Deutsch?*" he says. Here we were in . . . [he laughs], the dumb driver had left us in the row for the Germans because we didn't have any clothing on—I just had an army blanket around me—we didn't have any clothes on or any identification of any kind. But then somehow we got back to England.[514]

Later that month, early on the morning of 21 July, after nearly two weeks of naval bombardment, the 3rd Marine Division went ashore at Guam in the Pacific to find a "Welcome Marines" sign left by the Navy underwater demolition teams that preceded them. Five miles down the beach the Army's 77th Infantry Division also came ashore. Although the sign indicated that the Navy divers had done their job of clearing underwater obstacles, Buck Sergeant Al Bohnert and his fellow Marines, as well as the soldiers of the 77th Infantry Division, had their work cut out for them. It wasn't until 11 August, when Japanese Major General Toshiro Obata led a final last ditch suicidal *Banzai* charge in which he and 3,000 of his own troops and 1,500 Americans were killed, before organized resistance on the island was put down. Even then, pockets of resistance continued until the end of the war, with the last Japanese soldier not surrendering until twenty-seven years later in 1972.[515]

As Al was to write of his time on Guam, it was no picnic. "We had to cross over a coral reef; we used 'ducks' to propel over," he wrote. "When we reached the beach we were shot at by the Japanese." During the various landings that he was to make during the war, he would end up having to go back to the beachhead to bring up supplies. "Every time we went on some damn invasion," he stated, "then I'd get stuck on going down to the beach and bringing stuff up for our company. Everybody else was afraid to go down to the beach, I guess, because that wasn't too good a place." The Guam beachhead was to be no different; for that matter, it was an especially dangerous beachhead. As Al was to write explaining:

> I had to help bring all our equipment on shore. There were lots of holes from the navy shelling. So we crowded in one of them for the night. In the morning we crossed the road just as a mortar hit the hole we just left. I [had] returned to the beach to retrieve the equipment. The Navy had sent in hot coffee and boiled eggs for a snack. We were told [to] have just 2 or 3 guys sit together at a time. While we were there 3 fellows were sitting on a log when a mortar hit killing one and injuring the other two. Myself and another guy were standing just a little bit away and [I] had shrapnel go through my jacket. I wasn't injured, but could feel the heat from the metal.[516]

Nor was the beachhead the only dangerous place on the island. During the ensuing battle Al was to have several other close calls. As he wrote, "One morning I was shaving and using a stainless steel mirror. After I was done I bent over to wash my face and a bullet hit the mirror. We never found the sniper." As he continued, "The Japanese were dug into a 500 ft. hill, very well camophalged [*sic*]. To get to the top of the hill you had to wind your way up what used to be a road. It was a red clay and very slippery when wet. It was almost impossible to see them."[517]

And like at Bougainville, while on Guam Al and the rest of the cooks had to stand guard duty at night. In recalling this experience, he was to write, "[W]e were out on post duty 50 yards ahead. We were at the edge of a corn field and all at once we heard rustling. We asked for the password and all we heard was Japanese. We let them have a few hand grenades. In the morning all we saw was trampled corn."[518]

Back in the United States, Navy Signalman Carl Manthe, serving onboard his minesweeper in New York Harbor, was to witness a sister ship blown out of the water by a German mine. His ship, as he reported to his wife after the war, successfully cleared several other mines from the harbor. But as he also reported to his wife, one mine exploded so close to his ship that "the blast knocked a number of them [sailors] off the deck into the water."[519]

Of this timeframe, fifteen year old Cora DeMunck's memories were that of her family "getting letters from my brothers, and my mother sitting around the table reading those letters from their experiences and what they were doing in the war. And also reading letters from people that knew my brothers and who'd write my parents what nice people they were."[520]

At the Lawsonia POW camp near Green Lake, Wisconsin, young Edward Uecker had by now begun escorting the German prisoners from the camp to and from the canning company and various farmers' fields, as the draft board had recruited him to do. As Edward stated, the POWs would "pick corn, sweet corn, by hand of course, and they worked in the canning factory, worked and hauled peas. See, . . . as a farm boy I know where everyone works and lives [in the area], you know. That's the help [the draft board wanted me to do]. And the trucks were furnished mostly for hauling peas by Alex Lapier, he had a Chevy garage there" in Green Lake.[521] Edward wasn't formally a member of the military while he worked at the camp, but he did wear a kind of uniform, or as he related, "I guess you could call that a uniform. The only good thing, I had a combat jacket that wore like iron, *that* was new. But the rest . . . well, I had dungaree pants, but they all had been used, you know, and they'd all been re-done . . . some had grease on them, they had been cleaned but, but that's all."[522]

As for pay, Edward stated that he was paid while working at the POW camp through the canning factory, but when in the V-12 program he was "Never paid a cent for it." However, "rightly," as he stated, "we were [considered to be] in the service" then, although all of the records of it had been destroyed.[523] Apparently, all of the official records of his V-12 program involvement had been mistakenly destroyed by the government.

In referring to the American officers he encountered at the POW camp, Edward related:

> We had a few officers that should have been burnt. The first one, oh, he was terrible! I don't know, I think he was on pills or drugs or something. I don't think he ever slept.
>
> [We] Saved him from being killed one morning. Went into the mess hall and he—you always have a bunch of guys waiting on the tables, German prisoners—and you can see he was in kind of bad shape, so they [the POWs] dumped all his food and left his plate [Edward laughed]. And he went after the guy with a metal frying pan, a big frying pan. But the German got it away from him and was beating him over the head when we took it away from him [the German], or he would have killed him [the American officer], for Pete's sake!
>
> But they transferred him out, and then the next guy that came in, he was all business, boy. One meal a day; at noon.... No sweets. The only sweets that were there were the ones that probably the churches brought in, like that, you know. We couldn't eat those, they were just for the prisoners of war. "You got plenty to eat," [they'd say].[524]

Concerning the enlisted guards at the camp Edward related that

> we didn't have the best ones, I'm afraid. That's why they made us truck drivers guard too. Carried M-1s.
>
> They [the guards] were from all over . . . some were good . . . a lot of them were always involved with the women there. In Ripon [Wisconsin], Ripon College, Ripon. Some were drinkers, you know, heavy drinkers. We got them here though, they hadn't been in the quartermaster [hadn't had much training] and they'd look at the rifle and he'd say, "How do you shoot this gun?" [Edward laughed]. That's where I was lucky, I had hunted since I was what?, eight, ten years old, you know.

My uncle the Marine was expert, he had medals hanging on his chest for sharp shooting.

But they weren't the top. I meant, they weren't top grade. . . . Although, I met some goods ones. I met some that were good. But I met some that weren't.[525]

According to Edward, the local Wisconsin people took to the prisoners in different ways. As he explained:

Some were very receptive and some just the *opposite*! Boy, I'll tell yah, I was all but afraid. . . . You know, big hunting country, they all hunted deer, they all owned guns, rifles. Now we . . . would ride with the guys [POWs] in their trucks, you know. So all they [the farmers] had to do was sit up in a hay mound and fire in our direction, you know what I mean? A lot of them [the local farmers] had sons [in the war], some that didn't come back. One family I know where we went [had] two sons that were shot down and killed over Germany. And I thought, boy, I thought about that so often . . ., I thought about that so often.

Some of them [the farmers] would talk to 'em [the POWs in German], you know. But they [the German POWs] . . . weren't aggressive to the civilians.

The ones that really disappointed me was the women. As a farm boy we just couldn't figure out how those women would come there, hang at the fence early in the morning. And we were just shocked at that. They'd back up to the fence and flip their dress up and it happened right up through the fence. We just couldn't get over that.

Well, we had one—after we were married [Edward and his wife]—one girl, woman, that lived in the apartment we lived in. She had a baby girl by one of the German prisoners of war. She was only sixteen [at the time]. Farm girl. Worked in the fork and cans in a boxcar. "They [the machines] broke down a lot," she said. "In between times we'd lay on the cans and have sex," she said. She had a baby girl, the other girl [that worked with her] didn't [get pregnant].

But there were some of them, the women, oh, they'd hang around early in the morning.[526]

During many of Edward's trips escorting the POWs he had chances to talk with the prisoners, especially since he could speak German. Many of the prisoners the camp received had been in Erwin Rommel's Afrika Korps and were very well trained. As one of these stories that he heard goes, the tank gunners had practiced shooting at targets towed by boats, and, "If they want[ed] to, they could put it in your mess kit, they were so good," he was to recall. Many of these young men were, however, as Edward was to state, scarred with horrible looking phosphorus and other burns. As the POWs reported to Edward, their tanks ran on gasoline, and the Allied airplanes used phosphorous bullets, which ignited the fuel in the tanks.[527]

One German POW told Edward that he had lost almost all of his friends in a three day period of fighting. "Left them dead, burning outside the tank or burning hanging out of the tank," the POW had said. The same POW reported that he was captured in a village. Allied P-49 fighters "would come in sideways in that village . . . 'You poke your head out, they'd shoot your head off. That's how daring they were,'" related the prisoner. As Edward stated, the POW said that "when the American GI's came in with their Garand Rifles, that took care of them right there." The Germans "had light machineguns," stated the POW, "but when it was man on man . . . the GI's generally won." When the prisoner Edward was talking to left the village on a truck as a POW, as he related to Edward, "[H]e looked back, he said, and there was just a wind row, a double wind row of German dead all the way down the street, he said. The villagers had pulled them there and were going through their pockets and taking anything that was of value. And that's how he left."[528]

Edward recalled another German prisoner, but this POW was not really a *German*, he was an American caught up in the war on the wrong side. As Edward recalled:

> [W]e had a fellow from Milwaukee, sixteen years old. He was fully big as you, I mean [referring to the author's height and size]. His parents ran the Deutschland Dairy

in Milwaukee. That's one of the original delicatessens in Germany, in Milwaukee. His mother took him and his baby sister over to see her parents. Hitler stopped his visas and he ended up in the German Army as a paratrooper. The first jump he surrendered.

They were scaring 'em. They thought they were gonna jump at Malta, you know. The German's bombed Malta everyday. And the pilot told them, "Don't get captured," he said, "they skin captured airmen alive and put them on crosses so we can see," he said. So he surrendered to the British and ended up in America. I said [to him], "I heard you are from this part of the country." And he said, "Yes." I didn't want to get that friendly, but. And he says, "My parents used to spend summers at Eagle River." I said, "Alright, if you did," I said, "name some of the towns you had to go through." [Edward indicated that the young *German*/American had correctly listed the various towns between Milwaukee and Eagle River, Wisconsin.] . . . "My oldest sister and I would always guess what town would be next," he said. But he was sixteen years old . . . paratrooper.[529]

It was not always friendly relationships between Edward and the POWs, though. As Edward was to state:

Oh, I tell yah, we had trouble. Once I got . . ., one hit me. . . . That's why I got this bulge in here [he feels the back of his head with his hand]. I hit the back of a convoy truck, a Dodge, a big bumper, and it took a little chip out of my skull. And this thing was like an acorn for years, but all at once it got big. Now it's getting real big. But they don't want to operate on it because it's too many life given things they said up in there. But so far it hasn't bothered me.[530]

Across the Atlantic, on 15 August, *Operation Dragoon*, the invasion of Southern France, began. Seaman First Class Morris Page, participating in his fourth amphibious landing of the war, was to ferry troops and supplies ashore in his Higgins boat from the *USS Thomas Jefferson*. The remainder of the month Morris and the *Thomas Jefferson* would spend making numerous shuttle runs from either North Africa or Italy to Marseilles, France, bringing supplies and reinforcements to the Southern France beachhead.[531] That same month, on 23 August, word was received from the French Underground that German forces had withdrawn from Port de Bouc, France, which is located along the French Mediterranean Coast approximately twenty miles east of Marseilles. Ensign Howard Boyle was ordered to take his *PT 555* to the harbor to investigate. What follows is pieced together from an undated "rough log" of *PT 555* and "A report on the last mission of *PT Boat 555*," both written by Howard.[532]

The next day, 24 August, *PT 555* slipped from its moorings in the St. Maxine, France, harbor and cruised to the U.S. Navy flag cruiser *USS Augusta* (CA-31), about an hour's journey away. Once arriving at the *Augusta*, Howard received verbal orders to proceed to Port de Bouc to determine if it was indeed free of German soldiers. U.S. Navy Lieutenants Stanley Livingston, Squadron 29's Division Commander, and M. Walker, an intelligence officer, along with Commander Bataile of the French Navy, came aboard *PT 555* from the *Augusta* for the mission. Commander Bataile was in possession of secret mine charts of the harbor, which would assist in navigating the mined waters. *PT 555* set sail for Port de Bouc from the *Augusta* at 1230 hours (12:30 p.m.).

At about 1400 hours (2 p.m.) a U.S. minesweeper and destroyer were met coming out of the harbor. The minesweeper signaled *PT 555* that they had cleared a path of mines, marking the path with spars, but had been forced out of the harbor by shore battery shelling. It was later discovered that the shelling had come from a German railroad gun located several miles inland, east of the port. As a result, the minesweeper had to clear the mines while under the protection of a smokescreen, severely limiting its crew's visibility.

PT 555, flying a large white flag from its bow, continued into the harbor, being careful to keep within the spars laid down by the minesweeper. At about 300 yards from the breakwater they were met by several small boats manned by men of the Free French Interior [FFI] and Ensign Moneglia of the French Navy, along with a harbor pilot, who successfully piloted the PT boat through the submarine nets and into the harbor to the dock at Port du Bouc. The crew was greeted by what appeared to be the entire population of the town, all in a tumultuous mood.

While the boat's crew mingled with the jubilant crowd handing out cigarettes, candy, and food stuffs, and receiving in return bottles of wine and other gifts, the officers, including Commander Bataile and Lieutenant Walker, the intelligence officer, conducted their intelligence mission. Once they had received the information they had come for, *PT 555* again set sail back for the *Augusta*, getting underway at 1645 (4:45 p.m.) with French Navy Ensign Moneglia piloting and Howard's executive officer, Ensign Charles Stearns, steering. Howard had set general quarters upon leaving the pier—mainly because of the fear of the shore battery, but also to help keep the crew from sampling the wine they had received from the townspeople—as well as posting a mine watch. Fifteen minutes later, just as the boat sighted the innermost spar placed by the minesweeper, the aft end of *PT 555* suddenly exploded blowing six of the crew overboard and injuring a seventh. It was at first thought that a shell from the shore battery had hit the boat, but it was soon evident that the boat's screws (propellers) had hit a mine. The entire aft end of the PT boat had literally been blown away up to the 40 mm ammunition rack, and it was the 40 mm gun crew and a bow lookout that had been thrown into the harbor.

At first, the calamity had all seemed surreal. As Howard wrote, "The instant after the force of the explosion had subsided seemed to be locked in time. The sun shown brightly in the cloudless sky, the expanse of the sea was blue and calm, and utter silence prevailed."[533] Reality, however, suddenly came back as Howard and the rest of those left onboard heard the cries of the crewmembers in the water. Training and instinct quickly took over. Two crewmembers leaped into the harbor in an attempt to rescue some of those that had been blown overboard, life rafts were launched, ropes were cast to others that were floundering, watertight integrity was checked and set, the anchor was dropped, and torpedoes were jettisoned to lighten the hulk.

It was soon after this time that Howard and Seaman First Class Carmine Gullo noticed that the two swimmers, having reached one of the injured, were beginning to flounder in the strong current. Howard and Carmine instantly jumped into the water carrying a rope, and began swimming to the three crewmembers and the lifeless body of a fourth the other three had found. After what Howard related as nearly a last, super-human effort, he and Carmine were able to finally reach the other four with their rope, which was then used to tow all six back to what was left of *PT 555*.

Small French fishing boats from the town's pier soon appeared. After a head count was taken and all of the crew that could be located were accounted for, four crewmembers were found to be missing, besides the one known killed. Soon afterward, Lieutenant Walker and Commander Bataile, along with the body of the dead crewmember and two of the wounded, headed towards the pier onboard one of the fishing boats. No more than eighty yards from *PT 555* this fishing boat in turn hit another mine. Although the boat was lifted from the water and slammed back, upside down, onto the harbor, none of the occupants were injured. The body of the deceased sailor, however, was lost.

Commander Bataile and Lieutenant Livingston then took one of *PT 555's* rubber rafts and successfully rowed to shore to communicate their findings as well as coordinate a rescue. That night the remaining crewmembers of *PT 555* broke into three sections, each forming into bucket brigades keeping what was left of the boat afloat until the commander and lieutenant returned in the morning, 25 August, with a tow boat, which was successful in safely towing the remains of the PT boat and its crew to port at nearby Carro, France.

Just prior to the return of Commander Bataile and Lieutenant Livingston and their tow boat, however, at about 0700 hours, an unidentified vessel larger than a fishing boat was seen about five or six mile away approaching from the east. The shape and size of the vessel suggested a German E-boat, the German equivalent of a PT boat. All hands manned the only remaining arms on board *PT 555*—small arms and the forward twin-.50 caliber machineguns. The crew silently watched, knowing that if indeed the approaching craft was an E-boat, their fate was certainly in jeopardy. Suddenly, a column of water was seen engulfing the craft followed by the sound of a dull explosion. When the water flume settled, the vessel had disappeared. Apparently, the oncoming boat had also hit a mine, and, in its case, to the relief of Howard and his crew, was completely destroyed and no longer a danger.

Once towed to port, the remains of *PT 555* and several of the crew, including Howard, remained in Carro until 1 September when they were again towed, this time back to Port de Bouc. The boat remained in Port de Bouc until 8 September when *PT 212* attempted to tow the *555* back to the Squadron's home base in Calvi, Corsica. An hour out of port, however, the towing line parted and, in order to keep the *555* from being captured or becoming a hazard to other watercraft, it was sunk by

PT 212's guns. Howard and his remaining crew were not present to see their boat's final moments, having recently departed Port de Bouc for St. Maxine by truck.

Although in Howard's account, he stated the term 'E-boat,' which is what the Allies called enemy PT type boats, E for Enemy War Motorboat, the German equivalent of a PT boat was officially called an S-boat, for *Schnellboote*, literally meaning fast boat, or Fast Motor Torpedo Boat.[534] In addition, in the *PT 555* log Howard is listed as the boat captain, therefore, the skipper of *PT 555*. He is also listed in the outset of the log as a "Lt. Jg." (lieutenant junior grade); however, at the same time he is referred to in the contents of the log as Ensign Boyle. It could be surmised, therefore, that during the incident, Howard, as the skipper of *PT 555*, was an ensign, but had been promoted to lieutenant junior grade by the time of the writing of the log. Howard was also to receive the Bronze Star Medal for his actions during this operation.[535]

Late that same month, Marine Corporal Edmond Babler and over a thousand other Japanese held POWs were transferred to the *Noto Maru*, a Japanese built transport ship, moored at a Manila pier on the Philippine island of Luzon. All of the POWs were then crowded into two holds onboard for a trip through U.S. submarine infested waters to Japan. They would endure endless sufferings in these two holds for approximately twelve days, arriving in Moji, Japan, on 6 September.[536] Stanley Summers, having survived the Bataan Death March as well as some of the same infamous Japanese POW camps that Ed had, including Cabanatuan, would also be shipped to Japan around this same timeframe, but on a different ship.[537]

Ed recalled in very vivid detail his experiences in the hold of this "Hell Ship," as those POW ships were dubbed by the prisoners. "It was pitch dark in the hold," he wrote, "and a feeling of uneasiness would come over me. I would also get an inner feeling that at any time an American submarine might send a torpedo through the side of the ship; a man's chance of getting out of the hold was nil." As he continued, "It really did stink in the hold during the night because of all of the sweaty bodies and the gas released from the excreta," the latter which filled the floors of the holds. As Ed related, the Japanese would only send down buckets for this use, pulling them up overflowing, which would slosh back down on the POWs. Food and water, what little were provided, were sent down the same way, in buckets lowered by ropes.[538]

Once finally arriving in Japan, Ed and half of the POWs that were on the *Noto Maru* were marched to their new camp, Fukuoka Camp 05B-Omine, not far from a coal mine in the northwestern mountains of Kyushu, the southern large island of the Japanese main islands. It was in this coal mine that Ed and his fellow POWs were to work.[539] Many of the guards at both the camp and the coal mine were not military, but, as at many other mines, factories, and other institutions throughout Japan that utilized Allied POWs, were employees of the company that owned the mine. As was custom in Japan at the time, this company would also have provided, or not provided, what little housing, food, and clothing the prisoners were to be given.[540]

Across the world in Great Britain, things were much better for Charles Vellema. After recuperating from his wounds, Charles, along with five other sergeants and an officer, were assigned duty in England training American soldiers who had freshly arrived from the States for combat. As he jokingly recalled:

> This was a pretty sickly looking outfit, that six of us sergeants and one officer. He happened to be [a] first lieutenant, and he was from the First Division too, from Texas [the Big Red One]. We had good times. We were in brick buildings in England, and no heat in them. But there was some wood cupboards in there and a fireplace. So there was a fireplace but no wood cupboards left when we got done.[541]

Charles' 47th Infantry Regiment, 9th Infantry Division would fight either along side of the Big Red One (the 1st Infantry Division) or took turns with them leading the way through North Africa and Europe. As he stated:

> My outfit was fighting all the time. They fought all the way through to the end of the war, all the way through Germany. It seemed always to be that if they needed something done first, that's what our outfit was. [And then] The First Division from Texas, they were [would be] the number one, and then we were in reserve for them.[542]

In the fall, Radioman Petty Officer Third Class Irving Meyer would find himself onboard what he referred to as the Liberty Ship *USS Lafayette* in route to the Admiralty Islands in the Pacific Ocean. As he described his trip, "Well, first of all it was fine until we got beyond the gate [the Golden Gate Bridge]. Then ninety-five percent of over a thousand people got sick, me included. There is nothing worse than getting sick on a metal ship." As he related, the trip took "Twenty-eight days. Zoom, zoom, zoom, zoom [indicating a zigzag pattern with his hand]."[543]

On 20 October, General Douglas MacArthur's forces, the 7th, the 24th, and the 96th Infantry Divisions along with the 1st Cavalry Division, under the overall command of Lieutenant General Walter Krueger, conducted the initial landings on the Philippine Island of Leyte in their bid to retake the Philippine Island Chain. To avoid any confusions with the European Theater's more famous landing on 6 June 1944—"D-Day"—the Leyte landings were dubbed "A-Day." With these forces was Robert Daniels, having completed his training as a medic.[544]

The war would have different effects on different people. The military, of course, were seeing the horrors of war first hand, and the adults and young adults back in the States were dealing with it as best they could. But the young children had different views. As an example, back in Wisconsin, David Lyon, living in Waupun with his mother, grandmother, and aunts, and in only his third year of life, had a rather unique outlook on the war. As he recalled:

> It was strange, because having been born in 1941 I started growing up during the war, and my earliest memories are that all the men are gone. I had an uncle that was a medic in England in a hospital. I had another uncle that was in the Aleutians [Aleutian Islands, Alaska] building an airstrip. My dad was in the Pacific in the Navy. And later on when my mom and dad were divorced my stepdad was in [had been in] the Pacific in the Army. So my earliest memories was that there were no grown men around. There were old men and there were boys, but there were no grown men around. . . . [A]ll my aunts moved in with my grandma, and we all lived in one big house with my two aunts and my mother and my grandma. And

everything was done, you know, was basically done with the women.[545]

David also remembered listening to the news, as well as remembering that "everything was geared toward the military." He even recalled having an imaginary friend who he called Roger. Roger was a soldier in the Pacific who would write letters to David. Everyday David's mother and aunts would ask him how Roger was. David would always reply with stories of how his imaginary friend was doing, until one day, as David recalled, "I remember one day, this day after I had heard from Roger, and I said, 'No, he was killed.' I remember that."[546]

David also recalled having a toy gun from his earliest memories. "[A]nd we always, . . . you know, me and the neighbor kids, we were always playing army, we were always playing war. That I remember," he was to state. "It was a whole different world from now as far as firearms and everything were concerned. Those are my most vivid memories of my youth," growing up in the war.[547]

Jim Laird would summarize up his thoughts as a child during that timeframe by stating that as children during the war, "much of life is how it affects on us. . . . As children we are interested in *us* . . . the whole aspect pretty much was how it was effecting me. And the idea of death and the idea that there was something happening over there was very, very difficult to understand."[548]

Some of this not understanding may have been somewhat deliberate by parents and other adults. As Harriet Whiting related:

> I think they probably tried to keep us kids from worrying and so on. But we used to hear the adults talking sometimes, and we somehow picked up on some of the names like Adolf Hitler. They said his name was really what?, Schicklegroober or something like that. And we thought that was hilarious. And then, of course, we would hear about Tojo and Mussolini, and they were all such funny names, you know.[549]

As the young children tried to make sense of it all, the war continued. A few weeks after losing his PT boat to a German mine off the coast of southern France, Navy Lieutenant Junior Grade Howard Boyle was assigned to MGM Studios on special assignment to lead the PT boat crews in the filming of the John Ford movie *They Were Expendable*, which starred Robert Montgomery and John Wayne. Howard and his PT crews were to spend several months in Florida with the cast and crew in the filming of the movie. As his son, Dan Boyle, would relate, "[W]hen we watched that movie," his dad, Howard would always say, "'Those are my arms,' you know . . . when you see the guys steering the boats through the bombs blowing up."[550]

After seventeen weeks of schooling at OCS in Fort Benning, Georgia, Arnold Visser was commissioned an Army second lieutenant on 2 November and shipped off to Camp Blanding, Florida. Once there, Grace, once again joined him. Their time together in Florida, however, would not be long. The war in Europe was beaconing him.[551]

November would also find Fred Zurbuchen's 493rd Bomb Group, along with the rest of the Eighth Air Force, continuing to fly out of the Debach Airfield in England, bombing targets throughout Germany. Throughout the year, AnnaMarie Kretzer and her family had been watching from afar as these American bombers and their British counterparts were targeting the large German cities. One November day, however, all that would change. The Allies had recently begun targeting the smaller towns in her area of Germany. With her school in the neighboring town of Rudesheim, Germany, having given the children the day off, as AnnaMarie recalled, she was at the family home in Geisenheim preparing dinner for her family and cleaning the floors when she heard the warning of bomber planes approaching. AnnaMarie, with her aunt, uncle, and cousin, ran to the bomb shelter two houses away where they stayed for awhile. But after a period, with nothing happening, as well as several additional false alarms, they chose to ignore the last warning. After all, the lunch meal had to be prepared. This, however, would prove to be a mistake. The last warning was not a false alarm with the airplanes actually arriving and dropping their load of bombs in the area. The family was forced to quickly take shelter in the basement of their own home instead of risking the run to the stronger bomb shelter down the road.[552]

Although bombs had landed near enough to the family home to coat the kitchen and the meal they were preparing in dust, AnnaMarie and her family were fortunate; they had all survived without being injured. However, five other of the town's homes were destroyed and eighteen of its citizens were killed, and the town of Rudesheim, where AnnaMarie went to school, had been nearly wiped off the map. In addition, some of her school friends had been killed and another had run with her family, while covered with water-soaked blankets, through flames to safety; the home they had just left reduced to nothing but rubble.[553]

The Kretzer family was to spend most of the rest of the war "practically" living in a bomb shelter. As AnnaMarie stated:

> We had built it into a hill, it was like a mine supported with big beams. And there were only a few old men left and mostly women and children. And we went with picks and shovels and made some isles into the hill for shelter, and that's where we practically lived until the war was over in 1945.[554]

Not all wartime experiences for the troops would be centered on fighting the enemy. For example, during one of *USS Barnegat's* many port visits along the coast of Brazil where they would service their squadron of PBY's, according to Motor Machinist Mate Second Class Petty Officer Theron Mickelson, the ship's captain "wanted to go hunting."[555] Being assigned as the engineer of the captain's launch, Theron was to accompany the skipper up the Para River in northern Brazil. Besides Theron and the captain on this hunting trip were the boatswain's mate who piloted the boat, a chief petty officer, and one other person Theron did not identify. As he recalled:

> [W]e were going hunting for snakes. Well, *we* didn't go hunting for the snakes, but we dropped them off, and they picked up a guide that was going to take them out there with the snakes. And they picked up the guide and they went out. And you could hear 'em in the woods when they start[ed] firing. There must have been about ten shots fired, and then all of a sudden there was one that sounded different, and it was over with. They brought back a boa constrictor that, I'm not exaggerating, it was from here to there long [he pointed across the room] and was so big around [indicating the size of a basketball]. We had to go ashore in order to pick it up and pick them up. . . . [A]ll we got was the hide off of it, the skin. And

the captain asked the guide if he wanted the meat. And he [the guide] said, "That's one meat we don't eat." [556]

On 12 December, the 38th Photo-Reconnaissance Squadron, an intelligence gathering unit, became part of the 4th Photographic Reconnaissance Group stationed on the Island of Morotai, a small island in the Moluccas group nearly three hundred miles northwest of Sansapor, New Guinea, in the Pacific. Walter Riel was a member of this squadron. As he was to recall, their aircraft "took photos before, during, and after the raids. . . . And our planes didn't have no guns at all. Just four P-38's." Trained in the signal corps, Walter's job in the squadron was to set up and maintain the telephone system, including the switchboard. As he stated, "I was the only one with my MOS [Military Occupation Specialty] in our outfit."[557]

Recalling his trip over to the Pacific Islands, Walter remembered, much like Irving Meyer had been on his crossing, being seasick along with many of his fellow passengers. "Oh, was I sick, most of the time," he reported. "Finally, I got up . . . with the crew. It was twenty-eight days going over. And we stopped in New Zealand, Australia, and New Guinea. . . . And I worked in the kitchen then, and they let me sleep up on deck. Well, that made a lot of difference." His fellow passengers weren't as lucky, though. As Walter explained:

[E]veryone was sick . . . it was terrible! And the toilets weren't working good and the crap [was] all over, running. Good thing is they had little berms there that the water didn't run right onto the ship from the toilets, they ran over [the side]. It was a mess. Terrible! But what can you say. You're in it, and you do the best you can."[558]

The 38th Photo-Reconnaissance landed on Morotai Island, according to Walter, "shortly after the Marines" had landed.[559] Although Walter reported that Marines had taken the island, it was actually the Army's 31st Infantry Division, under General Douglas MacArthur, which had landed on the island on 14 and 15 September 1944.[560] Walter went on to relate some of his experiences on the island, stating that

The advance troops dug us some fox holes with a cover

on it. I spent many a night there during the air raids. So with the anti-aircraft and bombs falling it was noisy at times. Shortly after we landed we had a comrade we called Pops (he looked like it too). He would get up at night and holler "Japs! Japs!" They sent him to section 8. Later someone got a letter from him stating that he was back in photography, now who's nuts, you or me?[561]

Walter's unit was a part of the 13th Air Force, which, called the Jungle Air Force, consisted of a large variety of aircraft, including the B-17 Flying Fortress, B-24 Liberator, B-25 Mitchell, P-38 Lightning, P-40 Warhawk, and P-61 Black Widow, among others. During the early part of the war it was initially assigned a defensive role, but then took on a more offensive mission once the Allies were able to begin regrouping and organizing themselves into an effective fighting force in the region. With this switch, the Jungle Air Force's area of responsibility eventually ranged northeast from the Solomon Islands, to include New Guinea, the Admiralty Islands, Morotai, and the Philippine Islands.[562]

Across the world, with no further amphibious landings anticipated in the European Theater of the war, the *USS Thomas Jefferson*, with Morris Page still onboard as a crewmember, left Norfolk, Virginia, on 15 December for her trip through the Panama Canal and service in the Pacific Theater of the war. As Morris recalled, "I remember the Panama Canal. When we went though there they had piers out with bananas on every pier, and then my captain sent one of the landing craft and got a bunch of bananas, and we had bananas. Boy [he laughs], a lot of bananas."[563]

The year would come to a close with the alarming news that the war in Europe was at the brink of disaster for the Allies. Just four days after Walter's squadron became a part of the 4th Photographic Reconnaissance Group, and the day after Morris' trip through the Panama Canal, in a plan to destabilize the Allies, on 16 December, Adolf Hitler launched the Ardennes Offensive. The Allies would call this offensive the Battle of the Bulge. Ralph Bohnert, the youngest of Joseph and Linda Bohnert's sons, and brother to Al, Doris, and Lois, was one of the 600,000 American troops involved in the battle. Many of these, like Ralph, suddenly and without warning, found themselves literally surrounded and cut off by crack German troops and Panzer tanks.[564]

1945

As 1945 began, in January, a year after Walter and Catherine Riel were married, Catherine gave birth to their first child, a son. With the state of communications being as they were, Walter recalled that his son "was two weeks old before I knew he was born."[565]

That same month, after having secured the Philippine island of Leyte, General Douglas MacArthur launched the invasion of Luzon. On 8 January, the 37th and 40th Infantry Divisions of Major General Oscar Griswold's XIV Corps and the 6th and 43rd Infantry Divisions of Major General Inis P. Swift's I Corps came ashore at Lingayen, the same beaches on which, just over three years before on 21 December 1941, Japanese General Homma'a troops had waded ashore.[566] Robert Daniels and Leonard Schrank would both take part in this invasion. It would also be about this same time that, after having spent the last two months in the Admiralty Islands moving around boxes of radio equipment, Naval Radioman Irving Meyer was loaded aboard another transport and taken to Camp Logan on Leyte Island, where he would spend the following month copying radio messages.[567]

At the same time, in the Ardennes Forest (located mainly in Belgium and Luxembourg), Ralph Bohnert, as a result of being a cook and therefore having been somewhat in the rear echelons of the front lines when the German initial surprise attacks occurred in Hitler's Ardennes Offensive (the Battle of the Bulge), was to survive unscathed both the initial onslaught and the consequent fighting and siege. Over 81,000 other U.S. troops involved in the nearly month-long battle, however, would not, being either killed, wounded, or captured. Not until mid-January, with the German offensive stopped and the German army running out of gas, causing many of the its soldiers to literally abandon their tanks and other vehicles and walk back to their original starting positions and even beyond, did the battle end.[568]

For the first part of 1945, Sergeant Charles Vellema remained in England training young American soldiers fresh from the states. As he recalled:

> Now we got all the eighteen year olds. Some of them just were in service and came over there, and we had 'em six weeks and we flew them right into Belgium. This was in the winter, [around the time of] the Battle in the Bulge. So I was kind of fortunate that I had over a year of training before [I had gone into my first battle], and some of them had never had a rifle in their hand or anything—they went right in.[569]

Among his duties, Charles was also placed in charge of a building of troops that he did not know what they did. It was his job to issue them weekend passes to London; he had no other authority over them or, as he stated, "never did find out what outfit it was."[570]

Back in the United States, while attempting to keep pace with the all out war effort, including the rationing, and while their loved ones were off fighting in the war, people in the Waupun, Wisconsin, area, as people were throughout the country, also tried to keep things as much the same as it was before the war, while still fully and unswervingly supporting the war effort, the government, and the president. Although some things were bound to change, people, nonetheless, made do with what they had the best way they could. As Charlotte Mehlbrech, who was twelve years old at the time, was to recall:

> I think everybody got closer together during the war. You appreciated what you had more. Families got together more. There wasn't much other entertainment.
>
> You didn't go on trips. Of course, big families didn't anyway. But things did stay the same, a lot of it. We had school, we had church, we had, ... that part was the same. Food was a little bit different because . . . people that didn't have their own cow like we did, they went to olee margarine in the bag with a little berry in it because you couldn't get butter. And you'd squeeze this little bag and you'd have to punch that little berry 'cause it colored it

[the olee]—otherwise it was white—to look like butter. That was the olee margarine. Now [when] it all comes out [it] looks like butter, you know, the way it's made. But that was [the] differences then.

As far as things the same, I would think we tried to make things the same. We tried to have our family units, you know, close. I think we made an effort to stay the same, even though everyone would say for anything that came up, "There's a war on." That was what they said.[571]

Although DiAnna Reif was very young at the time, she did have some vivid memories of the era and how her father would help his neighbors whenever he could. Chuck, her father, was unable to serve in the military himself due to his previous bout with tuberculosis. Instead, he would spend the war working at the maximum security prison in Waupun as a guard. He did, however, do what he could to help those left behind. As DiAnna recalled:

[W]hen these guys were gone off to war I can remember my dad . . . a lot of times he'd go and he'd help the wives, you know, they'd need something done at their home or something. And I can remember very vividly Bill Schlei had contracted malaria [while at the war], and so he was hospitalized for a long, long period of time. But Jane [his wife] had gotten a call, and it was during the middle of the night, and she called my folks to tell them that Bill was going to be getting into Milwaukee by train. And so we kids were roused and we went over—they lived on Bly Street—and we went to stay with her children while my dad drove Jane down to Milwaukee to meet the train that Bill came in on, so. And, of course, there was a lot of celebrating, you know, when he came home. But he lived with the effects of malaria all of his life, you know. He never really got over everything.[572]

Like everyday people such as Chuck Reif helping their neighbors, nearly everyone also fully supported the President. As Charlotte Mehlbrech was to state, in those days

> We didn't . . . talk much . . . against the President or
> anything that was going on in the war effort. I actually
> think that if you were [did] . . . you would get in trouble.
> In fact, there was always rumors about somebody that
> hated the President, and then they would get in trouble
> with the FBI. And I don't know if this actually happened,
> but you would never hear a commentator talk like they
> do now about the President or any of the Congress, any
> of that. It just wasn't done 'cause you were aiding and
> abetting the enemy! That's what they said.[573]

Interestingly enough, in 1921, at the age of thirty-nine, Franklin Delano Roosevelt contracted polio (poliomyelitis). As a result, he was basically left crippled from his waist down.[574] At the time, however, it was not thought proper to show this, so most Americans were never aware of his affliction. As a matter of fact, he was elected President of the United States in 1932 and then reelected for an unprecedented three additional terms, all the while most Americans were oblivious of his condition. Whenever depicted in pictures or newsreels, he was either standing behind a podium or being assisted in standing by others, effectively concealing his need to use leg braces to stand or walk. This, of course, was prior to the invention of television, so it was much easier to conceal his condition. And it was prior to the modern tendency of gossip columns and sensationalism by many in the news media and others of today. Nonetheless, as Charlotte related to, at the time of the war it would have been considered unthinkable, even unpatriotic to have brought Roosevelt's condition to light.

Not aiding the enemy was also a common patriotic thought during the war. As Charlotte was also to explain:

> You wouldn't dare . . . you weren't supposed to gossip.
> If you were sure or had any idea where your loved one
> was you didn't tell. And when you went to the movie
> they would show in there "Don't Gossip." And then they
> would show pictures of this woman. Her son had told her
> where he was somehow and she told a neighbor and they
> told a neighbor. And then they went all the way and they
> showed the pictures on the screen in the movie house.

And then they would get to be looking more Asian and whatever. And finally at the end, the ship got blew up. And that was to let you know that you didn't need to aid and abet the enemy. You were not to help the enemy.[575]

The early part of the year also saw Army Tech-5 Gladys Jolly continuing to drive trucks at Fort Leonard Wood. By this time, however, she had the help of several German POWs from Rommel's desert forces. As she remembered them, they were

Plain, every day boys. Did their job, and they did it very well. Very military, very proud of them being in the military. We had the boys that were the kids—the SS boys were up on the hill; they had them fenced in. They were the goose-steppers. You couldn't trust them. I mean, I don't say trust them, but you couldn't . . . you didn't really accept them.

These boys [that worked with us] were the ones that were just kids. They were what?, sixteen, seventeen, eighteen years of age. They were just kids. Naturally they were scared. Their parents were upset. They left their sisters and brothers behind . . . [who] never knew if they were living or dead. And around the holidays we used to go out of our way and kinda, you know, give 'em a little extra candy or whatever we could do, whatever we could put in a compartment that would be theirs. We didn't have to, but we did because they were like us, actually. You know, they looked at us with a lot of love and respect.[576]

Across the Atlantic, as he had throughout 1944 from the time of the Normandy invasion, Fred Zurbuchen would fly bombing missions in his B-17. Besides being the ball turret gunner of his airplane, he was also responsible for arming the plane's load of bombs. "After we were airborne," he recalled, "I fused the bombs depending on what target was to be hit." If it was a target that required a contact fuse—the bombs exploding upon contact with the target or the ground—he would arm a nose fuse in the bombs. If the target required an air explosion, he would arm the tail fuse. "It had what they called an impeller on it," he stated, "and that would unscrew to the extent that wherever the bombardier wanted" the bomb to explode, "it would explode at that altitude."[577]

In his missions Fred took part in the bombings of the German cities of Düsseldorf, Dresden, Frankfurt, Kiel, and Berlin, and an aircraft factory deep inside of Czechoslovakia targeting "the main ball bearing factories, marshalling yards, aircraft factories, and such." As he recalled:

> The Germans had a huge submarine pen at Kiel, and I think we hit that . . . three times before we finally penetrated the top of the pens. The top of the pens were anywhere from fourteen- to sixteen-foot of cement, reinforced. And one [bombing run] didn't do it, so we went back another two times to finally penetrate that pen.[578]

In remembering his missions over Berlin, Fred was to state, "[W]e hit that three times, and the third time you couldn't see nothing but smoke." As he also recalled, his longest bomb runs were the two against the aircraft factories in Czechoslovakia: "I think we hit that twice, and that was one of the longest ones we had as far as a bomb run. That would run anywhere between six to eight hours, over and return."[579]

Fred would fly a total of twenty-five combat missions over Europe out of Debach, England, with the 493rd Bomb Group. As the ball turret gunner, he was to shoot down a German ME-109 fighter. He was also, as he related, "wounded once and returned to action after about two weeks of recuperation." For his part in these missions, among other awards, Fred would receive the Air Medal with three Oak Leaf Clusters. In describing those days during 1944 and 1945, Fred was to say:

> Well, that's a lonesome life over there, although we did have some advantages to some other people on the ground. We always had a place to come home to and a bed to sleep in. And the days . . . some days were very short and so were the nights—getting up at 3:00 to 3:30 in the morning to get this aircraft ready for a bomb run; it took some time. And then in between that, of course, you had to get your breakfast and so on.[580]

Since the pilot of Fred's B-17 was a captain, and, therefore, the lead aircraft pilot, his bomber would be one of the first to take off. They would then launch a colored smoke bomb. Each following plane was given the color of their lead aircraft, and once they too were airborne, they would form on their designated lead aircraft. Once assembled, the group would begin their flight over the English Channel for their bomb run.[581]

There were four squadrons in each bomb group. Each squadron would put up fifteen planes for each bomb run, making a total of sixty B-17s in one flight per bomb group. Each of these planes had a compliment of ten crewmembers—the pilot, co-pilot, navigator, bombardier, flight engineer, radio operator, armorer, two waist gunners, and a tail gunner—for a total of a 600-man aircrew. Fred related, however, that in the beginning they were short of one of the waist gunners for many of the planes in his squadron.[582]

As with Fred being wounded, these bombing runs were a dangerous business. It is reported that of the 158 combat missions flown by the 493rd Bomb Group, forty-one of their aircraft were lost with 234 crewmembers killed.[583] It was dangerous for those on the receiving end of the bombings as well. As AnnaMarie Kretzer, fourteen years old at the time and living in Geisenheim, Germany, about forty miles from Frankfurt, and on the receiving end of the B-17's bombs since November of 1944, poignantly pointed out, what she remembered most during this timeframe was "how *scared* we were with the bombing[s]."[584]

Back in the United States, on the twelfth of February, newly commissioned Second Lieutenant Arnold Visser received orders to report to New York City Harbor for his trip to the European Theater. On 15 February he said good-by to his wife Grace and headed for New York. Once there he boarded the *SS Aquitania*, a four stacked luxury cruise ship that had been converted to carry between 1,200 and 1,500 troops, for his trip across the ocean to England. As an officer, he was given duties onboard to ensure that no one smoked on the decks, since the lighting up of a cigarette could be seen for miles on the open ocean during the nights, and the scare of German submarines was still a very real threat. Because of these duties he was assigned a stateroom vice having to live in the holds with the thousands of other soldiers packed onboard the converted ocean liner.[585]

For the crossing, as Arnold lightheartedly recalled, he was given a sergeant to assist him; however, the sergeant became so seasick even before leaving the dock in New York that they had to assign him a different sergeant. The transit itself between New York and England would only take four days, and, because of the *Aquitania's* speed, the German submarines would not have much chance of intercepting her. For that matter, most of the Allied military ships could not even keep up with her. Therefore, according to Arnold, the only escort they had was one small airplane that would be seen from time to time throughout the voyage as it looked for enemy subs.[586]

On the same day that Arnold was saying goodbye to Grace, like Morris Page had just previously done onboard the *USS Thomas Jefferson*, as well as had the *USS Peto* and countless of the other submarines built in the Manitowoc Shipbuilding Company, Theron Mickelson and the *USS Barnegat* was also to go through the Panama Canal. First, however, Theron and the *Barnegat* paid a port visit to Montevideo, Uruguay, where they were to see the remains of the German cruiser *Admiral Graf Spee*, whose crew had scuttled her in 1939 to keep the ship from being captured by the British. As Theron recalled:

> We get in there [Montevideo] and we see the *Graf Spee*, it was where they had parked it, or sunk it themselves, what was left of it. And I was talking to some guys down there, and they said that when they got there the *Graf Spee* officers took I don't know how many caskets on shore. And somebody… was wondering about what's in those caskets. And they opened every one of them, and they were full of guns and ammunition. So those who did get off were planning on a little uprising down there, I suppose.[587]

After departing Montevideo, and after having sailed from port to port off the coast of Brazil and Uruguay servicing their squadron of PBY seaplanes, the *Barnegat* had sailed north and then west to the Canal Zone.[588] After about two weeks off the Atlantic side of the canal, on 15 February the ship entered the canal for its trip south to the Pacific Ocean. However, unlike Morris' trip, Theron's first experience in the canal was a bit more eventful. In recalling his duties as throttle man in the after engine room during their transit, he was to state:

> I hear "Full reverse." And so I pulled it into reverse. And my buddy in the forward engine room, he thought it

was full ahead. So we run into the chain, and that's a big chain. It knocked a hole about that big [he motions with his hands about the size of a beach ball] in the bow. [But i]t was up high enough it didn't leak anything.[589]

Theron's ship was to go through the canal several more times in the next few months. Exactly how many times he couldn't remember, but like Morris he was impressed with the canal. As Theron stated, ". . . that's really something going through that canal.[590]

Four days later, on the other side of the Pacific, after the most extensive shelling of any Pacific island during the war, on 19 February the Marines of the 4th and 5th Marine Divisions landed on the island of Iwo Jima. Right on schedule, five days later, the 3rd Marine Division joined the fight with the mission to secure the middle of the island.[591] Just prior to this, Marine Buck Sergeant Al Bohnert and the 3rd Marines had been on Guam, where, after the major fighting had died down, there had been some good times. As Al wrote:

> There was an airfield on the island. The air core [*sic*] was leaving and they were giving away supplies. So we were able to get a lot of stuff. We got powdered ice cream. The C.B. [Seabees ?] had an ice machine. We got a 50 gallon trash can filled with ice and with the powder managed to make a sort of "thin" ice cream. It was cold and tasty and everyone just loved it. When Guam was secured we had a pretty easy time of it.[592]

However, at the same time, as Al wrote, he and his fellow Marines "knew something was coming up. We didn't know what or where. We had heard rumors but no facts. Some of the higher ups knew but weren't talking. After we boarded the ship they gave us a map of the island we were heading to. We were being sent to Iwo Jima."[593]

Once at the island, as Al recalled, "The landing was very rough. Many Marines were killed. Once you were on the island there was no place to hide except in the caves, and the Japanese were already in them. So you had to dig about 6 inches into the sand so you could keep warm at night." On the island they were up against a very determined, very entrenched enemy. "We had 75 mm [cannons]. They had 150/155 mm [guns]. They were big," he wrote. The fighting was hand to hand and cave to cave at times. As Al continued his report:

> We fired at the caves and we had to make sure the air strip was safe for our planes to land. Then we were told to dynamite the caves, I carried about five sticks of dynamite and the guy next to me carried the fuses. We got to the first cave and [an] officer came up and said we didn't have to do that and sent us back to our outfit. Things [then] quieted down [for us] for awhile and I had a chance to make some doughnuts" [Al being the unit's cook].[594]

Keeping clean and getting drinkable water, as in any battle zone, was difficult. But on Iwo Jima it was especially hard. As Al wrote, "We had to wear leggings to keep the volcanic ash out of our shoes (it would rub your feet raw)," and "We weren't able to drink the water. It had to be hauled in. While we were there we hooked up a shower using the sulfur rich water. It was hot. You would run through, get soaped up and run through again."[595] Robert Daniels would also remember having to improvise in the taking of showers. He recalled that while in the Philippines one time he stood in a rainstorm—a literal downpour—and got all lathered up, just to have the rain suddenly and without warning stop, leaving him all lathered in soap with no water with which to wash it off.[596]

After its four-day crossing, once the *SS Aquitania* moored in England, it didn't take long for Arnold Visser to be quickly ferried across the English Channel to France where he arrived in Le Harve and was assigned to the 1st Army, XX Corps. Like Charles Vellema, Arnold spent the next few weeks as an instructor. However, unlike Charles, who was by that time an experienced combat veteran training nearly raw recruits prior to entering their first combat, Arnold, while he waited for orders for himself to go to the front, had no combat experience and was re-training *experienced* soldiers in the rear echelons that had been wounded. As such, giving instruction to combat hardened soldiers wasn't always easy for him. As Arnold recalled:

> I was fortunate to have an officer with me there that . . . he had already been . . . some place in Pearl Harbor or some place. . . . Because one time I started training 'em,

and here that one kid said to me, "Well,... what are you trying to tell us? We've been in combat, and here you come from the States trying to tell us...," you know what I mean. Then that other officer stood up and he says, "That's the last of you! I have got more medals than all of you put together! I have been in the war!" Did that ever help me [Arnold laughed]. They quiet right down. And he [the other officer] was the truth, you know.

When Arnold's orders finally arrived directing him to the front, they stated that he was to accompany the 9th Armored Division of the 1st Army as it entered Germany.[597]

On 3 March, after slugging their way through the island of Luzon, pushing the Japanese back, MacArthur's troops liberated what was left of Manila, the Philippine capital.[598] Once the capital was liberated, and after a month at Camp Logan on Leyte Island, Navy Radioman Third Class Irving Meyer was then shipped to the city, where he would finish out the war copying incoming messages. His base was on what had been Manila's polo grounds. As Irving related concerning his duties at the base, "[W]e only could copy [messages]. We could not transmit. We only copied messages coming in."[599] Most of these consisted of coded messages with four letter "names" for the ships or stations they were intended for. "We just copied them," he continued, "and the messenger takes 'em and deciphers 'em, who they were for, if they were for us," or others.[600]

While at the Manila polo grounds, Irving was housed in a Quonset hut barracks. When asked if there were still any Japanese soldiers in the area where he was, he related, "Not that I know of. . . . I doubt there were any Japanese running around [then]." However, to Irving's own admission, he did not leave his secure base while he was there.[601]

In Europe, on 7 March, the lead groups of the American 9th Armored Division discovered the lightly guarded Ludendorff railway bridge over the Rhine River at Ramegan, and rushed over it to establish a bridgehead on the eastern shore in Germany. Although damaged by several attempts by the Germans to demolish it, the bridge was still intact.[602] Lieutenant Arnold Visser crossed the bridge while it still stood.[603] Private First Class Robert Van Alstine and the 45th EVAC Hospital he was assigned to were also soon across the river at Ramegan and into Germany as well. As Robert recalled:

[T]he way the story goes, we came up to a place called Bad Noon Hour. You can't forget the name, you know. And we were told to stop there. It was about 10:00 at night, and nobody knew where we were, of course. And we stopped and set up pup tents with the idea in the morning we were going to move—we had already traveled for about 150 miles that day. And then all of a sudden the word come, "Pack up, we're gonna cross." And so everybody took down their tent again and got on the trucks. And . . . the idea, apparently, of which I have no factual data on, but the idea was that the colonel wanted to be cited for the first [hospital] to cross the Rhine, and we were. And for that we got a meritorious unit citation.[604]

However, unlike Arnold Visser, the 45th did not cross on the damaged railroad bridge, but by a pontoon bridge that had been thrown up nearby. As Robert was to state:

They were shelling at the time, and, of course, there were lights out there and the planes were strafing and whatever, you know. . . .

I wasn't a driver, I was in the back of the truck and there were probably maybe twenty other guys back there with me. But you don't know where you're going, you don't even know where you are, you know. And of course we ended up on the other side safely, fortunately. And the bridge fell down, I think, the next day. It was so weak, that's why they didn't want the traffic on it.[605]

The Ludendorff railway bridge was to finally collapse on 17 March, ten days after it had been taken by the Americans.[606]

Once across the river, the 45th sat up their hospital at Honnef, Germany. As Robert proudly stated, "We were the first hospital to cross the Rhine. While the bridge at Remagen was still in operation, we were on the other side already, setting up the hospital."[607]

Sometime after entering the Pacific Ocean from the Panama Canal, the *USS Barnegat*, with Motor Machinist Mate Theron Mickelson onboard, sailed to the Galapagos Islands. Once there, Theron had the opportunity to go ashore. As he recalled:

We went down to the Galapagos Islands. . . . And we were there for thirty some days. And while we were there the captain decided that he wanted to put the name of the ship on the side of one of the mountains. So I was one of the volunteers. I think there was eight of us.

We had to carry buckets of paint. And it took us from 7 o'clock in the morning to 2 o'clock in the afternoon to get up to the top to where we could do the painting, because it's all mountains and, you know, junk, other than the one place where we come down. That was just a slippery slide. . . . And we got it painted and came down. And on the way coming down I said, "I ain't walkin' down the way we come up, we won't get out of here until midnight." So I got the rest of the guys and we sat on our butt and slid down this. And I got just about to the bottom and I see this [he indicated with his hand sticking straight up as if it were a stick or stone] sticking up in front of me just like this, and it's coming right towards my centerline. Well, I was lucky enough, I put my foot over it and it connected on my foot and just flipped me right into the water. Yup.[608]

At the same time Navy Signalman Carl Manthe and the minesweeper he was on were still patrolling the waters around New York Harbor for German mines. And once Lieutenant Junior Grade Howard Boyle's part in the filming of the movie *They Were Expendable* was completed, he found himself transferred back to the war—this time to PT Squadron 8 in the South Pacific. Based in Tufi and Aitape, both on Papua-New Guinea, Squadron 8's operations consisted of attacking and harassing the Japanese naval forces in and around Papua-New Guinea and its many surrounding islands, as well as fighting in the Luzon, Philippines, area.[609]

On 1 April, the invasion of the Island of Okinawa, the largest amphibious operation in the Pacific and the last of the major campaigns of the Pacific Theater, began with two Marine Corps and two Army divisions (60,000 American troops) being ferried ashore. Taking a part in this landing was the USS *Thomas Jefferson* and her Higgins boat crews. As always, Seaman First Class Morris Page manned one of these boats. His task was to transport the troops and their supplies to the Hagushi beaches of Okinawa. It is reported that the *USS Thomas Jefferson's* Higgins boat crews did so well and with such a high degree of success that the ship was the first to be completely unloaded in her area. This would be the fifth and final combat landing that Morris would make in the war.[610]

This same battle also found Cora DeMunck's brother Bob, a trained mechanical engineer, on the island as an officer in an army engineering company. The fighting on Okinawa was so fierce that, as Cora related concerning Bob's experiences, "he was the only one of five officers in his unit to come out without a scratch . . . three of them were killed, one was wounded." Her oldest brother, Glen, was also serving in the Army, as an Army Air Corps pilot flying cargo planes.[611]

A little over a month after Robert Van Alstine and the 45th EVAC Hospital crossed the Rhine at Ramegan and sat up their hospital at Honnef, Germany, on 11 April the Buchenwald Concentration Camp near Weimar, Germany, was liberated by forces under General Patton. Upon arriving, Patton's forces had found that the camp had already been taken over by the inmates when most of the SS guards had fled. Nonetheless, many of the ex-inmates were in dire need of medical assistance.[612]

This is attested to by Arnold Visser. According to Arnold, he was one of, if not the first, U.S. soldiers in the camp. On orders and alone in his jeep, Arnold was headed towards the German city of Weimar when, not far from the city, he came across a fenced-in camp. Just as he arrived, a car sped out of the camp's opened and unguarded gates, followed by a thin man in "stripped pajamas," as Arnold described him, who walked out and just headed down the road. Arnold stopped his jeep and tried to talk to the man, even speaking Dutch to him, but the thin, pajama clad man just kept walking away from the camp. Alone and armed only with his service .45 automatic pistol, Arnold then ventured into the camp. In explaining his experience, Arnold stated:

> I went in this building and I stood there alone, and [then I] walked in, and all I saw was cubicles like this [he motions with his hands] and just heads looking at me; no motion. And the stench was out of this world. I mean, the stench and being quiet and. . . . You know what I mean, death in the eyes [that I saw], you know. And I walked down, you know, what could I do? I mean, I was on orders, but I stayed long enough to walk quite a ways in and . . . *alone*! And finally I left.[613]

According to Arnold, the man he saw leaving the compound and tried to talk to may have been French General Rene L'Hopital, who was an ex-Aide de Camp of WWI French Marshall Ferdinand Foch. L'Hopital had allegedly been sent to Buchenwald for refusing to command on the side of the Germans during the current war. It was reported that he weighed 180 pounds when he entered the camp—when Arnold saw him, he weighed approximately eighty-seven pounds. It is also reported that General L' Hopital would eventually assist the Allies.[614]

Arnold also believes, through viewing later pictures, that one of the concentration camp survivors he saw was Elie Wiesel. As he stated, "I saw where he was, because there was a partition, and I had to walk far enough in, you know. So at the 60th anniversary [of the liberation of the camp] I made contact with him, and he wrote me."[615]

The day after Buchenwald was liberated, on 12 April, President Franklin Delano Roosevelt, after four months into his thirteenth year—his unprecedented fourth term—as president of the United States, passed away from a cerebral hemorrhage.[616] Jim Laird, eight years old at the time, remembers walking down the street next to his mother when "a woman came running out of the house, 'Roosevelt's dead, Roosevelt's dead,'" she cried.[617] Harriet Whiting, also eight at the time, remembered it as well. As she recalled, her brother Walter would later state, "I can remember that. It was my birthday. And he died on my birthday, and nobody paid any attention to me the rest of the day. All the grownups were upset!"[618]

About the same time that Roosevelt died, according to Robert Van Alstine, the 45th EVAC Hospital was to take over caring for the Buchenwald Concentration Camp survivors. As he related, General Patton's men were not trained nor had the time to take care of these camp survivors, so the 45th EVAC Hospital received the word to "'Get over right away and take over the concentration camp.' So, we moved in there. It was about, oh, maybe the third week of April when we moved into Buchenwald where there was, oh, I think maybe 21,000 inmates, which most had tuberculosis." The 45th was instructed to evacuate those that could be and care for those that could not. "Fortunately," as Robert continued, "there was an airstrip not very far down the line there," so they could fly many of them out.[619]

After his experience at Buchenwald, on 17 April, Lieutenant Arnold Visser was finally assigned to his first combat role; a platoon leader in K Company, 47th Infantry Regiment, 9th Infantry Division, the same company that had landed with Charles Vellema's L Company at Safi in French Morocco two years before. During the next six days his company would see nearly continuous combat action until 23 April, fighting at the German cities of Aken, Wolfen, Chorau, Klienkűhnau, and Dessau, including attacking and clearing both an air field and a Junkers airplane factory. During this fighting, Arnold would receive the Bronze Star Medal for valor.[620]

Also battling against German troops, but around Eitensheim, Germany, was the 86th Infantry Division. On the 26th of April, Sergeant Bill Lees and his squad were sent to the front to pick up a wounded soldier. Under machinegun fire and a mortar barrage, the squad, including Medic Private First Class Emil Hopp, waded a river. As Lees explained, although Emil's face was "contorted with fear . . . he stuck with the patient which no ordinary man could have done. Emil is no ordinary man. His courage was as great as any hero of this or any other war." At about that time, Emil was hit in the right shoulder by a German sniper's bullet. "His calmness after being wounded," Lees would write to Emil's mother, "will never cease to amaze the three of us who were with him."[621]

Later that year, nineteen year old Joan Laandal was going into Damsteegt's Drug Store back in Waupun when she saw a soldier who, to her surprise, said, "Hello Joan." As she recalled, she

> looked at him, and my God, it was Emil Hopp who I went to school with. And I said, "Well, Emil Hopp, how are you?" And he said, "Well, I'm home on leave." He was wounded, and he says, "But I'm getting along okay." And just then, just then some guy—a lieutenant—he was going into the drug store and he looked at Emil and Emil looked at him and the lieutenant said something [like], "Did you forget how to salute solider?" And Emil, who could never hardly even say his own name, stood up like a . . ., I gotta show yah how Emil would stand, how he would stand to attention, you know how they stand [she stands at rigid attention], and he said the most—oh, I didn't know he knew those words—he said, "Sir, I was wounded in action and I am unable to salute with my arm." But he said it in such a . . ., more words than that and big words. And this, this lieutenant looked at him and he said, "I salute *you* solider!" . . . And then away he walked.

And I just stood like..., I couldn't believe this. I've never seen it. It was like the movies. You never saw that on a Waupun street where the lieutenant saluted this private or corporal or whatever he was.... And Emil didn't think twice about it, you know.... Oh, but it just flowed out of him, he was such a man right then.[622]

Three days after Emil was wounded and just six days after Arnold Visser's winning of the Bronze Star, on 29 April, Arnold was tasked with representing his regiment in meeting the advancing Russians near the town of Pratau, Germany, which is about a mile south of both the Elbe River and Wittenberg, Germany. As he recalled:

It was on a Sunday. Took my squad . . . we didn't have hardly anybody left because the unit was pretty well depleted. So we met the Russians. . . . Fortunately they didn't fire . . . because one of our units met 'em some other place and they got fired on by accident from other Russians, or whatever. . . . I had to meet their officers, make arrangements for our higher officers, regimental or division, to meet with them [in] two days or something like that. That was my job.[623]

This was also Arnold's last combat related mission of the war. Although only having served with his company for a short while, he proudly related that while he was with them they took 115 German POWs. As he stated, by that time the company "was down to about eighty, ninety people in there and three officers, you know, because the 9th Division lost a lot of men. We lost 4,400 men the 9th did, in their history of World War II."[624]

It was about this time that Dr. Leonard Schrank, having been promoted to captain, was practicing surgery in what he described as a MASH type of hospital on the main Philippine Island of Luzon, the same island Robert Daniels and Irving Meyer were also serving on at the time. He was later to report to his wife, Ges, that "it was the best thing that could have happened to him because he was forced to do it and things that he was not doing," she stated. "He would, you know, cut off an arm, whatever. And he said, 'I learned a lot of surgery during the year I was over there.'"[625]

But in a war torn country, even for a doctor, it wasn't always safe, and it was not just the Japanese that were always the source of this danger. As Ges continued to relate, Leonard

> was returning from an R & R [Rest and Relaxation] in Manila, and their jeep was only a mile or two from the camp, and someone shot the sergeant that was driving. And he [Leonard] said, "I just rolled right out the jeep and down into the bushes." And he said, "I just laid there and hid. And I watched what went on." And those Filipinos were after the gas cans and the gas. And he said, "That's all they took." They left the jeep there, they left the sergeant there, they didn't rob him, nothing. Just took the gas; because they had extra gas cans on the back of [the jeep] . . . because they never knew when they went out how many miles they were gonna have to go to pick up different people. But that was . . . he said, "A horrible experience." And he said that he stayed lying in this jungle, and he said, "I worried about snakes and animals, but nobody gave me away and luckily nothing made me scream or cry out." And he said he thought they looked for him for [just] about five minutes. They didn't spend any time . . . they just wanted that jeep with those gas cans. Cans of gas, you know.[626]

During this time of the year, back in Wisconsin, like the POW camp in Lawsonia near Green Lake that Edward Uecker was working at, and as there were in many of the towns and villages of the State as well as in other areas of the country during the war, there was a German POW camp located in Waupun. And like at Lawsonia, the POWs in Waupun were used as workers for local farms and factories. Many times the prisoners were just picked up by the farmer or a factory worker in the mornings and then dropped off again in the evenings. Sometimes guards would accompany the POWs to their daily work assignments, sometimes the POWs would just be under the 'guard' of the farmer or factory workers. In the summer of 1945, upwards of 150 German POWs were employed at the Waupun Canning Company, and another eighty or so by the Canned Foods, Inc., the two canning companies located in the town. Others worked in the nearby village of Brandon for the Stokely Foods Corporation, another canning factory. The POW camp itself was located on the southern outskirts of Waupun next to the Waupun Canning Company.[627]

Elmer Rigg, as manager of Canned Foods, Inc., which was located at the opposite side of town from the POW camp, related that "We'd send a truck up in the morning and get a load of prisoners and bring 'em down, and they'd work, and carrying them back at night." He recalled that they had "No problem at all [with them]. . . . Good help. The only problem I had, there was a fella here in town who could talk [speak] German, and he'd come down and call them off their work, you know, and talk German to them. Finally, I had to tell him to stay away because he was interfering with business."[628]

The local townspeople didn't seem to have much of a problem with German POWs in their midst. As Elmer stated, "I never heard any objection to them at any time." He does remember, however, that like the man that would come to his factory to talk to the Germans in their own language, others of the town also had 'relations' with the prisoners. "I remember one of them [a POW]," Elmer stated, "sneaked out of the prison and came down near the canning factory and met some woman down there.[629] Others corroborated this, relating that a German POW was indeed involved in an adulterous affair with a local woman, costing her her reputation and the prisoner quite severe punishment.[630]

Josephine Aarts, who was eighteen at the time and still working at the Huths and James Shoe Factory in Waupun, also recalled the POWs being in town, as well as some of the citizens' 'relationships' with them. As she stated:

> I know there were girls from the shoe factory . . . those guys were sneaking out, and these girls . . . had dates with them. Big talk shoe factory girls—I was not one of them! [she laughed, referring to not being one of the "big talk" girls]. But there were certain girls that were just that type of way. . . . Those guys would break out; they'd go to the cemetery [by the mill pond next to the Canned Foods, Inc. canning company] and did their thing.[631]

Joan Laandal remembered "going up there and going by it [the POW camp]. You couldn't be around there," she laughingly stated. "You better not be, you know, the first thing your dad would have whipped you if he knew you were up there by the prison camp." As she recalled, it was surrounded by a fence, although she could not recall what type of fence, and the prisoners lived in tents. Joan also recalled that on Sunday afternoons the soldiers would "march those guys [the German POWs] down Madison Street to the theater—down the Main Street, turn right to the Classic Theater—after, I suppose, the matinee was over for the [towns'] people, and showed them the propaganda films."[632] As she recalled seeing the prisoners marching from the theater, Joan was to state:

> And then they marched them back. And in the front row was the *exact* guy that Hitler was ever always talking about—the blonde, healthy looking, good looking, big German guy. Front Row. I just hated him. I didn't know him, but hated him because he was the enemy and they were killing our guys. We had a number of our class that were killed in ..., while they were still young men.[633]

According to Lois Bohnert, her father, Joseph, who could speak German, worked for a time at a local bindery, which supplied the canning companies, as a German translator for the POWs.[634] Having emigrated from Switzerland, Joseph could also speak French and Italian, besides German and English. Prior to emigrating to the U.S., he had worked in Cairo, Egypt, at the pyramids as a tour guide for European tourists.[635]

Josephine Aarts also recalled that the nearby town of Fox Lake as well had German POW camps.[636] In actuality, Fox Lake had two POW camps, one in 1944 housing 284 German POWs and then one again in 1945 holding 350 prisoners. They were both located in the community building and were surrounded by a snow fence. Their POWs worked in the Central Wisconsin Cannery plant in Fox Lake as well as on numerous farms in the area. Beaver Dam, about fifteen miles away, also had a POW camp in 1944 housing 300 German POWs.[637]

Charlotte Mehlbrech remembered that Marshfield, Wisconsin, also had a POW camp. As she recalled:

> We were not to speak to them on the way to the swimming pool. They were taking down something there with some

mallets in the hot sun, and hitting this great big thing that looked like a silo thing to me. It was just off of Main Street in Marshfield. And . . . my grandma said, "Do not talk to 'em." And they were whistling . . . whistling at me, a little girl walking along in her swimming suit. And I just marched right by.[638]

These POWs were Wehrmacht troops, not the hard core SS Storm Troops, the later which were extremely dedicated and loyal to Adolf Hitler and the Nazi Regime. The SS troops, as well as the relative few Japanese POWs, were to remain locked securely behind double barbed-wire fencing well within the boundaries of military installations, such as one that was located at Camp McCoy outside of Sparta, Wisconsin, guarded by well trained and led Army MPs and other military troops. These SS and Japanese troops could *not* be trusted.

Robert Daniels, who as an MP had guarded many German and some Japanese POWs, related that once the Germans were transported to the United States, especially once they actually set foot on the shores, with the exception of the SS troops, they could be, for the most part, trusted not to escape or do harm to civilians. For one thing, as he stated, they knew that there was no way for them to get back to Germany if they escaped. In addition, most were quite happy to be out of the war and, as such, had no more fight in them. They were also treated well by both their captors and the American public. The Japanese, on the other hand, Robert was to state, could not be trusted at all. One could not even to turn one's back to them without fear of being attacked.[639]

One of Robert's favorite war stories to tell was of German POWs. As he related, at one camp that he was a guard at, another guard loaded a group of German prisoners onto a truck and drove them to a nearby farmer's field for a day of work. Along with his rifle, the guard had also brought along a bottle of booze, and commenced to get himself drunk. Once inebriated, he began waving his rifle around at the POWs, who quickly subdued him, took away his gun, threw him in the back of the truck, then loaded themselves and the gun into the truck and drove back to the camp. Once back at the POW camp they handed the rifle over to the camp guards and pronounced that they would not again go on a work trip with that particular guard.[640]

While U.S. held POWs were well fed, and at times even 'entertained' by local women, across the Pacific Ocean in Japan, U.S. Marine Ed Babler, as a Japanese held POW, was still enduring extreme hardships struggling inside the coal mine near Fukuoka Camp 05B-Omine. Everyday he would have to walk each way to the mine with his fellow POWs through the bitter cold of winter and the heat of summer for a twelve hour shift of back breaking work mining and hauling coal. At the camp, the food was the same as the other camps, watery *lugao* and weak soup. As he was to record about the conditions in the mine itself:

> I believe that just about every mine has water in it, and this one was no different. Everyday inside the mine I would step in water; this ensured that my feet were constantly wet throughout the day's work. Besides the water being bothersome, the mine was constructed to accommodate the shorter Japanese, not someone like me at six feet tall.[641]

As a result, he always had to walk and work bent over when in the mine. Whenever he straightened up he would hit his head, which he calculated he did "an average of six times a day."[642] Stanley Sommers was also suffering as a Japanese held POW, working in a different coal mine in Japan.[643]

This same time saw Walter Riel, along with the others in the 38th Photo-Reconnaissance Squadron, still living in tents in the jungles of Morotai. Although Walter did not have to do any "hand to hand combat like the infantry," as he stated, he "had some trouble there with the Japs on this island infiltrating all the time, and air raids." As he recalled, this in itself

> was nerve-racking, very nerve-racking. We'd get these air raids and I'd have to shut down the generator because we couldn't have any lights—visibility, you know. And I had to keep the telephones going. You could say you had to sleep with your ears open and your eyes shut. . . . Air-raids or any Japs infiltrating, it was nerve-racking, that's what it was.[644]

The telephones that Walter took care of were battery operated and required stringing and maintaining wires throughout the squadron. But, as he indicated, it wasn't just the telephones he had to take care of. "[T]he first island that we landed on after the Marines," Walter stated, "then the lieutenant says, 'You're gonna have to get these generators going.' Well, then I said, 'I don't know anything about electricity. I never went to high school or anything like that.' He said, 'I don't either.'"[645] Because Walter could string telephone wires, they figured he could handle a generator as well. Nonetheless, and regardless of his lack of training on generators, Walter was able to figure out how to operate and keep the squadron's generators running, which would have a bright side. "[A]ctually," as Walter recalled, "my MOS only called for a corporal as the telephone operator and an installer. But because of what I was doing, he [the lieutenant] saw to it that I got an extra rank, because he says, 'You're doing an awful good job,' he says, 'you deserve one.' So he got me an extra rank, which was nice of him."[646]

In describing the incoming bombs during the many air raids he experienced, Walter would recall that "We'd hear 'em. 'Well, I guess that one didn't have our name on it.' You kind of humor a little bit too, you know. But just lay in that fox hole and just, just hope that the next one won't hit you, that's all."[647]

As Walter would write, "As the Japs were pushed back the air-raids became less," but what they called "Bed Check Charlie or Piss Call Charlie" would come around nearly every night at "1:00 am or 2:00 am" for a bomb run. Walter was also to relate that "During the war one of our planes ran out of fuel and crashed landed on the beach at the Halamahara Islands. After the war they went to see about the pilot. The natives told us that three days after the war the Japs beheaded the pilot, cruel."[648] Halamahara, also known as Halmahera, is the largest of the Moluccas group of Islands that Morotai was a part of.

The Japanese infantry, according to Walter, numbered "several thousand on the island with us when they surrendered." This caused the Americans, as Walter continued, "to keep forces on duty twenty-four hours a day. Especially at night to protect from the Japs from stealing equipment and food as they had none in the Jungle."[649]

The day after Arnold Visser had met the Russians near Wittenberg, on 30 April, Adolf Hitler committed suicide. Seven days later, on orders from German Admiral Karl Dönitz, General Alfried Jodl signed a general surrender of all German forces, effectively ending the war in Europe.[650]

"Easter, it was Good Friday when the Americans rolled into town," recalled fourteen year-old (at the time) AnnaMarie Kretzer of when the American soldiers entered her hometown of Geisenheim, Germany. In relating her feelings about the end of the war and the coming of the Americans, AnnaMarie was to state:

> Well, first of all, we were glad to be free now. And there was still very little to eat. And everybody knows Germany was divided into four sectors, the Russians got everybody off and then they were the French, and British, and the Americans. I lived in the American occupied zone. It was good; the Americans were good to us. The soldiers would give us some food and stuff.[651]

But things would not be back to normal for her for some time. There were still some struggles to come, however, things were certainly looking up. The family was getting leftovers from the Americans who now occupied AnnaMarie's old schoolhouse. As she reported, the American commander said to his troops, "'What you don't bite into, leave it whole if you don't want it, give it to the kids.' So we got a little extra there."[652] In addition, her mother sent AnnaMarie across the Rhine River—she had to use a boat since the American bombers had destroyed the bridge that had been there—each day into the French Zone to work at a flour mill, where she could then use the little money she earned to buy flour and other food stuffs for the family. However, the French were not as friendly and helpful as their American counterparts were. As AnnaMarie was to recall:

> French guards and soldiers were watching a little bit more. So if I had a suitcase on the back of the bike with some flour and a few other things in it I waited, hiding behind the building until the whistle blew for the ship, for the little boat, and then I dashed out, and the soldiers tried to stop us. I spoke French and I'd say, "No, no, I can't miss the boat," and they'd let us go.[653]

When asked about whether she or her family were aware of the concentration camps, AnnaMarie stated:

Not at all until after the war. I mean, we were all shocked. Now if, and that's a big *if*, my parents had heard about it, they never said anything. They were scared. But the concentration camps were hundreds of miles away from us. So we didn't live close enough to smell anything or see the smoke or see the trains coming. Nothing at all.

The only thing I was more aware of was . . . of course, Hitler killed all the mentally disabled people, and I heard my mother say one time, "What did they do with him?" And my dad said, "Shhh!" So disabled people in our town were gone, they disappeared.[654]

AnnaMarie was to report that anyone who would speak up against Hitler or the Nazis would disappear. A cousin of hers had done just that and "He disappeared, he was gone," she stated, "and his family didn't find out until after the war that he was in Dachau." Although he was "rescued" by the Allies, he soon died due to his advanced stage of starvation. In addition, as she related:

Ministers . . . a Lutheran minister spoke up in his sermons against some of the things that were happening, and he was warned not to keep his sermons like that. Well, he didn't stop, he wasn't quiet. He was gone. So it was a lot— mostly Jewish people—but a lot of others. Anything in politics, religion, whoever didn't agree and go along.[655]

AnnaMarie also recalled that Hitler had wanted the German women to bear as many children as they could. He would issue medals to mothers for the amount of children they bore: a bronze medal for up to four children, from five to eight they would receive a silver medal, and for baring over eight children mothers would get a gold medal. "Supposedly," she said, "it was an honor, because he did want a lot of children, and he wanted his race—if you were pure—to conquer, to spread out and take all of Europe. So he needed a lot of mothers and a lot of children. So that was his goal."[656]

While in school, AnnaMarie also had to show that she was of the pure race. As she recalled:

[W]hen I was in middle school, we had to make up a big family tree, like a big tree with all the branches, and we had to go back to the great grandparents if we possibly could. And there weren't that many records kept, but I got the tree all together, and on both sides of my parents, and this was to prove that there wasn't a bit of Jewish in us.

She kept this big poster in her bedroom for a few years, when finally her mother said, "'Get rid of this thing.' And I tore it up."[657]

Although the war in Europe ended, the B-17s of the 493rd Bomb Group did not stop flying missions. The payloads on these missions did, however, change. As Fred Zurbuchen recalled, "Germany had flooded Holland. They had broke their banks [dams and levies], it was a complete mess." He was to fly six "bread run[s]" over to Amsterdam, Holland. These "consisted of food, C-rations, K-rations, staples—flour, salt, whatever," he was to relate. Ground crews rigged wooden flooring to the bomb-bays so these foodstuffs could be loaded into the planes, then they would jettison the cargo over the large Amsterdam airfield.[658]

When the fighting ended, Robert Van Alstine and the 45th EVAC Hospital were still at Buchenwald treating the survivors of the concentration camp. And just prior to the end of the war, the Army took steps to insure the German citizens were fully aware of the atrocities of Buchenwald. As Robert recalled:

After Buchenwald had been pretty much secure, and, of course, the war was winding down pretty quick then, they took trucks back to Weimar, which is, I would guess, nine, ten kilometers outside of Buchenwald, and picked up all the people, the adults, and marched them through Buchenwald—all the German civilians—so that there would be no denying that this happened. Many of the [German] officers, particularly the high ranking officers, lived in Weimar, and yet these people claimed they didn't know the concentration camp even existed. And, of course, they were . . . at the time they were [had been] cremating bodies every day. The smell was terrible.[659]

About this same time, according to Robert, it was decided that the 45th would stay in Germany as part of the army of occupation. As he stated:

> [T]hey decided that because there was no way to get home anyway that we'd be in the army of occupation, and we were to set up the hospital in a city and take care of not only the American soldiers in the area but also civilians. So we operated as an occupation hospital.[660]

On the Fourth of July, Fred Zurbuchen and his B-17 crewmembers, after finishing making their humanitarian airdrops over Holland, landed in the United States at Bradley Field in Connecticut. Upon landing, his pilot, Captain Reynolds, came over the aircraft's intercom system and said, "If you gentlemen look out your starboard [right] side," recalled Fred, "you'll see a whole row of B-29s over there.... So when you guys get back from your furlough, you're coming back here and we're getting on board one of those B-29s and were going to go fight the Japanese."[661]

This was a real threat, since the war in the Pacific was still raging. As Robert Van Alstine stated concerning his hearing of the end of the war in Europe, "[Y]ou know, I see these pictures on television of the people dancing in the street. No, not where I was. Nobody really cared. And I think the reason they didn't care is because we were scheduled to go to Japan."[662]

That same month, July, found Arnold Visser re-assigned to the 405th Infantry Regiment of the 102 Infantry Division as the 1st Battalion S-2 officer. As such, he was assigned command of Stalag 7 near Moosburg, Germany, now a POW camp housing 2,400 German soldiers. Shortly thereafter, when returning to Stalag 7 from attending a short school in Paris, Arnold was to receive word that Grace had given birth to their first child, a daughter.[663]

With the war in Europe over, Charles Vellema was flown home to the United States from Great Britain on a large four engine aircraft. As he reported, "[T]here was only thirteen [of us] on the great big four engine thing. And they said that was the last plane that was flying out from there and it was done. But the war was [still] going in Japan by that time." Charles, however, was not to go to Japan. Instead, he received his discharge from the Army and went home to Waupun, arriving there on 31 July. He and Nova Wagner had not seen each other since a one short weekend furlough in December of 1941, nearly three and a half years before. Their only correspondence since then was letters, and although Nova wrote nearly every day, Charles would receive these in bundles, sometimes months apart. During the year, as in the previous years, Nova had continued teaching grade school. However, this year she had taken a new job teaching first and second grades at Oakfield, Wisconsin, approximately ten miles east of Waupun, which would be her first teaching position in a school with more than one room. Once together again, the couple wasted little time. On 4 August, just four days after Charles' return, they were married. In responding to a question of when they were married, Charles replied, "About as soon as I got home [he chuckled]. I got home on what?, July 31st . . . and we got married the 4th of August."[664]

Just two weeks later, on 14 August 1945, after the United States dropped a second atomic bomb on Japan, the Japanese agreed to surrender. Although the formal surrender did not take place until 2 September, 15 August was announced as V-J Day: Victory over Japan. The word quickly spread around the world. On the Island of Luzon in the Philippines, when Radioman Third Class Irving Meyer heard the news, as he was to state, he and his fellow navy radiomen "were thankful and glad to be going home."[665]

"Oh, boy! It was great! We just whooped and yelled," recalled Walter Riel, who was still on the island of Morotai in the South Pacific when he heard the news. "All the search lights went on. . . . In those days they had search lights to detect the planes so they could shoot them. All the search lights were on and everyone was just a yelling and whooping." As Walter continued to explain, it was not, however, totally unexpected. "[W]e had an inkling already because we had everything all packed up, because we were going to move further to the front. Of course, we didn't know where. And they dropped the first A-Bomb. Well, they suspected they might give up. Then they dropped the second one, then they cancelled our orders, and of course the war had ended."[666]

Back in Wisconsin people were also very excited. "Oh," recalled Doris Bohnert, living in Sparta at the time, "everybody threw stuff up in the air. We were happy."[667] Lois, her younger sister, remembered both surrenders, Germany's and Japan's. Although living in Waupun, she was in the county seat of Fond du Lac when she heard the news of Germany's surrender. "[T]hey were wild," she was to explain. "You know, everybody was whooping and hollering and running down around the main street." The same was true, she reported, in Waupun when the news arrived about Japan's surrender. "[E]verybody went wild. . . . I remember the people running around on the streets and stuff. . . . I remember the one girl ran and she fell on Main Street. Her dress went way over her head, you know," she laughingly recalled.[668]

As Dorothy Bal was to state, "I can remember my mother and dad and I were out on the front sidewalk. . . . And all of a sudden we saw this jeep coming with two servicemen in. So I waved at them and they stopped, and I told them, I said, 'The war just ended.' Boy, you should've seen the looks on their faces."[669] Bessie Douma, nine years old at the time, remembers being on the back lawn on her family's farm and hearing the sound of horns blowing in the nearby village of Friesland, Wisconsin. As she stated, "I thought they were car horns, but my brother said that the trains were blowing their horns in celebration."[670] "What a thrill, what a thrill," recalled Fred Zurbuchen. He had only been home in Burnett, Wisconsin, on furlough a short while and looking at the prospect of returning to Bradley Field in Connecticut to man a new B-29 bomber, which he would have soon been flying in the Pacific against the Japanese, when word of Japan's surrender reached him and his oldest brother, Ewald, who was also at home from the Army on furlough. Ewald had spent the last few years as one of General Patton's tank commanders in both North Africa and Europe.[671]

Ges (Mintzlaff) Schrank and her two sons, which had been born during the war years, had recently moved from her parents home in Grafton to the Waupun area and was living with her husband's, Leonard Schrank's, family. As she recalled:

> Berty and I, Mrs. Neugent, and Eva Hayes all got together the night the war ended, and we decided to go to Beaver Dam to celebrate. And we went up and down the streets and we finally found a tavern we thought we would be safe in [she laughed]. And we went in and had a beer, and, oh, we were home by 10:30 [p.m.]. And grandma Schrank stood at the door; she said, "You naughty girls, you are not to go out and drink to celebrate the end of the war." Oh, grandma was so angry at us! And we were

her daughter-in-laws, you know. Her sons were the boys that were in the service. So that was funny [she again laughed]. But she got over it.[672]

Charlotte Mehlbrech, twelve years old at the time, also vividly remembered the excitement in Waupun:

Oh, everybody was just [excited]. . . . See, my mother was a history buff, we have to go down[town]. My dad was always working shift work. We had to get in the car and we had to go down to the victory parade. And then we left because it got unruly. But everyone . . . people were blowing their horns all the way when you were going around. The church bells were ringing. Everybody was so happy. Everybody was crying. Everybody was dancing around. "The war was over! The war was over!"

And we didn't even know what it was going to mean that the war was over. We'd been so long with it. It seemed my lifetime was all about wars because I was born in '33 and it was soon there. But everyone was just elated. And then everybody first wanted to know about their loved one that was in the service. When were they gonna hear? When were they gonna get out?[673]

Young four year old David Lyons remembered that his mother, aunts, and grandmother

all celebrated because they knew that everybody was gonna come home then. And their husbands were coming back and, you know, everything was gonna get back to normal. We no longer had to worry about the Japanese and the Germans and everything. Everybody at that time thought that Harry Truman was a great president. [674]

Harry S. Truman, as Franklin Delano Roosevelt's vice president, had recently become the president upon Roosevelt's death, and it was he who had authorized the dropping of the two atomic bombs on Japanese cities.

Although just two years old at the time, DiAnna Reif even remembered the end of the war. As she recalled:

> I still do remember the day the war ended, when the church bells rang, the whistles blew, and all of that. I can still hear that. I mean, it was scary to me too, I guess. I know I couldn't figure it out. And I remember mom and dad telling us, "Well, the war is over, the war is over." And people went out on the streets and actually . . . celebrated in the streets. I can remember we walked to the downtown area.[675]

Joan Laandal remembered that the army captain in charge of the POW camp in Waupun came driving down the street in his jeep. Joan's sister knew the captain, and their bother John's little daughter Judy, "who was four or five years old, if that," as Joan recalled, "got to ride in that jeep. But she was the only civilian in Waupun that got to ride in that army jeep. And there she was. It was cute." Joan also recalled that her dad's bar was "very busy that evening. . . . Neighbors were over and, you know, people coming in." Joan also related that "we had fun that night because we were dancing in the middle of the street on Main Street. Right smack in the middle. I don't know where the music was coming from, but . . . it was just like heaven, you know. Such a relief." She stated that the dancing went on late into the night. "[I]t was two, three in the morning and it was still going. We walked, you know, to our homes then. And my dad had closed the tavern [*Laandal's Lunch* restaurant-tavern], but my folks were still up. . . . It was just unbelievable . . . such a joy."[676]

Jim Laird recalled talking amongst his fellow eight year old schoolmates about hearing about the dropping of the atomic bomb: "Did you feel the earth shake last night? Did you feel the earth shake? They blew up a big, big, big, big bomb, and the whole earth shook." A few days later he would go downtown in Cuba City and help celebrate, "Marching up and down the street," he stated, "and I believe I had a flag—a flag, a little flag—bells ringing and that sort of thing, you know. How exuberant and happy the people were."[677]

Just like Walter Riel and Irving Meyer, Gladys Jolly was also still deployed, in her case at Fort Leonard Wood as and Army truck driver. But her reactions on hearing the news were a bit different. "I don't remember how we really reacted," she recalled. "I think we all just looked at each other. It's like we were on this big merry-go-round, now it's stopped and now we are gonna get off. I don't know. I can't remember what I felt and how I acted."[678]

The end of the war found Marine Al Bohnert stationed at Newport, Rhode Island. After Iwo Jima was secured, he and his fellow Marines had been shipped back to Guam. He was then shipped to San Diego where he was given a thirty-day furlough, his first since boot camp. He spent this furlough back home in Waupun, after which he reported for duty at a torpedo base in Newport where he resumed his duties as a cook. When the news of the Japanese surrender broke, "People were going nuts," he recalled. "They were trying to break into liquor stores . . . other stuff. So we were assigned to keep them away." As he stated, "[E]verybody in the base that was a sergeant or above were ordered to go on MP duty. So we all handled our MP duty for about, let's see . . . two or three weeks we all had to go out and keep law and order." When asked if the Marines had to deal with civilians also, Al replied with a laugh, "Well, if they tried to break in, yeah. Some of them did, though, and they got a little bit *discouraged*."[679]

Motor Machinist Mate Theron Mickelson, once the USS *Barnegat* had again crossed through the Panama Canal re-entering the Atlantic Ocean from the Pacific, had also been given thirty days leave. This placed him back home in Neenah, Wisconsin, when the war ended. As he recalled upon hearing that the Japanese had surrendered:

> I and my buddy, both about the same age within about six months of one another, we were in Neenah, Wisconsin. If you've ever been there, there was only one bridge that separated Neenah from Menasha. And when we heard on a little radio in the kind of convertible that I had, which was a Ford, we had a case of beer. And we stopped right in the middle of the intersection [on the bridge]. We handed everyone a bottle of beer that come to us. And when the beer was gone, we left. Never nothing by no cops, no nothing. Yet this was the only way [speaking of being on the only bridge between the two cities], the cars were lined up like you wouldn't believe. Yup.[680]

No one was more excited about the end of the war than Ed Babler who vividly remembered hearing about its ending on the evening of 15 August at his POW camp on the Island of Kyushu in Japan. Sitting in his room with the doors open, he could hear the radios in the nearby civilian homes. At about 7:30 p.m., after over three years of brutal captivity, including the last year mining coal under slave-labor conditions, as Ed reported, "[T]hese radios began repeatedly announcing, '*Senso wari, senso wari,*" which meant the war was over." He immediately became both excited and overwhelmed, and it wasn't long before the whole camp also became aware of the end of the war. "Although we hadn't yet received any word from the Japanese camp commander, official or otherwise, and we had to be careful not to jump to conclusions too quickly," he was to write, "it was a tremendous relief to know that this horrible ordeal was about to end."[681]

The next day things were different. Although the guards were still there, for the first time in years, the normal *bango* (roll call) was not held, and not only were the POWs not marched to the mine, the normal wake up also never happened. Ed and his fellow POWs, however, were up and wide awake by 3 a.m., eagerly waiting news. Then, around 8 a.m., the Japanese camp commander announced to the POWs that the war was indeed officially over, but the American Command had informed him to await further orders. "All that day, 16 August," Ed recalled, "we did nothing but talk about how soon American forces would come in to take us out. . . . We just wanted to get out of Japan as quickly as possible" and get to the States. The next couple of days saw wave after wave of American aircraft fly over the camp dropping provisions to the POWs. As Ed related concerning the first day of these airdrops, "That was probably the happiest day of my life up to that time, not only did I receive some real food, and a lot of it, but I finally realized the war was over."[682]

Within a couple of days, the POWs were placed on a train and taken to a Japanese resort near the town of Omuta to recuperate. There they ate well, bathed in mineral water baths, and were cared for by Japanese girls. From there, they were again placed on a train to the coastal city of Kanoya, where they were checked over by American military doctors and placed on transports back to the States. While onboard the transport, Ed was treated nearly as royalty by the ship's crew. As he recalled, "While on my way to Guam I was treated like a long lost dog. The Navy crew served me steak and ice cream, the first of both I had had since early 1941."[683]

After a short stay in Guam, Ed was then shipped to San Diego,

California. At San Diego he would undergo several medical tests and evaluations at the San Diego Naval Hospital. He recalled getting upwards of fifty penicillin shots to help combat all of the dysentery and unclean food he had eaten during his nearly forty months of captivity. It was also the first time he was able to call home and talk to his parents since he had left for Shanghai, China, five years earlier in 1940.[684]

Stanley Sommers of the U.S. Navy, who also spent nearly three and a half years in the same conditions, even in some of the same POW camps that Ed had been in, who ate the same type of watery *lugao* and same non-nutritious millet soup, who also worked in a coal mine in Japan and was regularly beaten for no reason, who had also survived the horrors of a Hell Ship, and had endured the Bataan Death March, was also released from his Japanese captors. Like Ed, Stanley was treated extremely well on his transit back to the United States. As his niece Charlotte Mehlbrech was to relate, "They would try to fill it [his wishes] one way or another. And he wanted peaches. And he ate a whole can, I suppose it was, of peaches. Of course, [he] got sick. But . . . that's how nice they were to him." And like the Bablers, the first Stanley's parents heard of their son coming home was a phone call. "[M]y grandma did not even know," Charlotte related. "The letter didn't come quick enough. He called on the phone . . . he says, 'Hi, ma.' And, you know, she was just hysterical and my grandpa had to talk."[685]

Although the war had ended, the work was not over for many of those in the military. Morris Page was one of those. The USS *Thomas Jefferson*, which he was still a crewmember of, participated in transporting American occupation troops to Sasebo, Japan, arriving in Sasebo on 22 September 1945.[686] Prior to this, as Morris pointed out, from time to time when his ship was not involved in an invasion or ferrying replacement troops and supplies to the front lines and Pacific islands, the ship would anchor off an island and allow the crew to go ashore for some rest and relaxation. As he related:

> When we was in the Pacific we'd pick an island and then take like a horse tank, you know, [a] water [tank]? Fill it full of ice, and then they gave us beer then. And you'd be surprised how many guys couldn't drink beer, and you'd get a case of beer for two guys. And you'd pick a guy that didn't drink and then get stinking drunk . . . they'd

take you over to an island, and then when you got drunk they'd haul you back.[687]

Back in the United States, as Al Bohnert was to recall, after receiving his honorable discharge from the Marine Corps on 3 October, he had his wallet stolen while on a train travelling back home to Waupun. "All my papers and everything was stolen out of it. Never did find it." When he got home he attended an American Legion meeting. "When they heard about my troubles getting home," he stated, "they chipped together and gave me some money." He also went to visit his sister Lois at Shaler's National Rivet and Manufacturing Company where she still was working. As he laughingly explained, "[T]hey wouldn't even let me in because 'That was *security*.' I said, 'Hell, you guys don't know what security is around here.' I walked right in anyway. And they didn't do anything."[688]

Also in October, Private First Class Robert Van Alstine and the 45th EVAC Hospital received orders "to turn in the hospital equipment to the Army . . . and pack up ready to go home, which we did," he recalled. "And we shipped out to what they call cigarette camps, which were really just assembly areas to get ready to ship out." However, with the lack of transport ships available, they were not to leave their cigarette camp for a while.[689]

At about 9:30 p.m. on 16 November 1945 newly promoted Marine Sergeant and ex-POW Edmond Babler arrived at the train station in Green Bay, Wisconsin. His mother and father, as prearranged, were to meet him not far away at the Y.M.C.A. As he recalled, "I took a cab to the Y.M.C.A. and paced the floor of the lobby until about 10 p.m. when my folks walked through the door. Although it had been almost six years, we recognized each other immediately and I embraced each of them."[690]

Around the same time, ex-POW Stanley Sommers also came home. As his niece Charlotte Mehlbrech related:

> [B]ecause they [Stanley's parents] didn't know when he was coming . . . he had to bust in the house. And he could always get on the porch. And then there was one window that never would . . . didn't lock or they couldn't lock it, but that went into the living room. So they heard some noise. And then my grandma came down . . . there was her Stanley. And he had been eighteen when he went in

the service, and when she saw him he was four years older and had been through all of that.[691]

As Charlotte remembered, once home Stanley at times would "Just stare at the wall. And the first Thanksgiving that he came home, I remember that dinner. . . . We all sat around the table and he came there and he was real thin. He had had malaria, and he just burst into tears."[692]

The day after Thanksgiving Robert Van Alstine, finally able to catch a transport back from Europe, returned home as well, to Kenosha, Wisconsin, after turning down an invitation to re-enlist. According to Robert, of the 220 members of the 45th EVAC Hospital, he only knew of one that re-enlisted. Robert had telegraphed his family from Boston that he was coming home, but had first to travel to Fort Sheridan in Chicago. Of coming home he recalled that

> The Army did their darnedest to get, I think, everybody out of Fort Sheridan before Thanksgiving, and I just missed it by a shade, you know. At any rate, when I got home I took this taxi from the [train] depot and walked in. I had my duffle bag and gear, you know, and threw it down.
>
> Actually, I was very disappointed. Sure, my mother was glad to see me; my dad was working, of course. I don't even recall what day of the week it was. I don't know where my sister was. She probably was working too, I imagine. By the time everyone got home for supper— this was in the afternoon I got there—by the time they got home for supper is was kinda like, "ho-hum" type of thing, "The war is over, been over for months." There was no cheering, there was no nothing.
>
> My butt was dragging. So I went in for the next few days, sat down, turned on the radio, which I hadn't had anything like that [in the Army], you know, and my mother said, "You're not gonna set there for the rest of your life are yah?"[693]

Likewise, Gladys Jolly had also recently been sent home from the

Army. She travelled from Fort Leonard Wood to Ripon, Wisconsin. "[M]y mother had gotten ill," Gladys recalled, "and I had to really come back because dad just couldn't handle it anymore. Not that I wanted to. No, I wanted to stay, I wanted to go on into whatever. But I had to sign up for the reserves, too. That was a must."[694] Walter Riel as well came home. After first being shipped from New Guinea to the Philippines for a three month stay, the liberty ship that Walter was riding on docked in San Francisco on Christmas Eve. Unlike on his trip over to the southwestern Pacific a year earlier, he was not seasick on this return trip.[695]

While others were coming home, Theron Mickelson, still in the Navy, and with his thirty-day leave over, was shipped to Treasure Island in San Francisco, California. There he would spend six weeks as a "kind of a head honcho" in a barracks set up in a large building that also, as he stated, "housed railroad cars, and not just cars but the engines and all the rest of that stuff inside that building."[696]

Theron, being a second class petty officer at the time, was second in command of the barracks under a first class petty officer. The two of them, instead of simply telling the men living in the barracks how to maintain the barracks, would both also pitch in and help in the daily chores. One day their chief petty officer came in to inspect and saw what the two of them were doing, and quickly said, "What the hell is going on here?" reported Theron. "You're not supposed to be doing it. You're supposed to be telling *them* to do it." And I thought, Theron added, "Kiss my ass, buddy. But I didn't tell him that." After his six weeks at Treasure Island, he was also mustered out of the service and sent home. As he recalled about the people in Neenah when he finally got back home for good, "I would say they were happy it was over with 'cause, like that little town I came from, there wasn't too many kids that were in the war but they knew friends and relatives that had, and I think they were happy. I know I was. My father was, my mother was."[697]

In Waupun, David Lyon remembered when the men began to come home how happy everybody was. As he was to state, his mother, grandmother, and aunts who he was living with were saying:

> "Uncle Ray [Ray Ruhland] and Uncle Dick [Richard Leonard] and dad were coming home." And I remember coming home . . . my mom and my aunts and I were downtown, and we came home and grandma said, "I've

got a surprise for you." And we said, "What is it?" And she said, "Go to the bedroom and open the door." And we opened the door and my Uncle Ray was back from England. And he was the first guy to come back [of David's family].[698]

David also remembered his Uncle Dick coming back home, who had been a military cook stationed in the Aleutian Islands. In recalling one of his uncle's stories, David said his uncle Dick related that

they got up to this island, I believe it was Kiska, and there was nothing there but a Russian cemetery. And he said, "We didn't have anything to do so we dug up the graves and everybody had a skull hanging outside their tent." And he said, "Then the officers came around and made us bury everything again." [699]

Joan Laandal also vividly recalled the men coming home, but one or two at a time. "Well, they didn't come home as a big group," she said. "They came home . . . you just kinda know that they were home." She remembered that when a boyfriend of one of her girlfriends came home from the Navy, he took his girlfriend and all of her friends, including Joan, down to the Bon Ton Tavern in Waupun for drinks, "and he paid for 'em," she stated. "It must have been his whole total savings" [700]

It wasn't until around March of 1946 that Irving Meyer finally came home, having sailed from Manila in the Philippines on what he referred to as the Liberty Ship *MacArthur*. He would be honorably discharged from the Navy on 11 April of that year at the Naval Station Great Lakes north of Chicago.[701] Like Irving had, others would also come home in 1946.

The long, trying war was over and the troops were returning. Although things were going back the way they had been . . . or at least the best that they could, those that served in the military had changed; so had, to some extent, those who held down the home front.

Picking up the Pieces

With the end of the war and the returning of many of those who fought it, also came the end of the country being on an all out war footing. This included the mass production of war materials and rationing. As such, many factories soon began to re-tool once again, this time back to their pre-war status. The two shoe factories in Waupun, Wisconsin, the Ideal Shoe Factory and the Huth and James Shoe Factory, both discontinued making combat boots and converted back to making loafers and other everyday shoes, the Speed Queen factory in Ripon, Wisconsin, converted back to making washing machines and dryers from warplane parts, and the Manitowoc Shipbuilding Company in Manitowoc, Wisconsin, stopped building submarines and landing craft and began once again building civilian ships.

With these re-toolings, as well as the returning of the men who had previously worked in these plants, many people soon also found their war-time employment at an end. Having been working at Aluminum Goods in Two Rivers, Wisconsin, inspecting welds on navy aircraft parts being manufactured by Grumman, Jeanette Rochon was one of these. As she was to state, "[W]hen the war ended, my job ended." She would then take a job "at a place called Schwartz's" making milk filter discs. "God," she recalled, "it was just a bunch of dust all over the place."[702] Lois Bohnert also found herself out of work, her war-time job at the National Rivet and Manufacturing Company in Waupun reverting back to the man who had held it before he went off to the war. She then worked for the Waupun Canning Company for one pea season. Just as the corn season was about to begin she had to stop working to have her tonsils out. Upon recuperating from her operation, Lois then took a job in the office of East Central Breeders, a company located on the southern outskirts of Waupun which specialized in farm animal artificial insemination (now called East Central—Select Sires), where she would work for the next seven years.[703]

Along with many of the local jobs reverting back to their pre-war workers, the Waupun area, much like the rest of the country, would change somewhat with the returning of the troops and their war experiences. At a time prior to the diagnosis and subsequent treatment of Post-Traumatic Stress Disorder, or PTSD, for some it would be easier to re-adjust than it would be for others. It was also somewhat different for those who had held down the home front during the war who, albeit enthusiastically, had to make due without their loved ones and suffer under the hardships of rationing. Most of these hardships were now gone and money in the post-war times was much better than it had been for nearly everyone prior to the war. The Great Depression, which everyone had to endure in one form or another prior to the war, was over, and the economy was booming. Most of Americans living in the mid- to late 1940's now had access to more money than they had ever seen and even dreamed of before, with many people even having savings accounts from funds earned during the war that, with rationing, they could not or did not spend during the war.

In most cases, times were good. But, it was also a time to, or in many cases at least attempt to, put the war behind them and carry on with their lives. And as we will see, patriotism and the willingness to serve one's country did not necessarily stop with this greatest of generations.

With the return of Charles from the war, Nova and Charles Vellema settled down on the Vellema family farm on State Highway 26 a few miles north of Waupun. Charles originally worked the farm with his father, starting "right in where I left off," as he was to state. But eventually he would take over the entire operation. Nova continued working as a teacher from time to time, even taking summer classes in Oshkosh, Wisconsin, to bring her two-year degree up to where she could teach in Waupun, where she taught sixth grade part-time (half days) at Washington Elementary School. The Vellemas were also members of the local Grange and, as Nova was to state, "My big thing at that time was the 4-H Club, I was general leader for that and I did a lot of work for them, and I enjoyed every bit of it."[704]

Charles became a member of the American Legion, and has recently been awarded his sixty year certificate. When asked if he ever fully recuperated from his war wound, he answered, "No. . . . I'm still classified disabled, twenty percent or whatever. I have a fragment right in the bone of my ankle." In summing up his experiences in the war, he, the recipient of the Bronze Star Medal for valor, modestly stated, "It was rough, but it was interesting." At the time of their interview, Charles and Nova still lived on their farm. They had four children, one boy and three girls, who provided the couple with eight grandchildren and ten great-grandchildren. Their son Dennis served in the Army during the Vietnam era; however, being stationed in Germany, he was not to actually serve in the Vietnam Conflict.[705] Sadly, Nova was to pass away on 18 July 2009.

In 1960, with the Canned Food Incorporated canning company "having trouble selling their goods, and the schools . . . having a problem finding a math and a science teacher," as Elmer Rigg related, after eighteen years as superintendent of the canning company, Elmer went back to teaching. He taught math and science at the Waupun High School. After a couple of years of his teaching in the school, the school system built a new high school and split off the junior high to its own school—the old high school. Elmer was selected as its principle. As he jokingly stated, "I guess I did such a poor job teaching they made a principal out of me." He would hold this job until his retirement in 1972. Elmer and his wife Gertrude had one child, a son, who would join the Navy the same year Elmer retired, 1972. He would go on to retire from the Navy as a commander and then teach at a college in Virginia. In 2005 when interviewed, Elmer, now a widower, was ninety-nine years old and living comfortably and unassisted in his own apartment in Waupun.[706] At his 103rd birthday, living in an assisted living home, Elmer was recognized for his outstanding contributions to education. A few months later, on 15 October 2009, he passed away.

Ed Babler, like many veterans of the war, had some difficulties settling down after arriving back in the States after his 1,220 days in Japanese POW camps. As he related, "For about the next [first] six months [home] all I wanted to do was relax. I wanted to be able to sleep late and not have to get up for *bango* or be forced to do anything I didn't want to do. I just wanted to sleep as late as I chose, smoke cigars, and drink beer, and to be able to do these things whenever I wanted to."[707]

As he continued:

> I stayed at my family home in Maplewood [Wisconsin] for about six months. I needed the rest and time to regain

some of my strength and weight that I had lost during my captivity. I didn't go to the village to help my father in the blacksmith shop until I had enough strength back that I could be of some help to him. . . . I soon realized that it might take longer than I anticipated to become adjusted to my old normal way of living . . . there were quite a number of people that I didn't feel as if I wanted to speak to because their outlooks on life were now so much different than mine.[708]

While recuperating, Ed was to meet Jeanette Rochon. In recalling their first meeting, Jeanette was to state:

His cousin, Curley Babler and Beah, his wife, had one of those little neighbor bars. You know, everybody knew everybody that walked in there. And we were in there, both of my brothers were in there and I was with my girlfriend. We [two girls] were sitting in the back there in a booth, and all of a sudden—it was on Sunday, 13th of January—and all of a sudden beers started coming, and we thought, "Gosh, we can't drink all of that." And first thing you know, my two older brothers came in and they brought this big Marine, a big, quiet Marine. Click! Just like that, click, that was it.[709]

As soon as it was possible, Ed would go to the Naval Station Great Lakes naval base just north of Chicago, Illinois, where he was honorably discharged from the Marine Corps on 16 March 1946. Soon thereafter he was able to find employment at a shipyard in Manitowoc. Ed and Jeanette were married a little over a year later in May of 1947, and soon afterward moved to Waupun where Ed had been accepted, ironically, as a prison guard at the Wisconsin State Maximum Security Prison. Ed was to work at the prison for the next twenty-six years, first as a guard and then as an industries technician, until his health became so bad that he was forced to retire on full disability. In his spare time he created a boxing club, which trained young men to box for the Golden Gloves. Jeanette became a housewife and mother for their two sons, both of which, Joseph and John, were also to enter the military, both serving in the Vietnam Conflict. Joseph received two Purple Heart Medals while there as a member of the Army, and John, as his father had gone to war over two decades earlier, went to Vietnam as a Marine. Keeping the tradition of the Marines alive, one of Ed and Jeanette's grandchildren, Christine, one of Joseph's daughters, also served in the Marine Corps. Ed was to pass away on 29 January 1994.[710] Jeanette just recently joined him on 21 October 2010.

Stanley Sommers was to remain in the Navy, making it a career. He never forgot his fellow prisoners, however. Upon attending a reunion for American POWs, he discovered that a "lot of them," as his niece Charlotte Mehlbrech was to write, "didn't come and those that were there had just terrible health, hearing and sight and, of course, the malaria and emotional problems and trouble with marriages. Some of 'em weren't even married anymore. Alcoholics. And there's nobody to help 'em."[711] He would take this to heart, and upon his retirement from the Navy he became a medical researcher for American ex-POWs, where he collected evidence and information supporting long term effects of being incarcerated. At the time he received and answered nearly three thousand letters a year from ex-POW's, some requesting information, some requesting advice, and some even threatening suicide.[712] He would also become the National Commander of the POWs and MIA Association.[713]

Stanley eventually married "Central." As Charlotte was to relate, in those early days of the telephone, long distance phone calls would entail the call being routed from one telephone company to another through a set of operators. As she stated:

> [Y]our phone would ring, and she'd say, "Central," [as] they called her [the operator]. And she would say, "You have a call from" such and such and it was long distance.... That is what they called her. And if you're going to place a long distance call also, you had to call central. And then you gave your number and then they connected you and they would connect the other side.[714]

As Charlotte explained, it was one of the operators, the "Central" that had placed Stanley's call to his mother when he first called home after returning to the United States upon being released from his Japanese POW camp, that he married.[715]

Charlotte Mehlbrech herself was to graduate from high school in 1951. She was married the next year to a high school friend that had joined the Navy and was stationed in Hawaii. She saved up just enough money for the flight. As she was to state, "I had worked at root beer stands and [the] dime store, and I saved $310.00, and it took $309.87 to fly over there." They were married at her Uncle Stanley's house, who at the time was still in the Navy and also stationed in Hawaii.[716]

Charlotte and her husband soon moved back to Wisconsin Rapids, Wisconsin, where they had three children, although a daughter was stillborn and her first son, who had suffered from a brain injury, passed away at the age of seven and a half. The marriage would not last, however, and in 1964 Charlotte married Vernon Hagen. The two had a daughter together, and the four of them, including Charlotte's surviving son from her first marriage, moved to Waupun in 1968. As she stated concerning her son and daughter, "[T]hey were brought up as brother and sister, and they speak of each other as brother and sister."[717] Charlotte still resides in Waupun.

Upon returning from the war, Walter Riel was to rejoin his wife Catherine in Randolph, Wisconsin, where he met his one year old son for the first time. He used the G.I. Bill to become an electrician, receiving $90.00 a month to go to school one afternoon each week in nearby Beaver Dam. He worked for Van's Electric in Randolph for a while, where he, his wife, their son, and their second child, a daughter, lived. At one time the family moved to California for a short period where Walter again worked as an electrician. However, after three years, as Walter related, "It was good but, I didn't like the busy-ness. It was rough. So then we moved to Waupun [in 1959], and I worked for Mink Brothers." He was to work there for eighteen years "managing the store, doing the selling and buying and everything" until it burned down. He then took a job at Waupun Supply, a wholesale plumbing business, until his retirement.[718]

Although Walter's life was fulfilling after the war, his return from it was not without incident. He was one of many that would be tormented for years to come by his memories. As he stated, "I was a nervous wreck when I came home. . . . [Y]ou kind of pick up like from when you left, you know. For myself it wasn't that way. I mean, up here [pointing to his head], see. You try, but it didn't work that way. I had an awful time when I came home, to adjust to it."[719]

"I know when I came home," he explained, "I just had, I had an awful time. I'd hear a little noise and jump out of bed, you know . . . hit the fox hole." In addition, he was also plagued with "nightmares, nightmares always thinking the Japs was coming in or bombs were dropping."[720] He also told of an incident of not long after he came back when one of his co-workers thought it funny to throw a fire cracker at him. As he related:

> Oh, I jumped and said, "Don't you ever throw one again!" But half hour later, he threw another one. I grabbed him around the neck and I said, "You SOB," I had a hammer in my hand, you know, I was hanging wire, "you do that again I'm gonna kill you." And I was going to hit him on the head. You know, that's your reaction, you're taught that way. Good thing I didn't hit him because I'd have probably killed him, hit him on the head with the hammer, you know. But that's the way it was, your reflexes.[721]

Although going to the Veterans Administration, until the 1980's after the Vietnam Conflict, they never really did anything for those in Walter's condition. As he stated, "They didn't have the P[T]SD or whatever, Post-Traumatic Stress Disorder, at that time, see. They gave us the three hundred bucks and you were on your own, see. No, it wasn't until the early '80's, I think, that I first got good help."[722]

In summarizing his experiences in the war, Walter related that "I think it helped me, you know, to learn to be self-sufficient, to take care of yourself, and be innovative and doing things . . . to survive. So I think it's helped me throughout my life, so it's not been a wasted time when I think back." In ending, he added, "It is just one of those things, you know, . . . it's a million dollar experience, but I wouldn't give a nickel to go through it again."[723]

On 21 October 2000, Walter was called to Milwaukee where the Philippine Ambassador to the United States pinned the Philippine Liberation Medal on him. As Walter wrote, "It was a great honor after 55 years after the war."[724] Walter still lives with his wife Catherine in Waupun enjoying their retirement, children, and grandchildren. Their son was to serve in the Army during the Vietnam Conflict, but like Dennis Vellema, he served his time in Germany and would not actually see combat in Vietnam. Their grandson, their daughter's son, also served in the military, joining and being in the Navy during the 1983 Lebanon Crisis.[725]

When Robert Daniels returned from the war and received his discharge from the Army, he indeed, as was promised, had his old job waiting for him at the Wisconsin State Child Center in Sparta, Wisconsin, where Doris Bohnert was waiting for him. He and Doris were married on 9 March 1947. Upon their marriage, Doris quit work at the Child Center and settled into life as a housewife and homemaker for the four children they would have: three sons and one daughter. Robert continued to work at the Child Center in Sparta until late in 1965, when, with the constant threat of the closing of the Center hanging in the air, he took a job at the Wisconsin State Maximum Security Prison in Waupun as a mason. The family moved to Waupun on New Year's Day of 1966. Prior to their move, Robert had the distinction of being the first World War II veteran to join the Sparta branch of the Veterans of Foreign Wars (VFW). Robert would retire from the State after twenty-five years of service on a medical retirement. He passed away on 10 September 1994. Doris was to pass away nearly fifteen years later on 13 August 2009. [726]

Robert and Doris' three sons all joined the military out of high school. Their eldest, Richard, served in the Army, including a year stint in Vietnam where he experienced the infamous Tet Offensive. Robert Charles joined and made the Navy a career, while David did the same in the Army. One of Robert and Doris's granddaughters, Brenda, their son Robert's daughter, is currently serving in the Coast Guard. [727]

Doris' sister Lois Bohnert was to marry Frank Schleicher from Almond, Wisconsin, in 1953. Frank had been in the Army during the war as a mechanic, serving time in the European Theater. They settled in Waupun where Frank would work at the Standard Gas Station on Main Street until his retirement, while Lois became a housewife and homemaker to their family. The couple had five children together; however, their first child, Charles, would die at age six months. Their eldest son, Ronald, upon graduating from Waupun Senior High, joined and served a tour in the Air Force during the late 1970's. [728] Frank has since passed away, however, Lois currently lives in an apartment complex on the site where the old Lincoln Grade School once stood, the same grade school she attended as a young girl.

According to Lois, like Walter Riel and Ed Babler, it would take a little while for her brother Alfred Bohnert to get re-acclimated back into civilian life. As she recalled:

[W]hen I went to wake him. Well, I sent . . ., we had a little dog, you know. I sent the dog in the room to wake him up—that was the wrong thing to do. He knocked him [the dog] off the bed, you know. He thought he was in the war yet. . . .

And then one time I went to wake him and I shook him, I guess, or something, touched him; anyhow, and he grabbed like this [she motioned grabbing for a gun] for his rifle. He didn't have one, but he grabbed for it, you know. So he said after this, talk to him. So it took a while [for him] to kind of adjust that you weren't fighting anymore.[729]

Al was, however, eventually able to successfully re-adjust, and he met Vergeana McNeil on a blind date sometime later. The two were married in 1948. Vergeana, who went by Jean to her family and friends, became a housewife and homemaker for their two surviving children; their second child, Katherine, having died when just over a year old. Upon first returning from the war, Al went back working for his uncle at the Waupun Bottling Works until 1950 when he sold his share in the company for a down payment on their home and, having been a cook in the Marines, took a job at the Wisconsin Central State Hospital for the Criminally Insane in Waupun as a chef. He would work at the hospital for thirteen and a half years, after which he worked as a butcher in a local grocery store until his retirement. Al passed away on 6 December 2006. Jean still resides in Waupun in the house they originally purchased.[730]

Ralph Bohnert, Doris, Lois, and Al's brother, was to come home from the war already married. He had met Marion Brown after Germany's surrender when he was stationed in Massachusetts, and the two were married prior to coming back to Waupun. They were to eventually move to Oshkosh, Wisconsin, where Ralph would work at a State hospital until his retirement. Marion, like her sister-in-laws, stayed home as the family's homemaker. The couple would have four children, one daughter and three sons. Their eldest son, David, would serve a tour in the Navy in the early 1970's. Upon his retirement, Ralph was to have some difficulties in initially obtaining his Social Security benefits because of confusion over his actual date of birth. This was directly related to his having lied about his age to join the Army at age seventeen. Marion passed away in 1998, and Ralph would follow her in 2002.[731]

Ironically, like her best friend Lois (Bohnert) Schleicher, Dorothy Bal would marry a man from the same small community of Almond, Wisconsin, that Lois' husband had come from. Also like Frank Schleicher, Lois' husband, Dorothy's husband was named Frank, Frank Vroman, and had served in the Army during the war. But, unlike Frank Schleicher, Frank Vroman served in the Pacific Theater as a medic with the combat engineers. The two were married in 1949 and were to have three children. Although Frank has passed away, Dorothy still resides in Waupun, spending time with her childhood friend, Lois.[732]

After his furlough, Fred Zurbuchen would return to his squadron, then move on to Fort Dix in New Jersey. In late October 1945, Betty Lidtke, his fiancé, who had written to him every day of the war, took leave of absence of her teaching job—her sister stood in for her, teaching Betty's classes—and came out to Trenton, New Jersey. The two were married on 27 October 1945. Once Fred was discharged, on 2 February 1946, he and Betty moved back to Burnett, Wisconsin, where Betty again took up her teaching position and Fred went back working for his father in the family dairy. Later, Fred opened his own dairy, but within five years applied for and received a job at the Wisconsin State Prison in Waupun, where he worked for thirty-two years until his retirement. Fred and Betty would eventually have three children, and in 1994 would visited Debach, England, for the dedication of a monument at his old airbase. Both now live a comfortable retired life in Waupun.[733]

Fred's younger brother, Melvin, like Fred, joined the Army Air Corps, but was too young to see action in World War II. As an aero-photographer on a B-29, however, he was to photograph all of North Korea prior to the outbreak of the Korean War.[734]

Morris Page was released from the Navy on 11 January 1946, after which he returned and settled in Beaver Dam, Wisconsin, and began working with the local electric company as a lineman. In 1947 he married Luella Helmer. The couple were to have six daughters and eventually nine grandchildren, and Morris would join and be active in both the American Legion and the VFW. He also attended one of the first of the USS *Thomas Jefferson's* post-war reunions, which was held in Berlin, Wisconsin. He retired from the electric company in 1987.[735] Morris would live in Beaver Dam until his passing on 30 March 2008.

After the war Cora DeMunck graduated from Alton High School in Alton, Iowa, in 1946 and entered college at Iowa State University in Ames, Iowa, where she was to receive her two-year degree. She then attended a university in Iowa City where she received a degree in Economics. As she stated, "Enrollments really increased because the service men were back. And some of those were starting college on the GI Bill." As a matter of fact, as she recalled, "There was like one or two girls in the class at that time. All the rest were men."[736]

From college she went to Washington, D.C., in hopes of getting an advertised job as an airline hostess. However, as she related, "They were interviewing fifteen people for one position, and I didn't get the position."[737] But not being daunted, she applied for a job with the Armed Forces Security Agency, an agency of the Department of Defense, which she was accepted for. Upon being granted a top secret security clearance and receiving eight to nine months of training, she would work in this position up to and during the Korean War.[738]

Carl Manthe had been discharged from the Navy on 9 December 1945. While he was in the service he managed to take a few college courses at Butler University in Indianapolis, Indiana. Once he got out of the Navy he used the G.I. Bill to finish his degree in correctional administration at the University of Wisconsin Madison in Madison. He then moved to Washington, D.C., and worked for the Hecht Company. While there, he and Cora DeMunck met. They were married on 5 April 1952 and moved to Wisconsin where Carl again attended the University of Wisconsin Madison, receiving a Master's Degree in social work. In 1961 he took a job at the Wisconsin State Maximum Security Prison in Waupun as a psychiatric social worker, and the family settled in Beaver Dam. Over the next twenty-three years he worked at the prison in various positions, including a half of year as the acting warden while the actual warden was recuperating from a heart attack. Cora, meanwhile, became a housewife and mother for their two sons, but would always dabble in investing, buying a building on the corner of Fond du Lac and Main Streets in Waupun, which she held onto for many years renting both the store front as well as the several upstairs apartments.[739]

During this time, Carl was also an active member of the Naval Reserve unit at Oshkosh, retiring from the Reserves in 1982 as a Signalman Chief Petty Officer. A year later, in 1983, he retired from the prison. Carl was to pass away in December of 1987. Cora still lives in their home in Beaver

Dam where she enjoys playing rounds of golf and travelling around the globe.[740]

A few days after listening to his mother state, "You're not gonna set there for the rest of you life are yah?," Robert Van Alstine used the GI Bill to enter college at Bradley University in Peoria, Illinois, where he would earn a degree in mechanics. While there, he met Mary Elizabeth Alden, who was also a student at Bradley. According to Mary, before the great influx of ex-GIs after the end of the war, there were very few men at the university. The only ones there were those that were 4-F or discharged wounded GIs.[741] With this great influx of ex-GIs, as Robert recalled, the university did not have the room for student housing, so they set the men up in a type of barracks. "Didn't make any difference, you know," as Robert was to state:

> There was Navy and Air Force people there, and everybody was used to living under the same conditions, so who cared, you know. You had to walk, I guess it was two blocks, to take a shower. There was a bathroom downstairs that they put in this old building that had three or four sinks in, something like an army barrack, you know. Nobody cared. The idea was, "We're out; we're home." Everybody got along real good, you know. They were all on cots; just like in the Army, lined up ... all over the place; they'd mop the floor, whatever. Really, it wasn't any different than being in the Army, except you went to school all day.[742]

Robert and Mary were married on 18 June 1948, and were to have four children, one daughter and three sons. In 1962 Robert was hired on at the Wisconsin State Correctional Facility in Fox Lake, and the family moved to Beaver Dam. Robert worked at the prison for twenty-five years, first teaching prisoners basic mechanics and then auto mechanics, retiring in 1987. In summing up his time in the military, Robert stated that

> [M]ost of the time you were very lucky if you knew what day of the week it was. You didn't know what country you were in. You didn't know where you were going next. And the name of the game was pretty much "Get the war

over." I think that was . . . because when it's over we can go home, so let's just get the thing over, and then if we have to go to Japan then we'll go to Japan. But, of course, fortunately, we were left out on that one. . . .

I do think what I learned in the Army, while it wasn't combative, in a way, it certainly was very good for working in the prison system—dealing with people, patience, you know, that type of thing. And the training that you get in the military . . . helped me, because the inmates, a lot of inmates have the idea of "Poor me, I'm in jail," and I had the idea you're lucky they're not shooting at you, you know. So it was a big help.[743]

Mary passed away on 1 February 2009, Robert joined her on 4 August of that same year.

After being shipped to Battle Creek, Michigan, to recuperate from his wound, Emil Hopp would be in and out of the hospital for nearly two years. During this period of time he traveled to and from Waupun to visit not only his mother, but also Josephine Aarts, whom he had met on one of these trips. As Josephine remembered the first time they met, it was

Under a pump, an old fashion pump that you pump the water out of. My sister went out with him once. He [Emil] went over and picked her up and she didn't care so much for him, I guess, or whatever. And he asked me. We were all standing around there outside around the pump there.[744]

The two were married on 15 March 1947 while Emil was still in the Army waiting for operations on his shoulder to fix his deformed hand. But Emil seemed to always get the run-around from his doctors, with the Army continually postponing his operation. As Josephine explained, "There is a couple of times when they let him go when they was going to operate on his hand, because he had a tendon in his arm, his hand," that caused his right hand to be crumpled and nearly useless. As she stated, "[T]wice over the doctor had cancelled on him. The doctor wanted to go to a ball game or whatever it was. Then they gave him a ninety-day furlough."[745]

When out in public, Emil would hide his deformed hand in his pocket. As Josephine recalled, "I don't think he was ashamed of it, because he was fighting for his country, too, you know. I think more or less it was of a habit of his of doing that. . . . But they [the people Emil would meet on the street] always wondered why he stuck that hand in his pocket." However, one of Josephine and Emil's daughters remembers hearing that the citizens of Waupun, when meeting Emil in the streets, would welcome him home from the war and tell him that "he did not need to hide his hand or be ashamed of it."[746]

The Army was never able to fix Emil's wound, nor would the wound ever heal properly. After two years of waiting, Emil finally accepted a discharge from the Army on 5 February 1948 as a corporal. Although he was to receive a pension from the Army, getting jobs would become difficult for him due to his hand. His job at the National Rivet and Manufacturing Company was indeed waiting for him when he returned as promised, "But," recalled Josephine, "they didn't treat him very kindly because of his hand. That was the main thing, I guess, because of his hand—that he couldn't put out work the way the other people could." And when attempting to get a job at the John Deere plant in nearby Horicon, Wisconsin, "They said," Josephine was to state, "'They couldn't get water out of a dry well,' meaning that they couldn't use him because of his hand." Emil was able to get a job, however, working in a Waupun filling station. And from time to time he worked for the City of Waupun raking leaves and such in the city's parks. As Josephine related, "He wasn't the type to sit around."[747]

Over the years Josephine would assist Emil in dressing himself, because, being right handed and having his right hand crippled, he had difficulty doing such things. As she explained, "I had to help him tie his shoes and then button his shirts, too. But then we got him shirts with snaps on. Then he got—that's later on—then he got slippers that he could slip right on."[748]

Although the war left Emil crippled, the following letter, post marked 26 May 1945, to Emil's mother from his squad leader explaining how Emil was wounded sums up how highly esteemed he was by his fellow soldiers:

> Dear Mrs Hopp:
>   First I believe it proper to introduce myself. I was

your son's Squad Leader. As you know by now, Emil has been wounded in action; thank God the wound isn't serious and he shall recover quickly.

Emil, and we who were with him that day, would like to forget it, but never will. Our squad was sent out to the front to pick up a man who was wounded. We had to wade a river, undergoing a mortar barrage, were pinned down by a machine gun whose bullets landed never farther than a yard from us; God knows men never came so close to Hell before. Only the prayers of our loved ones saved our lives.

I saw Emil's face contorted with fear; that we'll never forget; but he stuck with the patient which no ordinary man could have done. Emil is no ordinary man. His courage was as great as any hero of this or any other war.

He was shot from behind by a sniper while on the performance of a duty I, the Company Commander, or anyone else but God could ask him to do. His calmness after being wounded will never cease to amaze the three of us who were with him. Emil always told us how proud he was to be your son, believe me Mrs Hopp, you can always hold your head high and be proud he is your son.

We of Emil's squad have asked that he be decorated for bravery. I realize it cannot undo what has been done, but believe it will show his loved ones what a wonderful and courageous man he is.

We miss Emil a great deal; his good humour [sic], everything about him. Myself, and the other two men who were with him, consider it a great privilege to know your son and to have served with him.

Yours sincerely,
Sgt Bill Lees[749]

Emil and Josephine were to have four daughters and numerous grandchildren and great-grandchildren. Emil passed away in March of 1979. At his funeral, the American Legion Honor Guard, after rendering honors, handed Josephine an American flag.[750] Josephine was to pass away on 8 November 2006, less than eight months after interviewing for this account.

When Arnold Visser returned home to Waupun from the war he did not return to the job at Johnson Truck that he had left, but worked with his brothers in construction like their father before them. Arnold attended and graduated from the State of Wisconsin's Carpenter's Technical School, earning his Journeyman title, and he and Grace were to have a second daughter. Arnold also was to remain in the Army Reserves and eventually retire as a captain in 1963, but, as he stated, he would be considered on call until 1980. Today, although Grace has passed on, Arnold is still peaceably living in Waupun.[751]

Captain Leonard Schrank came home on 2 January 1946. According to his wife, Ges, the ship he was on was held at sea over New Year's Eve to keep the troops from having "too much of a wild party." As she stated, "By that time the guys were anxious to get on a train and get home. I think I saw him [Leonard] on the 2nd of January when he got home." In continuing, she was to say that "it was quite an adjustment [for Leonard] to make. He had seen an awful lot of war injuries and he did a lot of surgery." And once the TV show *MASH* became popular, "We watched [it] a lot. He [Leonard] says, 'Oh, I remember those days.'"[752]

They and their growing family—eventually three boys, and, eleven years after the birth of their third son, a daughter—would settle in Waupun where Leonard and his brother Raymond, also back from the war, would open the Schrank Clinic. Although the Schrank Clinic still exists today, both Leonard and Raymond have passed on and the clinic now has new owners. But, with medicine in the family blood, two of Ges and Leonard's sons today are dentists and a granddaughter is an M.D. Their youngest son, Thomas, was to volunteer and serve six years in the National Guard.[753] Ges would pass away on 2 March 2007.

After the end of the war, Howard Boyle returned to Fond du Lac, Wisconsin, upon being discharged from the Navy. But soon after he took a teaching job at a college in Minnesota, which he held for a couple of years. He then attended Marquette University in Milwaukee, where he received a law degree and became a lawyer in the Milwaukee Law Firm of Brooks-Tibbs. By this time he had married Elizabeth Jagdfeld from Fond du Lac, whom he had known since childhood. They were to have seven children and eventually move to Beaver Dam where Howard practiced law and ran for several political offices, including state senator, state attorney general, court of appeals, circuit court of Dodge County, and state supreme court justice. One of his sons, Dan, was to state that "most of his elections were very close. One he got 49.5 percent of the votes. But he was never elected."[754]

Howard was also to author several books, including two law books—*Wisconsin Safe-Place Law* and *Wisconsin Safe-Place Law Revised*—and a police book—*Wisconsin Law Enforcement Manual*—as well as co-authoring two other police books—*Illinois Law Enforcement Manual* and *Ohio Law Enforcement Manual*.[755] He passed away on 14 October 1991.[756]

Gladys Jolly would soon be joined in Ripon by John Hritsko, whom she had met while serving in the Army at Fort Leonard Wood where he had managed the base recreation hall and was an assistant postmaster. John's father had emigrated from Russia and his mother from Yugoslavia.[757]

When Gladys was twenty-nine years old the two were married and, with John's background of being an assistant postmaster, he was able to get employment with the post office in Ripon. They would have three children, two sons and a daughter. Their oldest son, Mike, would join and spend several years in the Air Force in electronics.[758]

As Gladys recalled concerning her husband John and their life together:

> [H]e came from the melting pot of the world of steel. The melting pot would be Pittsburg [Pennsylvania]. Huge steel mills. Very hard, hard working background, you know. Very religious background. And that was a lot of our problems of me being a Protestant and him being a Catholic. And immediately when he notified them that he was wanting to get married, his mother took a downward swing. She never liked me because I was not Catholic. But I was English. I laid it right there [to him]. I was English. "Well, don't you think you could change?" No. "Are you gonna change for me?" "No." But we did raise our children and we raised them well, and we got along. He went his way and [I went] my way in so many of our social lives, but we were always together.[759]

While John has been deceased for over twenty years, until her retirement, Gladys kept herself busy working at Ripon Good Cookies. Gladys was also very active in the local American Legion branch, even having served as one of the few women to hold the Legion's office of state vice commander. She also visited local high schools giving lectures to the students about her time in the military. In October of 1993, Gladys attended a reunion of her old outfit where several of the ex-German POWs she had worked with during the war attended.[760] She was to pass away on 23 July 2010.

When the war ended, Theron Mickelson had already started working in the machine shop where his dad worked back in Neenah, Wisconsin, when he was home on his thirty-day leave. As Theron stated, he did this to pick up some extra money

> 'cause what did we get back then?, $96 a month. That was for a second class [petty officer]. When I went in [the Navy] it was $54 ... once a month. ... Anyhow, they were short of help. And when I was aboard ship I run the machine shop, and anything they wanted they brought it up to me. And it wound up that I got the name of Botch, because I could botch anything together. So I get home [on leave] and needed a little extra money, so I worked in the machine shop there for, I don't know, a week or a week and a half.[761]

So when he finally received his discharge from the Navy, Theron was able to pick up a job again at the same machine shop on the night shift from 4 p.m. to midnight.

After about a year and a half on the job, as Theron stated, his foreman was shot by his own wife. "Blew his arm apart. She missed him where she wanted to hit him and blew his arm apart ... so ... they took a guy off of the day crew to be the night foreman, and he lasted for about three months and said, 'I don't want no part of that.' So he recommended me."[762] Theron then filled the position of night foreman for another couple of years before asking for a vacation to go deer hunting. As he recalled:

> [I]t was a week before I would have had my vacation time in ... [and] they says, "We can't do it." And I says, "Okay, I can't do it either." I give 'em two week's notice and laid

down my keys and walked out the door. So I went over to Apple Machine Company. Worked there for five years, off and on, you know. I went off to purchase machines for 'em because they knew that I had run these kind of machines before then.[763]

Just over five years with the Apple Machine Company, Theron's superintendent came to him one day and asked if he would be willing to go into business for himself, basically, asking if he was willing to join a few others in a joint venture in Green Bay, Wisconsin. He sold his house in Larson, Wisconsin, and moved to Green Bay. Another five years went by when he read a notice in a newspaper that a position was available for a machine shop instructor at the new Fox Lake Correctional Institution being built outside of Fox Lake, Wisconsin. As Theron stated, "I knew welding and machine shop and blueprint reading and all the rest of that. So I applied for the job." He received a letter telling him to report to Madison to take a test. "Well," he explained, "come to find out there was ten guys ahead of me that had taken the test and everything else. I was the eleventh one, the last one. I get back home and got a phone call, 'Your hired.' Then you had to prove yourself for six months, which I guess I did."[764]

Actually, when Theron showed up at the Fox Lake Correctional Institution for work the facility was not yet completed. "Well," as he recalled, "I was out there as a teacher before the machine shop was ever built, or before we ever had any inmates. So I was setting up a machine shop in the basement of the academic school. I had bits of this, a little of that, all the rest of that. And they finally got our building finished there."[765] It was at the correctional facility that Theron was to meet Elva (Drews) Voss.

After twenty-two years of marriage, moving from the Weber Dairy to become the head cheese maker at the Alto Co-op, and fathering a son and four children with Elva, Arthur Voss passed away from his long bout of kidney problems in 1965, leaving Elva a widow. Not long thereafter Elva found employment with the Wisconsin State Prison System at the Fox Lake Correctional Institution. At the facility she began as a secretary at the same school that Theron taught at, but would eventually move up to the position of a registrar, fingerprinting inmates and signing parole releases for the parole board of the prison.[766]

Both being widowed, Theron having also lost his wife, the two soon began dating and eventually married, joining Theron's three daughters to Elva's family. Theron would eventually work at the facility for nineteen years, retiring to help care for Elva when she came down with cancer. Elva's cancer, however, would go into remission for twenty years. They both declared that it was a result of eating rather large qualities of raw garlic. Between the two of them, Theron and Elva have twenty great-grandchildren and eighteen grandchildren. Three of their grandsons were in the military as of the date of their interview for this writing, one being a lieutenant commander in the Navy.[767] Elva, sadly, passed away on 17 February 2008.

Joan Laandal would never marry, but she had an interesting life as a secretary to several local prison wardens, including the wardens at the Fox Lake Correctional Institution, the State Maximum Security Prison (the Walls, as she called it), the Central State Hospital for the Criminally Insane, and the Dodge Correctional Institution for forty years before she retired from the State of Wisconsin. Two of the more interesting prisoners she has seen come through the gates of these facilities were Ed Gein and Jeffery Dahmner.[768]

Joan mentioned that when the soldiers, airmen, and sailors came back from the war:

> They didn't talk about their experiences. . . . I don't remember any of them saying how god awful it must have been on their ships when they were under attack, and that sort of thing. They didn't talk about it. They were so glad to be home and so glad to see you, you know. We just sort of picked up where we left off. But not really, you know, everybody had, you know, gone through a lot.[769]

Both of Joan's two brothers were to come home safely from the war. "Bob never left the States," she was to recall." "He was a first lieutenant and he trained flyers in Texas all through the war. . . . [A]ll the good flyers you ever heard of, Bob trained 'em." Her other brother, John, as she continued, "was stationed in Honolulu through the whole war as a postmaster, and never left there. So my brothers were relatively safe." Joan now lives in quiet retirement just outside of the Waupun city limits.[770]

After the war Tillie Dykstra would meet Steve Brotouski from

Markesan, Wisconsin. Steve had landed on the beaches of Normandy on D-Day as a member of M Company, 28th Infantry Regiment, 8th Infantry Division. He had fought in France until being wounded. After recuperating in England, Steve returned to his outfit where he finished out the war. They met while they both worked at the National Rivet and Manufacturing Company in Waupun. On 16 March 1946 the two were married. As Tillie recalled about the different jobs Steve would hold, "Seems like all of a sudden people . . . some people were laid off sometimes. . . . And it always seemed like he got laid off. . . . [H]e worked at the shoe factories and different places. . . . [But] then later on he worked at May Steel" in Mayville, Wisconsin.[771]

After living in Waupun for a while, Tillie and Steven first moved to Markesan and finally to Fox Lake. They would have one daughter. In telling about Steve's experience in the war, Tillie stated that Steve "never got over it. Never. It was really terrible because he hit the beach at Normandy. He was one of the only ones left in his whole outfit that got through the whole thing. Said he never knew how he did it."[772] Although Steve has passed away, Tillie still resides in their home in Fox Lake.

With the war over, Edward Uecker took up plumbing, including attending a vo-tech school and an apprenticeship before becoming a master plumber. After marrying his wife Shirley, the couple first lived in Brandon, where she was from, for eight years. They then moved to Waupun where Shirley, a registered nurse, worked at the Waupun Memorial Hospital for thirty-six years, including in the polio ward. They had four children, three sons and one daughter. Their two oldest sons were to serve in the military. Bruce, the oldest, served in the Air Force. Larry, their third child, enlisted in the Army and served in a preventative medicine unit with the Green Berets in Vietnam, including, like Richard Daniels, during the Tet Offensive.[773]

In summarizing his days during the war, Edward stated, "[P]eople make due, people can make due, you know. Its surprising what you can do when you put your mind to it."[774] Edward was to pass away on 29 December 2007.

After obtaining his discharge from the Navy, Irving Meyer regained his job with the Milwaukee Railroad, working as an agent and telegrapher for forty-two years in various towns throughout the Wisconsin area, including Waupun and Beaver Dam. He and his wife, Jean (Harlab), were married in 1948. They were to have two sons and a daughter, who would eventually present to them four grandchildren and four great-grandchildren.[775] Irving passed away on 6 February 2007.

Shirley Karmann would graduate high school with the Waupun class of 1948. She had worked for a while during school at the Super Ice Cream Shop in Waupun, but after graduating found work at Guth's Candy Store until she was hired on at the National Rivet and Manufacturing Company in the order department. Moving up to better positions at the factory, she eventually worked directly for William Coles, the factory's vice president. While dating a service member on and off, mostly through letters while he was in the service, and then in person after he was released from the service, she met his friend at a basketball game in Brandon. As she related:

> I was so impressed with this new guy . . . well, to make a long story short, after a while I didn't go with the first guy anymore, seems he met some one else and didn't tell me, just stop dating. His friend moved in with his brother in Oshkosh, found a job, and when I heard where he was, I wrote him a letter inquiring about the first guy and wondered what happened to him. I belonged to a bowling team and was at one of our team's events when I turned around and here stood the friend of my former boyfriend, his name was Arthur [Bartow]. We talked and he asked if he could give me a ride home, which he did, and from there on we became a couple, and a year or so later we were married.[776]

The two first moved to Oshkosh, but within the year they were back in Waupun, where Arthur worked as a lineman for the local utility company. They were to have five sons and one daughter. Two of their sons were to serve in the military, both in the Army. John served for four years, spending two of them in Germany and was on the way to Grenada when the fighting there ceased. Robert, joining right out of high school and, making the Army a career, spent twenty-two years in the service before retiring, including serving in both Operation Desert Storm and Afghanistan.[777] Although Arthur has passed away, Shirley still lives in Waupun.

In 1951, Marshall Mclean graduated from Oakfield High School and joined the Air Force, where he was trained to repair office equipment. After training he would be transferred for a short while to France, then to Wiesbaden, Germany. While there, he met AnnaMarie Kretzer, who was by then working for the United States Air Force as a secretary. She had learned French, English, and Latin while in high school and taken a course in English shorthand after graduating. Marshall and AnnaMarie were married on both 14 *and* 17 April 1955. As Marshall explained:

> In Germany, you have to get married by someone like a mayor, or a person who is hired to do just that, marry you. And then you can arrange your church ceremony, which we couldn't do on the same day. So, we said, "Well, let's get married on the 14th and go get married in the church on the 17th." We actually got two of 'em [anniversaries], but 14th is official.[778]

For the convenience of the government—so the Air Force would not have to pay for the birth of their expected baby—in 1956, Marshall was discharged a few months early, and the two of them moved to Fond du Lac. They lived there until Marshall began working at the State Maximum Security Prison in 1962, when they moved to Waupun. Marshall worked at the prison for twenty-nine years as a guard and then a foreman for the prison's metal furniture factory until his retirement in August of 1988. He had also joined and served in both the Army National Guard and the Air National Guard, which he would retire from in 1991 after twenty-one years of service.[779]

AnnaMarie worked for ten years in the Waupun Middle School as a teacher's aid. While there she began being a guest speaker when the sixth graders were studying the Second World War. As she related, "That's my volunteer thing, I always go back. And the students were very attentive." The couple have two children, a son and a daughter, and still reside in Waupun.[780]

When he was twelve years old and after the war ended, Lambert De Jager and his family immigrated to the United States from Holland, settling in Wisconsin near Randolph. Once there, he was to meet Bessie Douma. In 1954 Bessie graduated from Randolph High School, and just over two years later, on 6 July 1956, the two were married. For awhile the couple farmed near Fox Lake on Lakeland Road, but as interest rates rose, so did the cost of farming. Selling their farm, they moved to Alto, Wisconsin, where Lambert became a truck driver, driving semi-tracker trailers. Bessie would become a certified nursing assistant and work as such, between the Christian Home and the Homestead, both assisted living residencies in Waupun, for twenty-one years. The couple have three daughters and two sons, and as of this writing thirteen grandchildren. As Bessie stated, "I didn't want to be grandma, but it sure is fun." Recently retired, Bessie enjoys playing the piano, organ, auto harp, and harmonica, as well as writing poetry.[781]

Harriet Whiting completed high school, graduating from Waupun High School in 1955. She then attended a three-year nursing program at Saint Agnes Hospital in Fond du Lac, after which she began working as a nurse at Waupun Memorial Hospital. Jim Laird graduated high school that same year from the same school he had attended since kindergarten in Cuba City, Wisconsin. After attending and graduating from the University of Wisconsin Platteville in Platteville, Wisconsin, with a teaching degree in mathematics, he moved to Waupun and taught at the Waupun Senior High School for six years until a teaching position opened up at the Fox Lake Correctional Institution, where he began teaching math to the inmates.[782]

Jim and Harriet caught the eyes of matchmakers at their church in Waupun who, according to Jim, "decided that we should get married, so they introduced us and that's how the whole thing started." They were married on 8 June 1968 and have one birth daughter and an adopted son. They are both now retired and living in Waupun. Jim is also the president of the town's historical society and manages Waupun's history museum, currently located in the old Carnegie Library.[783]

Soon after the war, David Lyon's mother and father divorced. His mother would then marry Bernie Schwalenberg, who had served in the Army in the Pacific Theater of the war. Although David's father was in the Navy during the war, his father being divorced from his mother, David "never had a chance to talk to him a lot about the war. But," as David related, "I have some pictures of him and everything." David also has an ornate silver belt buckle his father had made out of coin silver while serving in the Philippines, which he then gave to David. Remembering when the military men of his family first came back, David recalled:

[N]obody had a house, so everybody kinda moved in, my

aunts and uncles and everybody. My grandma's house was quite large, it was over at Olmstead Street. And everybody had one room that was a bedroom. I thought this was great 'cause every morning I got to run upstairs and wake up all my uncles, you know. That was pretty neat I thought. It was different. Then over the years everyone moved out, got their own home and went away.[784]

When asked about any perceived changes when the military came home, David, although quite young at the time of the end of the war, stated that "a lot of the guys that came back drank a lot, and that was the height of the bar business, I guess, because everybody was going downtown. It was like one big party for a long time. I think everybody was kind of unwinding."[785] Waupun's downtown district, which is centered on Main Street, was at the time and still is today about three blocks long and one block deep. At the time of the end of the war and well into the 1970's, this strip contained numerous small bars; to the extent that nearly one in every three or four establishments in the downtown area was a bar, which was typical of numerous other small towns in the area.

Being born just before the American involvement in the war and growing up during and just after the war, David had a unique outlook on the subject. As he was to relate:

> Well, a lot of the guys that went to school that time—I think because of when we were born and when we were brought up and how we were brought up—we almost worshiped war. We talked about it, we talked about the war a lot. And we talked to a lot of the people that had been in the war, and they related a lot of their experiences. And I was fortunate enough to work with a lot of guys who had served in the military.[786]

David also learned about the war in school. As he stated:

> There was a man that lived outside of town [outside of Waupun] named Frank Kittell, which was one of my teachers. And he would talk a lot about World War II. And he served not only in World War II, but he served

233

[also] in Korean [the Korean War]. And in school he'd tell us guys about the war, about World War II. And he talked about [the] Korean [War], and he said, "Yeah, I walked down the streets of Berlin," he said, "and I walked down the streets of Seoul, and some day I'm gonna walk down the streets of Moscow." You know, it almost brought tears to your eyes. It was so intense the feeling of patriotism and the pride in your country, and everything was so fantastically intense. It was . . ., it really . . ., really formed a lot, I think, a lot of the character in the people that grew up in those days.[787]

David told of yet another teacher, Sesper Jasper Casper, who would also tell about the war:

He helped fly the hump in World War II in India and Burma. . . . And Mr. Casper said, "You know, I never flew after the war." He never flew in a plane, he never rode in a plane, "That's it, that's enough flying," [he said]. But they would talk about, you know, the war, and talk about flying the hump and talk about the Japanese and that. . . . I think a lot of them talked because we asked. And I think in some respects it was good for 'em to talk, you know, get it out. And it was certainly good for us because they shared. They were sharing, you know, what they had seen and done. It gave you more of a personal concept of the history that you had lived through.[788]

David was to graduate from Waupun High School with the class of 1959, and in a little less than a year later, in January of 1960, join the United States Air Force. During his stint in the Air Force, which included the timeframe of the Cuban Missile Crisis, he was to receive another perspective of World War II. Trained in electronic counter-measures, David worked on B-52 bombers in Carswell Air Force Base in Fort Worth, Texas. While there, one of his supervisors was a technical sergeant by the name of Elmer Burkhart. Burkhart had been in War World II, but not on the side of the Allies, as a German soldier. He had also been a member of the Hitler Youth. As David related, Elmer would talk about Adolf Hitler.

"You know," he'd say, "Hitler was not all bad." And it was just a total different perspective, you know. And then after the war, we won, and he decided to get on the winning side. He came here and he went into our Air Force. And the man . . . loved anything technical. And I asked him once, "Do you read?" And he said, "Only technical manuals." And he was good. I mean, he knew electronics, and he knew the systems on the plane backwards and forward. If you had problems, you got Sergeant Burkhart and he'd straighten things out. But that was something. I guess a lot of people don't have the opportunity to work with somebody who was actually on the other side. That was, I thought, interesting.[789]

After leaving the Air Force, David returned to Waupun and worked for a few months at a factory before moving onto the Central State Hospital for the Criminally Insane as a guard. While there, almost all of his supervisors were World War II vets of one sort or another. As David recalled:

There was Lavern Hendricksen who had been in the Marines in the Pacific. Basel Kroniger was in the Marines in the Pacific. Everybody. . ., Norman Eugene Tophand was a little old to be in the service, but he worked for Badger Ordinance. . . . [I]t seemed like everybody you worked with almost at that age group had either been in the service or worked in some war related industry.[790]

David was to marry twice and has two children, a son and a daughter. His son, Matthew, served in the Army during Operation Desert Storm. David and his wife currently live in Waupun.[791]

Although born on 22 September 1943 in the middle of the war and only two years old at its end, DiAnna Reif, even at that age, had several vivid memories of the rationing and the blackout drills conducted in Waupun, as well as the celebrations at the end of the war. After the war, DiAnna's father, Charles, who always felt bad about not being able to serve in the military due to having contracted tuberculosis as a child, always made it a point to assist the men who would become known as

235

bums, feeling that a lot of these were veterans that were having a hard time adjusting to society after their war experiences. The Reif family home was next to the train tracks in Waupun, and many of these individuals would ride the rails from town to town. As DiAnna related:

> And if the bums were on the train and if they came to the door, my mother always had strict orders to feed them, because my dad used to say, you know, "There but for the grace of God go I," you know. Because he . . ., he always felt bad because he couldn't serve in the Army. He put in his time in [a] CC[C] camp, but, you know, he wanted to do everything and anything he could to help the people. And after the war there were a lot of men came back and they were rather lost, you know, and they took to riding the rails. They had a hard time adjusting to civilian life. And I can remember, my mom could never let them in the house, but we used to have a big front porch with steps and a rail around, and she used to make them a meal and take it out and give it to them on the front porch. And if dad was home, I can remember dad always sitting out there and talking with them, and that kind of thing.[792]

DiAnna went on to graduate from Waupun Senior High School in 1961. Shortly thereafter that same year she married Donald Mueller from Livingston, Wisconsin. They were to have two children, a daughter and a son, and subsequently four grandchildren. Donald and DiAnna still live in Waupun where DiAnna recently retired from the *Fond du Lac Reporter* newspaper as a reporter.[793]

Epilogue

During the Second World War the United States had sixteen million of its citizens in uniform; 407,000 of these never came home.[794] Wisconsin alone was to send 332,200 off to the military. This figure represents one in every ten Wisconsinites—8,149 of these would not come home, representing a loss ratio of one in forty-five.[795] Others would return suffering from what is today referred to as Post-Traumatic Stress Disorder, but would receive little, if any, medical or psychological help for it. But then, few of that generation would expect or ask for it.

The small rural Wisconsin town of Waupun, like many small and large cities, if not all of them, throughout the United States, did its share of fighting as well, both actually in the war and at the home front. The townspeople willingly sacrificed as they could, sending 862 of their men and women off to the war; a good ten percent to fifteen percent of its 1941-1945 population—twenty-two of whom would not return—while those that stayed behind put aside personal comforts, simply because their country and president called for it. They followed the government and its leaders' many requests without questioning their motives, without protesting, and, most remarkably, with enthusiasm and even pride in doing so . . . for not doing so would have been considered unpatriotic.

Wisconsin farms and factories, like farms and factories all over the country, also stepped up and put out massive quantities of vital food stuffs and war materials. For example, the National Rivet and Manufacturing Company in Waupun produced and shipped rivets that were instrumental in the production of virtually every military aircraft built in the United States during the war. In addition, of the twenty-eight submarines built by the Manitowoc Shipbuilding Company in Manitowoc, twenty-five saw service in the Pacific Theater, the last three arriving in the war zone after hostilities ceased. Their contribution to the war effort was exceptional with the combined sinking of 132 large enemy ships totaling approximately

500,000 tons. These figures do not include the many smaller vessels downed with the use of the submarines' surface guns, nor the rescue of numerous Navy and Marine Corps pilots. This achievement, however, was not without loss. Of the fifty-two American subs lost during the war, four of these were Manitowoc built boats, and their crews.[796]

It was a time when the entire country went to war, with nearly every factory, small and large alike, re-tooling in some fashion or another to produce war materials. It was also a time before many of our modern day conveniences. The people of the era lived their lives and produced their products, both the war materials and the basics simply required for living, without the use of smart phones, television, computers, air-conditioning, electric refrigerators . . . and in many instances central heating, indoor plumbing, and electricity. A time when even having toilet paper was a luxury, and many farms still used horses to pull plows and other farm equipment. It was a time when doing even basic household chores, such as washing clothes, was very labor intensive.

It was also a time that all Americans fully supported the war effort, not just those and their families that were actually fighting in it. It was a time when young children spent their days gathering needed raw materials for the war effort, and working in the fields alongside their parents and siblings instead of simply playing. And when they did play, it was outside, not in front of a computer or electronic toy—and this was in between attending school, which they had to *walk* to and from, sometimes two or three miles each way, and in all forms of weather. It was a time when everyday Americans helped each other when the need arose, and without being asked to do so. And it was a time when many of these things were done without wanting or expecting compensation for their efforts. It was truly a different generation than it is today. As Joan Laandal very aptly summarized the war and her generation:

> Nothing compares, I don't think, to that generation to have that war. We just assimilated it. It was ours, you know. And still we feel that way. It's our war. It was important to us and . . . nobody, *nobody* shirked their duty. The kids that went to service and the ones that were left home; nobody shirked their duty. And I don't think you ever found that in a war since, you know. We were attacked.[797]

This book was never designed to be a history of the war, or the story of a famous general, war hero, or battle. I leave that up to others. From its inception to the writing of these parting words, these pages were and are intended solely to tell the story of how the average American viewed, witnessed, and lived their lives during the Second World War. What have been represented within the covers of this book are the stories of those individuals interviewed, many times in their own words. It represents how they spoke during their interviews and what and how they remembered experiencing and living their lives during the war years. Any miss-quotes of the interviews, misspellings of personal or place names, or editing, spelling, or punctuation errors are solely my responsibility, for which I humbly apologize.

It is my sincere hope that I have related these accounts in the manner, form, and accuracy that those interviewed would have wanted them related, the average of whom was seventy-nine years old at the time of their interview—the youngest being sixty-three and the oldest ninety-nine.

Since time can erode the memories of the best of us, and wanting to ensure the most accurate representations of their stories as possible, I attempted to corroborate as many of the facts presented as possible. With this said, it should be pointed out that although the *USS Lafayette* and the *USS MacArthur* were related as being liberty ships, research could not identify either *Lafayette* or *MacArthur* as names of liberty ships, nor could any U.S. naval ship during World War II be identified by the name of *MacArthur*. The name *Lafayette*, on the other hand, was given to the ex-French luxury liner the *Normandie*, which was rechristened the *USS Lafayette (AP-53)* and was planned to be converted to a troop transport. However, a fire broke out onboard the ship as it was tied to a pier on the Hudson River in New York City that was so intense that it damaged the ship to the point where it would never be used during the war.[798] The name *Lafayette County* was given to a Landing Ship Tank (LST), the *USS Lafayette County (LST-59)*, commissioned on 6 January 1945. The *Lafayette County* saw service in the Pacific Theater from 8 March until after the end of the war ferrying troops.[799]

This does not mean, however, that a mistake was made concerning the names of the ships or what type of ships were sailed on to and from the Pacific war zone. It just means that *research* could not identify the two ships named as being World War II liberty ships. The two ships may certainly have been liberty ships, and, as remembered, these liberty ships may indeed have been named the *USS Lafayette* and the *USS MacArthur*.

– Robert C. Daniels

Selected Bibliography

Published Books and Articles

Bendall, Katie, Bob Ferrell, Rhonda Fleming, Alyce M. Guthrie, Alyce F. Newberry, Boats Newberry, Don Rhoads, and Dave Turner, eds. *Knights of the Sea*. Dallas, TX: Taylor Publishing Co., 1982.

Cooper, Bryan. *PT Boats*. New York: Ballantine Books, Inc., 1970.

Costello, John. *The Pacific War 1941-1945*. New York: Parennial, 1981.

Cowley, Betty. *Stalag Wisconsin: Inside WWII prisoner-of-war camps*. Oregon, WI: Badger Books, Inc., 2002.

Daniels, Robert C. *1220 Days: The story of U.S. Marine Edmond Babler and his experiences in Japanese Prisoner of War Camps during World War II*. 2nd ed. Bloomington, IN: AuthorHouse, 2011.

"Dr. R. E. Schrank." Un-sourced newspaper clipping, undated.

Fritz, Sue, ed. "Reach Out: With a little help from friends." *Clinic People* vol. 1, no. 3 (November 1979): 7.

Griess, Thomas E., ed. *The Second World War: Europe and the Mediterranean*. Garden City Park, NY: Square One Publishers, 2002.

Holmes, Linda Goetz. *Unjust Enrichment: How Japan's companies built postwar fortunes using American POWs*. Mechanicsburg, PA: Stackpole Books, 2001.

Keegan, John. *The Second World War*. New York: Penguin Books, 1990.

Kerr, E. Bartlett. *Surrender and Survival: The Experience of American POWs in the Pacific 1941-1945*. New York: William Morrow and Company, Inc., 1985.

Knox, Donald. *Death March, Survivors of Bataan*. New York: Harcourt Brace & Company, 1981.

Miller, Michael J. *From Shanghai to Corregidor: Marines in the defense of the Philippines*. Washington, D.C.: Marine Corps Historical Center, 1997.

Milwaukee Journal article about AnnaMarie (Kretzer) McLean. (Milwaukee, WI). 7 December 1975.

Morris, Eric. *Corregidor: The American Alamo of World War II*. New York: First Cooper Square Press, 2000.

Nelson, William T. *Fresh Water Submarines: The Manitowoc Story*. Manitowoc, WI: Hoeffner Printing, 1997.

Nesbit, Robert C. *Wisconsin: A History*. 2nd. ed. Revised and updated by William F. Thompson. Madison, WI: The University of Wisconsin Press, 1989.

"PFC Emil Hopp." Unsourced newspaper clipping, undated.

Side Boy. Twelfth Class. New York: United States Naval Reserve Midshipmen's School, 1943.

Whitlock, Flint and Ron Smith. *The Depths of Courage: American submarines at war with Japan, 1941-1945*. New York: Berkley Caliber, 2007.

Electronic Sources

Bartow, Shirley (Karmann). Email to author, 31 January 2011.

Bohnert, David. Email to author, 3 March 2008.

Clancey, Patrick, "USS PT 555." http://www.ibiblio.org/hyperwar/USN/ships/PT/PT-555.html, accessed on 15 November 2009.

Daniels, Richard. Email to author, 27 February 2008.

Daniels, Robert C. "MacArthur's Failures in the Philippines, December 1941-March 1942." http:/www.militaryhistoryonline.com/wwii/articles/macarthursfailures.aspx, accessed on 17 October 2007.

"Debach Airfield – home of 493rd BG(H) – Helton's Hellcats - USAAF." http://493bgdebach.co.uk/dahistory.htm, accessed 4 December 2007.

Donellan, Sandy. "Third Marine Division Association – History Bougainville." http://www.caltrap.org/history/Bougainville.asp, accessed on 22 November 2007.

"Franklin D. Roosevelt." http://www.whitehouse.gov/about/presidents/Franklindroosevelt, accessed 6 December 2009.

"History Shots." http://www.historyshots.com/usarmy/backstory.cfm, accessed 9 August 2011.

"History of the 3rd Marine Division." http://1stbattalion3rdmarines.com/div-hist-index_files/history_3rddiv.htm, accessed on 22 November 2007.

"History of the *USS Thomas Jefferson* (APA-30)." http://lrwbf.com/USSTJ/history.html, accessed 4 January 2008.

"History of Two Rivers: Growth of Manufacturing." http://www.tworiverseconomicdevelopment.org/relocation/history-growth.htm, accessed 2 November 2007.

Keefer, Louis E. "The Army Specialized Training Program in World War II." http://www.pierce-evans.org/ASTP%20in%20WWII.htm, accessed 3 December 2009.

"Lafayette." http://www.history.navy.mil/danfs/l1/lafayette.html, accessed 4 December 2009.

"Lafayette County LST-859." http://www.historycentral.com/NAVY/LST/lafayette%20county.html, accessed on 4 December 2009.

Miller, Kimberly J. "Third Marine Division Association – History Iwo Jima." http://www.caltrap.org/history/iwojima.asp, accessed on 22 November 2007.

Morison, Samuel Eliot. *History of US Naval Operations in World War II, Vol. II: Operations in North African Waters,* as quoted by Brad Smith. http://navweaps.com/index_oob/OOB_WWII_Mediterranean/OOB_WWII_Casablanca.htm, accessed on 1 October 2007.

"Naval Amphibious Base Little Creek." http://www.globalsecurity.org/military/facility/little_creek.htm, accessed 2 January 2008.

"Pacific Air Forces, 13th Air force." http://www.pacaf.af.mil/library/factsheets/factsheet.asp?id=3608, access on 22 December 2007.

"Rationed Items." http://www.ameshistoricalsociety.org/exhibits/ration_items.htm, accessed 25 July 2011.

"Rationing on the US Homefront during WWII." http://www.ameshistoricalsociety.org/exhibits/events/rationing.htm, accessed 25 July 2011.

"The Battle of the Bulge." http://www.historylearningsite.co.uk/battle_of_the_bulge.htm, accessed 2 August 2011.

"The 4-F Classification for the Draft during World War II." http://www.nebraskastudies.org/0800/stories/0801_0106.html, accessed on 25 October 2007.

"The Milkweed." http://newton.dep.anl.gov/natbltn/100-199/nb162.htm, accessed 4 December 2009.

"The Normal Schools." http://www2.lib.virginia.edu/finearts/guides/brown-normal.html, accessed 26 July 2011.

"USS Barnegat (AVP-10)." http://www.history.navy.mil/photos/sh-usn/ usnsh-b/avp10.htm, accessed 27 October 2009.

"USS PT 555." http://uboat.net/allies/warships/ship/10385.html, accessed on 15 November 2009.

"Views of Germany's West Wall (The Siegfried Line)." http://www. 63rdinfdiv.com/siegfriedlinepage1.html, accessed 18 August 2011.

"V-12 Program." http://homepages.rootsweb.com/~uscnrotc/V-12/v12- his.htm, accessed 3 December 2009.

"Women in the Military." http://www.mscd.edu/history/camphale/ wim_001.html, accessed on 31 August 2011.

Walden Geoffrey R. "The Third Reich in Ruins." http://www. thirdreichruins.com/buchenwald.htm, accessed on 5 March 2008.

"World War II Statistics." http://www.angelfire.com/ct/ww2europe/ stats.html, accessed 9 August 2011.

"86th Infantry Division." http://www.history.army.mil/documents/eto- ob/86ID-ETO.htm, accessed on 10 March 2008.

Unpublished Reports and Documents

Bohnert, Alfred. Written essay to author of his WWII experiences. Undated.

Boyle, Howard. H. Jr. "A report on the last mission of PT Boat 555." Undated.

_____. "Rough Log of PT 555." Undated.

Brickson, Melinda. "My Grandma and World War II." Undated. Photocopied.

De Jager, Bessie (Douma). Pre-interview questionnaire. Undated.

Hagen, Charlotte (Mehlbrech). Pre-interview questionnaire. Undated.

Hopp, Carol. Pre-interview questionnaire written for her father, Emil Hopp. Undated.

Hritsko, Gladys (Jolly). Pre-interview questionnaire. Undated.

Lees, Bill, Sgt. Letter to Mrs. Hattie Hopp. 26 May 1945.

Manthe, Cora (DeMunck). Letter to author. 20 January 2006.

_____. Pre-interview questionnaire. Undated.

_____. Pre-interview questionnaire for Carl Manthe. Undated.

McLean, AnnaMarie (Kretzer). Written essay to author of her WWII experiences. Undated.

McLean, Marshall. Written essay to author of his WWII experiences. Undated.

"Navy Department, Bureau of Naval Personnel Service Schools graduation certification NAVPERS 674 (REV. October 1942)" form for Irving Meyer. Undated.

"Notice of Separation From U.S. Naval Service NAVPERS-553 (REV. 8-45)" form for Irving Meyer. Undated.

"Notice of Separation From U.S. Naval Service NAVPERS-553 (REV. 8-45)" form for Morris Page. Undated.

Riel, Walter. Written essay to author of his WWII experiences. Undated.

Schrank, Gertrude (Mintzlaff). Pre-interview questionnaire written for her brother-in-law, Dr. Raymond Schrank. Undated.

Scott, Edith Moul. "The First Hundred Years: A History of Waupun 1839-1939." Prepared by Jim Laird. Waupun Historical Society: Waupun, WI, 2004.

Van Alstine, Robert. Pre-interview questionnaire. Undated.

Visser, Arnold. Pre-interview questionnaire. Undated.

Zurbuchen, Fred. Written essay to author of his WWII experiences. Undated.

Interviews

Babler, Jeanette (Rochon). Interview by author, 16 March 2006.

Bohnert, Alfred. Interview by author, 30 November 2005.

Bohnert, Vergeana (McNeil). Interview by author, 30 November 2005.

Boyle, Dan. Interview by author, 2 December 2005.

Brotouski, Tillie (Dykstra). Interview by author, 1 December 2005.

Daniels, Doris (Bohnert). Interview by author, 3 April 1997.

_____. Interview by author, 30 November 2005.

De Jager, Bessie (Douma). Interview by author, 15 March 2006.

Hagen, Charlotte (Mehlbrech). Interviewed by author, 28 November 2005.

Hopp, Josephine (Aarts). Interview by author, 13 March 2006.

Hritsko, Gladys (Jolly). Interview by author, 28 November 2005.

Laandal, Joan. Interview by author, 16 March 2006.

Laird, Harriet (Whiting). Interview by author, 16 March 2006.

Laird, James. Interview by author, 16 March 2006.

Lyon, David Allen. Interview by author, 1 December 2005.

Manthe, Cora (DeMunck). Interview by author, 28 November 2005.

McLean, AnnaMarie (Kretzer). Interview by author, 28 November 2005.

McLean, Marshall. Interview by author, 28 November 2005.

Meyer, Irving. Interview by author, 15 March 2006.

Mickelson, Elva (Drews). Interview by author, 30 November 2005.

Mickelson, Theron. Interview by author, 30 November 2005.

Mueller, DiAnna Kay (Reif). Interviewed by author, 14 March 2006.

Page, Morris. Interview by author, 29 November 2005.

Riel, Walter. Interview by author, 2 December 2005.

Rigg, Elmer. Interview by author, 30 November 2005.

Schleicher, Lois (Bohnert). Interview by author, 29 November 2005.

Schrank, Gertrude (Mintzlaff). Interview by author, 30 November 2005.

Uecker, Edward. Interview by author, 29 November 2005.

Van Alstine, Robert. Interview by author, 2 December 2005.

Vellama, Charles. Interview by author, 4 March 2006.

Vellema, Nova (Wagner). Interview by author, 4 March 2006.

Visser Arnold. Interview by author, 15 March 2006.

Vroman, Dorothy (Bal). Interview by author, 29 November 2005.

Zurbuchen, Fred. Interview by author, 29 November 2005.

Endnotes

1   Robert C. Daniels, *1220 Days: The story of U.S. Marine Edmond Babler and his experiences in Japanese Prisoner of War Camps during World War II*, 2nd ed. (Bloomington, IN: Authorhouse, 2011), 17.

2   Charles Vellema, interview by author, 4 March 2006.

3   Doris (Bohnert) Daniels, interview by author, 30 November 2005.

4   Nova (Wagner) Vellema, interview by author, 4 March 2006.

5   Edith Moul Scott, "The First Hundred Years: A History of Waupun 1839-1939," prepared by Jim Laird (Waupun Historical Society: Waupun, WI, 2004), 2.

6   Ibid., 1.

7   Ibid.

8   Ibid.

9   Ibid., 6.

10 Robert C. Nesbit, *Wisconsin: A History*, 2nd. ed., revised and updated by William F. Thompson (Madison, WI: The University of Wisconsin Press, 1989), 273.

11 Scott, 30-33.

12 John Costello, *The Pacific War 1941-1945* (New York: Parennial, 1981), 52-53.

13 Ibid., 55-56.

14 John Keegan, *The Second World War* (New York: Penguin Books, 1990), 243.

15 Doris Daniels, 30 November 2005; Doris (Bohnert) Daniels, interview by author, 3 April 1997; and Lois (Bohnert) Schleicher, interview by author, 29 November 2005.

16 James Laird, interview by author, 16 March 2006.

17 Doris Daniels, 3 April 1997.

18 Ibid.; and Doris Daniels, 30 November 2005.

19 Ibid.

20 Schleicher.

21 Ibid.

22 Doris Daniels, 3 April 1997.

23 Dorothy (Bal) Vroman, interview by author, 29 November 2005.

24 Ibid.

25 Joan Laandal, interview by author, 16 March 2006.

26 Shirley (Karmann) Bartow, email to author, 31 January 2011.

27 Ibid.

28 Ibid.

29 Josephine (Aarts) Hopp, interview by author, 13 March 2006.

30 Ibid.
31 Edward Uecker, interview by author, 29 November 2005.
32 Ibid.
33 Ibid.
34 Ibid.
35 Ibid.
36 Nova Vellema.
37 Ibid.
38 Ibid.
39 "The Normal Schools" (http://www2.lib.virginia.edu/finearts/guides/brown-normal.html, accessed 26 July 2011).
40 Nova Vellema.
41 Ibid.
42 Ibid.
43 Elva (Drews) Mickelson, interview by author, 30 November 2005.
44 Tillie (Dykstra) Brotouski, interview by author, 1 December 2005.
45 Marshall McLean, interview by author, 28 November 2005.
46 Cora (DeMunck) Manthe, letter to author, 20 January 2006; and Cora (DeMunck) Manthe, interview by author, 28 November 2005.
47 Manthe, interview.
48 Ibid.
49 Robert Van Alstine, interview by author, 2 December 2005.
50 Ibid.
51 Dan Boyle, interview by author, 2 December 2005.
52 Theron Mickelson, interview by author, 30 November 2005.
53 Ibid.
54 Ibid.
55 Gladys (Jolly) Hritsko, interview by author, 28 November 2005.
56 Ibid.
57 Charles Vellema.
58 Gertrude (Mintzlaff) Schrank, interview by author, 30 November 2005.
59 Ibid.
60 Ibid.
61 Elmer Rigg, interview by author, 30 November 2005.
62 AnnaMarie (Kretzer) McLean, interview by author, 28 November 2005.
63 Robert Daniels, *1220 Days,* xix, 1.
64 Ibid., 1, 3, 4.
65 Nova Vellema.
66 Alfred Bohnert, interview by author, 30 November 2005; and Doris Daniels, 3 April 1997.
67 Van Alstine, interview.
68 Vergeana (McNeil) Bohnert, interview by author, 30 November 2005.
69 Fred Zurbuchen, interview by author, 29 November 2005.
70 Arnold Visser, interview by author, 15 March 2006.
71 Ibid.

[72] Ibid.

[73] Ibid.

[74] Morris Page, interview by author, 29 November 2005.

[75] Cora (DeMunck) Manthe, pre-interview questionnaire for Carl Manthe, undated; and Boyle.

[76] Elva Mickelson.

[77] Charlotte (Mehlbrech) Hagen, interview by author, 28 November 2005.

[78] Ibid.

[79] Ibid.

[80] Ibid.

[81] William T. Nelson, *Fresh Water Submarines: The Manitowoc Story* (Manitowoc, WI: Hoeffner Printing, 1997), 11-12, 24-26.

[82] "History of Two Rivers: Growth of Manufacturing" (http://www.zztworiverseconomicdevelopment.org/relocation/history-growth.htm, accessed 2 November 2007); and Jeanette (Rochon) Babler, interview by author, 16 March 2006.

[83] Babler.

[84] Ibid.

[85] Walter Riel, interview by author, 2 December 2005.

[86] Ibid.

[87] Ibid.

[88] Nesbit, 480.

[89] Riel, interview.

[90] Irving Meyer, interview by author, 15 March 2006.

[91] Ibid.

[92] Ibid.

[93] Bessie (Douma) De Jager, interview by author, 15 March 2006.

[94] Robert Daniels, *1220 Days*, 11-12.

[95] AnnaMarie McLean, interview.

[96] David Allen Lyon, interview by author, 1 December 2005.

[97] Eric Morris, *Corregidor: The American Alamo of World War II* (New York: First Cooper Square Press, 2000), 21; and Robert C. Daniels, "MacArthur's Failures in the Philippines, December 1941-March 1942" (http:/www.militaryhistoryonline.com/wwii/articles/macarthursfailures.aspx, accessed on 17 October 2007).

[98] Charles Vellema.

[99] Ibid.

[100] Robert Daniels, *1220 Days*, 12-14.

[101] Uecker.

[102] Ibid.

[103] Charles Vellema.

[104] Ibid.

[105] Ibid.

[106] Ibid.

[107] Nova Vellema.

[108] Robert Daniels, *1220 Days*, 17.

[109] Ibid., xiv, and Robert Daniels, "MacArthur's Failures in the Philippines."

[110] Babler.

[111] Riel, interview.

[112] Doris Daniels, 30 November 2005.

[113] Alfred Bohnert, interview.

[114] Vroman.

[115] Ibid.

[116] Schleicher.

[117] Vroman.

[118] Laandal.

[119] Schrank, interview.

[120] Ibid.

[121] Vergeana Bohnert.

[122] Brotouski.

[123] Ibid.

[124] Meyer.

[125] Bartow.

[126] Hritsko, interview.

[127] Ibid.

[128] Elva Mickelson.

[129] Visser, interview.

[130] Zurbuchen, interview.

[131] Theron Mickelson.

[132] Uecker.

[133] Ibid.

[134] Ibid.

[135] Marshall McLean, interview; and Hagen, interview.

[136] De Jager, interview.

[137] Van Alstine.

[138] Josephine Hopp.

[139] Harriet (Whiting) Laird, interview by author, 16 March 2006.

[140] James Laird.

[141] Manthe, interview.

[142] Robert Daniels, *1220 Days*, 17-18.

[143] Michael J. Miller, *From Shanghai to Corregidor: Marines in the defense of the Philippines* (Washington, D.C.: Marine Corps Historical Center, 1997), 1-3.

[144] Morris, 3-4.

[145] E. Bartlett Kerr, *Surrender and Survival: The Experience of American POWs in the Pacific 1941-1945* (New York: William Morrow and Company, Inc., 1985), 19-20.

[146] Morris, 22.

[147] Kerr, 22. Much of this paragraph, as well as the proceeding two paragraphs, was also taken either directly or paraphrased from the authors' essay entitled "MacArthur's Failures in the Philippines."

[148] Robert Daniels, *1220 Days*, 19.

[149] Morris, 136.

[150] Robert Daniels, *1220 Days*, 20.
[151] Ibid.
[152] Ibid.
[153] Michael Miller, 9.
[154] Morris, 137.
[155] Robert Daniels, *1220 Days*, 20.
[156] Nelson, 50.
[157] Michael Miller, 14.
[158] Robert Daniels, *1220 Days*, 21.
[159] John Costello, 172.
[160] Morris, 169-174.
[161] Keegan, 266.
[162] Robert Daniels, *1220 Days*, 22.
[163] Ibid.
[164] Michael Miller, 13-14.
[165] Robert Daniels, *1220 Days*, 23.
[166] Michael Miller, 18.
[167] Robert Daniels, *1220 Days*, 23.
[168] Morris, 31.
[169] Robert Daniels, *1220 Days,* 23-24.
[170] Ibid., 24.
[171] Hagen, interview.
[172] Nova Vellema.
[173] Hritsko, interview.
[174] Ibid.
[175] Laandal.
[176] Visser, interview.
[177] Hritsko, interview.
[178] Ibid.
[179] Elva Mickelson.
[180] "Women in the Military" (http://www.mscd.edu/history/camphale/wim_001. html, accessed on 31 August 2011).
[181] Elva Mickelson.
[182] Hritsko, interview.
[183] Morris, 23.
[184] Robert Daniels, *1220 Days*, 25.
[185] Ibid., 26.
[186] Bessie (Douma) De Jager, pre-interview questionnaire, undated.
[187] Nelson, 35.
[188] Babler.
[189] Nelson, 36, 53-55.
[190] Ibid., 149.
[191] Ibid., 122-123.
[192] Riel, interview.
[193] Ibid.

[194] "The 4-F Classification for the Draft during World War II" (http://www.nebraskastudies.org/0800/stories/0801_0106.html, accessed on 25 October 2007).

[195] Josephine Hopp; and Brotouski.

[196] Doris Daniels, 30 November 2005.

[197] Ibid.

[198] Theron Mickelson.

[199] Schleicher.

[200] Vroman.

[201] Marshall McLean, interview.

[202] Schrank, interview.

[203] Elva Mickelson.

[204] Hagen, interview.

[205] Ibid.

[206] Harriet Laird.

[207] DiAnna Kay (Reif) Mueller, interviewed by author, 14 March 2006.

[208] James Laird.

[209] Ibid.

[210] AnnaMarie McLean, interview.

[211] Ibid.

[212] AnnaMarie (Kretzer) McLean, written essay to author of her WWII experiences, undated.

[213] AnnaMarie McLean, interview.

[214] Hagen, interview.

[215] Costello, 228; and Keegan, 266.

[216] Costello, 228.

[217] Keegan, 266.

[218] Hagen, interview.

[219] Morris, 359-363.

[220] Robert Daniels, *1220 Days*, 27.

[221] Ibid., 28.

[222] Ibid., 29.

[223] Keegan, 266.

[224] Robert Daniels, *1220 Days*, 29.

[225] Michael Miller, 42.

[226] Robert Daniels, *1220 Days*, 30.

[227] Ibid.

[228] Ibid.

[229] Schrank, interview.

[230] Nova Vellema.

[231] Ibid.

[232] Lyon.

[233] Ibid.

[234] De Jager, interview.

[235] Ibid.

[236] "The Milkweed" (http://newton.dep.anl.gov/natbltn/100-199/nb162.htm, accessed 4 December 2009).

[237] Marshall McLean, written essay to author of his WWII experiences, undated.

[238] Harriet Laird.

[239] James Laird.

[240] Hagen, interview.

[241] AnnaMarie McLean, essay.

[242] "Rationing on the US Homefront during WWII" (http://www.ameshistoricalsociety.org/exhibits/events/rationing.htm, accessed, 25 July 2011); and "Rationed Items" (http://www.ameshistoricalsociety.org/exhibits/ration_items.htm, accessed 25 July 2011).

[243] "Rationing."

[244] Nova Vellema.

[245] Schrank, interview.

[246] Hagen, interview.

[247] De Jager, interview.

[248] Ibid.

[249] Vroman.

[250] Marshall McLean, interview.

[251] Harriet Laird.

[252] Josephine Hopp.

[253] Elva Mickelson.

[254] Marshall McLean, interview.

[255] "Rationing."

[256] Nova Vellema.

[257] Vroman; and Schleicher.

[258] Josephine Hopp.

[259] Schleicher.

[260] Hagen, interview.

[261] Harriet Laird.

[262] Mueller.

[263] Hagen, interview.

[264] Josephine Hopp.

[265] Hagen, interview.

[266] Schrank, interview.

[267] Ibid.

[268] Mueller.

[269] Laandal.

[270] Ibid.

[271] Harriet Laird.

[272] James Laird.

[273] Manthe, interview.

[274] Josephine Hopp.

[275] Brotouski.

[276] Harriet Laird.

[277] James Laird.

[278] AnnaMarie Mclean, interview.

[279] AnnaMarie McLean, essay.

[280] AnnaMarie Mclean, interview.

[281] Robert Daniels, *1220 Days*, 31-32.

[282] Ibid., 33.

[283] Ibid., 33-34.

[284] Ibid., 35-36.

[285] Ibid., 36-38.

[286] Ibid., 39-40; and Hagen, interview.

[287] Linda Goetz Holmes, *Unjust Enrichment: How Japan's companies built postwar fortunes using American POWs* (Mechanicsburg, PA: Stackpole Books, 2001), 44-45.

[288] Uecker.

[289] Ibid.

[290] Ibid.

[291] Rigg.

[292] Ibid.

[293] Nelson, 58.

[294] Page.

[295] Visser, interview.

[296] Alfred Bohnert, interview.

[297] Schleicher.

[298] Ibid.

[299] Doris Daniels, 3 April 1997.

[300] Van Alstine, interview.

[301] Ibid.

[302] De Jager, interview.

[303] Ibid.

[304] Robert Daniels, *1220 Days,* 40-42.

[305] Ibid., 46-48.

[306] Ibid., 49.

[307] Manthe, letter; Manthe, interview; and Manthe, for Carl Manthe.

[308] Hritsko, interview; Gladys (Jolly) Hritsko, pre-interview questionnaire, undated; and "Women in the Military."

[309] Alfred Bohnert, interview.

[310] Ibid.

[311] Schleicher.

[312] Doris Daniels, 30 November 2005.

[313] Zurbuchen, interview; and Fred Zurbuchen, written essay to author of his WWII experiences, undated.

[314] Ibid.

[315] Page.

[316] Van Alstine, interview; and Robert Van Alstine, pre-interview questionnaire, undated.

[317] Lyon.

[318] Laandal.

[319] Thomas E. Griess, ed., *The Second World War: Europe and the Mediterranean* (Garden City Park, NY: Square One Publishers, 2002), 171-172.

[320] Charles Vellema.

[321] Ibid.; and Griess, 171-172.

[322] Charles Vellema.

[323] Ibid.

[324] Ibid.

[325] Ibid.

[326] Samuel Eliot Morison, *History of US Naval Operations in World War II, Vol. II: Operations in North African Waters*, as quoted by Brad Smith (http://navweaps.com/index_oob/OOB_WWII_Mediterranean/OOB_WWII_Casablanca.htm, accessed on 1 October 2007).

[327] Charles Vellema.

[328] Ibid.

[329] Ibid.

[330] Riel, interview.

[331] Ibid.

[332] Charles Vellema.

[333] Ibid.

[334] Ibid.

[335] Ibid.

[336] Ibid.

[337] Ibid.

[338] Hritsko, interview.

[339] Ibid.

[340] Riel, interview.

[341] Ibid.

[342] Carol Hopp, pre-interview questionnaire written for her father, Emil Hopp, undated; "PFC Emil Hopp," unsourced newspaper clipping, undated; Sgt Bill Lees, letter to Mrs. Hattie Hopp, 26 May 1945; and "86th Infantry Division" (http://www.history.army.mil/documents/eto-ob/86ID-ETO.htm, accessed on 10 March 2008).

[343] Hritsko, interview.

[344] Alfred Bohnert, written essay to author of his WWII experiences, undated.

[345] Alfred Bohnert, interview.

[346] Ibid.

[347] Ibid.

[348] Nelson, 132.

[349] Visser, interview.

[350] Griess, 175.

[351] Charles Vellema.

[352] Ibid.

[353] Ibid.

[354] Ibid.

[355] Ibid.

[356] Ibid.

[357] Author's recollections of his father's war-time experiences.

[358] Van Alstine, interview.

[359] Ibid.

[360] Theron Mickelson.

[361] Ibid.

[362] Nova Vellema.

[363] Babler.

[364] Josephine Hopp.

[365] Hagen, interview.

[366] Laandal.

[367] Uecker.

[368] Laandal.

[369] Harriet Laird.

[370] Page.

[371] "Naval Amphibious Base Little Creek" (http://www.globalsecurity.org/military/facility/little_creek.htm, accessed 2 January 2008).

[372] Page.

[373] Ibid.

[374] Ibid.

[375] Robert Daniels, *1220 Days*, 49.

[376] Ibid., 49-50.

[377] Ibid., 51-52.

[378] Ibid., 52-53.

[379] Manthe, for Carl Manthe.

[380] Riel, interview.

[381] Zurbuchen, interview.

[382] Schrank, interview.

[383] Doris Daniels, 30 November 2005.

[384] Schrank, interview.

[385] Hagen, interview.

[386] Doris Daniels, 30 November 2005; Vroman; and Schleicher.

[387] Laandal.

[388] Schleicher; Josephine Hopp; and Brotouski.

[389] Laandal; Schleicher; and Bal.

[390] Laandal.

[391] Ibid.

[392] Brotouski.

[393] Ibid.

[394] Ibid.

[395] Laandal.

[396] Dan Boyle; and *Side Boy*, Twelfth Class (New York: United States Naval Reserve Midshipmen's School, 1943), 12.

397 Robert Daniels, *1220 Days, 54.*

398 Kerr, 212-215.

399 Hritsko, interview.

400 Theron Mickelson.

401 Ibid.

402 Ibid.

403 Ibid.

404 Ibid.

405 Flint Whitlock and Ron Smith, *The Depths of Courage: American submarines at war with Japan, 1941-1945* (New York: Berkley Caliber, 2007), 194.

406 Schleicher.

407 Whitlock, 195.

408 Ibid.

409 Charles Vellema.

410 Page; and "History of the USS Thomas Jefferson (APA-30)" (http://lrwbf.com/USSTJ/history.html, accessed 4 January 2008).

411 Page.

412 Robert Daniels, *1220 Days, 55, 57.*

413 Ibid., 56.

414 Harriet Laird.

415 Ibid.; and James Laird.

416 Harriet Laird.

417 Ibid.

418 Ibid.

419 Ibid.

420 Ibid.

421 James Laird.

422 Manthe, interview.

423 Nova Vellema.

424 "History of the 3rd Marine Division" (http://1stbattalion3rdmarines.com/div-hist-index_files/history_3rddiv.htm, accessed on 22 November 2007); and Alfred Bohnert, essay.

425 Charles Vellema.

426 Page; and "History of the Thomas Jefferson."

427 Van Alstine, interview.

428 Ibid.

429 Ibid.

430 Ibid.

431 Dan Boyle; Patrick Clancey, "USS PT 555" (http://www.ibiblio.org/hyperwar/USN/ships/PT/PT-555.html, accessed 15 November 2009); "USS PT 555" (http://uboat.net/allies/warships/ship/10385.html, accessed 15 November 2009); and Katie Bendall, Bob Ferrell, Rhonda Fleming, Alyce M. Guthrie, Alyce F. Newberry, Boats Newberry, Don Rhoads, and Dave Turner, eds., *Knights of the Sea* (Dallas, TX: Taylor Publishing Co., 1982), 162-163.

432 Meyer.

[433] Sandy Donellan, "Third Marine Division Association – History Bougainville" (http://www.caltrap.org/history/Bougainville.asp, accessed on 22 November 2007).

[434] Alfred Bohnert, essay.

[435] Ibid.; and Alfred Bohnert, interview.

[436] Ibid.

[437] Ibid.

[438] Theron Mickelson.

[439] "USS Barnegat (AVP-10)" (http://www.history.navy.mil/photos/sh-usn/usnsh-b/avp10.htm, accessed 27 October 2009).

[440] Author's recollections of his father's wartime experiences; and Richard Daniels, email to author, 27 February 2008.

[441] Van Alstine, interview.

[442] Ibid.

[443] Alfred Bohnert, interview.

[444] Robert Daniels, *1220 Days*, 59-60, 62.

[445] Ibid., 60-61.

[446] Elva Mickelson.

[447] Ibid.

[448] Ibid.

[449] Riel, interview; and Walter Riel, written essay to author of his WWII experiences, undated.

[450] Nova Vellema.

[451] Hagen, interview.

[452] Rigg.

[453] Ibid.

[454] Ibid.

[455] Babler.

[456] Vroman.

[457] Schleicher.

[458] Josephine Hopp.

[459] Laandal.

[460] James Laird.

[461] Laandal.

[462] Ibid.

[463] Bartow.

[464] Uecker.

[465] Ibid.

[466] Ibid.

[467] Ibid.

[468] Ibid.

[469] "V-12 Program" (http://homepages.rootsweb.com/~uscnrotc/V-12/v12-his.htm, accessed 3 December 2009).

[470] Louis E. Keefer, "The Army Specialized Training Program in World War II" (http://www.pierce-evans.org/ASTP%20in%20WWII.htm, accessed 3 December 2009).

[471] Uecker.

[472] Ibid.

[473] James Laird; and Harriet Laird.

[474] James Laird.

[475] Ibid.

[476] Ibid.

[477] Schrank, interview.

[478] Gertrude (Mintzlaff) Schrank, pre-interview questionnaire written for her brother-in-law, Dr. Raymond Schrank, undated; and "Dr. R. E. Schrank," un-sourced newspaper clipping, undated.

[479] Schrank, interview.

[480] Ibid.

[481] Ibid.

[482] Harriet Laird.

[483] Uecker.

[484] Zurbuchen, interview.

[485] Ibid.; and "Debach Airfield – home of 493rd BG(H) – Helton's Hellcats - USAAF" (http://493bgdebach.co.uk/dahistory.htm, accessed 4 December 2007).

[486] Van Alstine, interview.

[487] Melinda Brickson, "My Grandma and World War II," (undated, photocopied), 7.

[488] Hritsko, interview.

[489] Theron Mickelson.

[490] Ibid.

[491] "USS Barnegat."

[492] De Jager, interview.

[493] "Debach Airfield."

[494] Page; and "USS Thomas Jefferson."

[495] Page.

[496] Van Alstine, interview.

[497] Ibid.

[498] Charles Vellema.

[499] Ibid.

[500] "Navy Department, Bureau of Naval Personnel Service Schools graduation certification NAVPERS 674 (REV. October 1942)" form for Irving Meyer, undated; and Meyer.

[501] Uecker.

[502] Ibid.

[503] Betty Cowley, *Stalag Wisconsin: Inside WWII prisoner-of-war camps* (Oregon, WI: Badger Books, Inc., 2002), 138.

[504] Ibid., 138-140.

[505] Charles Vellema.

[506] Ibid.

[507] Ibid.

[508] "Views of Germany's West Wall (The Siegfried Line)" (http://www.63rdinfdiv. com/siegfriedlinepage1.html, accessed 18 August 2011).

[509] Charles Vellema.

[510] Robert Daniels, *1220 Days*, 77-79.

[511] Ibid., 84.

[512] Visser, interview.

[513] Richard Daniels.

[514] Charles Vellema.

[515] Costello, 485-486.

[516] Alfred Bohnert, essay; and Alfred Bohnert, interview.

[517] Alfred Bohnert, essay.

[518] Ibid.

[519] Manthe, for Carl Manthe; and Manthe letter.

[520] Manthe, interview.

[521] Uecker.

[522] Ibid.

[523] Ibid.

[524] Ibid.

[525] Ibid.

[526] Ibid.

[527] Ibid.

[528] Ibid.

[529] Ibid.

[530] Ibid.

[531] Page; and "USS Thomas Jefferson."

[532] Howard H. Boyle, Jr., "Rough Log of PT 555," undated; and Howard H. Boyle, Jr., "A report on the last mission of PT Boat 555," undated.

[533] Howard Boyle, report.

[534] Bryan Cooper, *PT Boats* (New York: Ballantine Books, Inc., 1970), 11, 15.

[535] Dan Boyle.

[536] Robert Daniels, *1220 Days*, 87, 93; Holmes, 154; and Donald Knox, *Death March, Survivors of Bataan* (New York: Harcourt Brace & Company, 1981), 365.

[537] Hagen, interview; and Charlotte (Mehlbrech) Hagen, pre-interview questionnaire, undated.

[538] Robert Daniels, *1220 Days*, 87-94.

[539] Ibid., 97

[540] Holmes, xxi and 149.

[541] Charles Vellema.

[542] Ibid.

[543] Meyer.

[544] Costello, 502; authors recollections of his father's wartime experiences; and Richard Daniels.

[545] Lyon.

[546] Ibid.

[547] Ibid.

[548] James Laird.

[549] Harriet Laird.

[550] Dan Boyle.

[551] Visser, interview.

[552] Article about AnnaMarie (Kretzer) McLean published in the *Milwaukee Journal* (Milwaukee, WI), 7 December 1975.

[553] Ibid.

[554] AnnaMarie McLean, interview.

[555] Theron Mickelson.

[556] Ibid.

[557] Riel, interview; and Riel, essay.

[558] Riel, interview.

[559] Ibid.

[560] Whitlock, 302; and Costello, 495.

[561] Riel, essay.

[562] "Pacific Air Forces, 13th Air force" (http://www.pacaf.af.mil/library/factsheets/factsheet.asp?id=3608, access on 22 December 2007).

[563] Page; and "USS Thomas Jefferson."

[564] "The Battle of the Bulge" (http://www.historylearningsite.co.uk/battle_of_the_bulge.htm, accessed 2 August 2011); and authors recollections of his uncle's wartime experiences.

[565] Riel, interview.

[566] Costello, 531.

[567] Meyer.

[568] "Battle of the Bulge."

[569] Charles Vellema.

[570] Ibid.

[571] Hagen, interview.

[572] Mueller.

[573] Hagen, interview.

[574] "Franklin D. Roosevelt" (http://www.whitehouse.gov/about/presidents/Franklindroosevelt, accessed 6 December 2009).

[575] Hagen, interview.

[576] Hritsko, interview.

[577] Zurbuchen, interview.

[578] Ibid.

[579] Ibid.

[580] Ibid.; and Zurbuchen, essay.

[581] Zurbuchen, interview.

[582] Ibid.

[583] "Debach Airfield."

[584] AnnaMarie McLean, interview.

[585] Visser, interview; and Visser, pre-interview questionnaire, undated.

[586] Visser, interview.

[587] Theron Mickelson.

[588] Ibid.

[589] Ibid.

[590] Ibid.

[591] Kimberly J. Miller, "Third Marine Division Association – History Iwo Jima" (http://www.caltrap.org/history/iwojima.asp, accessed on 22 November 2007).

[592] Alfred Bohnert, essay.

[593] Ibid.

[594] Ibid.

[595] Ibid.

[596] Author's recollections of his father's wartime experiences.

[597] Visser, interview.

[598] Costello, 534.

[599] Meyer.

[600] Ibid.

[601] Ibid.

[602] Keegan, 519; and Griess, 398.

[603] Visser, interview.

[604] Van Alstine, interview.

[605] Ibid.

[606] Griess, 398.

[607] Van Alstine, interview.

[608] Theron Mickelson.

[609] Manthe, for Carl Manthe; Dan Boyle; and Cooper, 126, 131, 145.

[610] Page; and "USS Thomas Jefferson."

[611] Manthe, interview.

[612] Geoffrey R. Walden, "The Third Reich in Ruins" (http://www.thirdreichruins.com/buchenwald.htm, accessed on 5 March 2008).

[613] Visser, interview.

[614] Visser, interview; and Visser, pre-interview questionnaire.

[615] Visser, interview.

[616] "Roosevelt."

[617] James Laird.

[618] Harriet Laird.

[619] Van Alstine, interview.

[620] Visser, interview; and Visser, pre-interview questionnaire.

[621] Lees.

[622] Laandal.

[623] Visser, interview.

[624] Ibid.; and Visser, pre-interview questionnaire.

[625] Schrank, interview.

[626] Ibid.

[627] Cowley, 257.

[628] Rigg.

[629] Ibid.

630 Cowley, 258.
631 Josephine Hopp.
632 Laandal.
633 Ibid.
634 Schleicher.
635 Author's recollections of his grandfather.
636 Josephine Hopp.
637 Cowley, 77, 116-117.
638 Hagen, interview.
639 Author's recollections of his father's wartime experiences.
640 Ibid.
641 Robert Daniels, *1220 Days*, 104.
642 Ibid.
643 Hagen, interview.
644 Riel, interview.
645 Ibid.
646 Ibid.
647 Ibid.
648 Riel, essay.
649 Ibid.
650 Keegan, 528, 533.
651 AnnaMarie McLean, interview.
652 Ibid.
653 Ibid.
654 Ibid.
655 Ibid.
656 Ibid.
657 Ibid.
658 Zurbuchen, interview.
659 Van Alstine, interview.
660 Ibid.
661 Zurbuchen, interview.
662 Van Alstine, interview.
663 Visser, interview; and Visser, pre-interview questionnaire.
664 Charles Vellema; and Nova Vellema.
665 Meyer.
666 Riel, interview.
667 Doris Daniels, 30 November 2005.
668 Schleicher.
669 Vroman.
670 De Jager, interview.
671 Zurbuchen, interview.
672 Schrank, interview.
673 Hagen, interview.
674 Lyon.

675 Mueller.
676 Laandal.
677 James Laird.
678 Hritsko, interview.
679 Alfred Bohnert, interview; and Alfred Bohnert, essay.
680 Theron Mickelson.
681 Robert Daniels, *1220 Days*, 128-129.
682 Ibid., 129-131.
683 Ibid., 132-134.
684 Ibid., 135.
685 Hagen, interview.
686 Page; and "USS Thomas Jefferson."
687 Page.
688 Alfred Bohnert, interview; and Alfred Bohnert, essay.
689 Van Alstine, interview.
690 Robert Daniels, *1220 Days*, 136.
691 Hagen, interview.
692 Ibid.
693 Van Alstine, interview.
694 Hritsko, interview.
695 Riel, interview.
696 Theron Mickelson.
697 Ibid.
698 Lyon.
699 Ibid.
700 Laandal.
701 Meyer; and "Notice of Separation From U.S. Naval Service NAVPERS-553 (REV. 8-45)" form for Irving Meyer," undated.
702 Babler.
703 Schleicher.
704 Nova Vellema; and Charles Vellema.
705 Ibid.
706 Rigg.
707 Robert Daniels, *1220 Days*, 137.
708 Ibid., 138.
709 Babler.
710 Babler; and Robert Daniels, *1220 Days*, 141-142.
711 Hagen, pre-interview questionnaire.
712 Sue Fritz, ed., "Reach Out: With a little help from friends," *Clinic People*, vol. 1, no. 3 (November 1979), 7.
713 Hagen, pre-interview questionnaire.
714 Ibid.
715 Ibid.
716 Ibid.
717 Ibid.

[718] Riel, interview.

[719] Ibid.

[720] Ibid.

[721] Ibid.

[722] Ibid.

[723] Ibid.

[724] Riel, essay.

[725] Riel, interview.

[726] Doris Daniels, 30 November 2005; and author's personal recollections.

[727] Author's personal recollections.

[728] Schleicher.

[729] Ibid.

[730] Alfred Bohnert, interview; and Vergeana Bohnert.

[731] Pieced together from Schleicher; Alfred Bohnert, interview; Doris Daniels, 30 November 2005; an email from David Bohnert—son of Ralph and Marion—dated 3 March 2008; and the author's personal recollections.

[732] Vroman.

[733] Zurbuchen, interview; and Zurbuchen, essay.

[734] Zurbuchen, interview.

[735] Page; and "Notice of Separation From U.S. Naval Service NAVPERS-553 (REV. 8-45)" form for Morris Page, undated.

[736] Manthe, interview; and Cora (DeMunck) Manthe, pre-interview questionnaire, undated.

[737] Manthe, interview.

[738] Ibid.; and Manthe, pre-interview questionnaire.

[739] Manthe, interview; Manthe, letter; and Manthe, for Carl Manthe.

[740] Manthe, interview; and Manthe, for Carl Manthe.

[741] Van Alstine, interview.

[742] Ibid.

[743] Ibid.

[744] Josephine Hopp.

[745] Ibid.

[746] Ibid.; and Carol Hopp.

[747] Josephine Hopp.

[748] Ibid.

[749] Lees.

[750] Josephine Hopp.

[751] Visser, interview.

[752] Schrank, interview.

[753] Ibid.

[754] Dan Boyle.

[755] Bendall, 162.

[756] Dan Boyle.

[757] Hritsko interview; and Brickson, 6.

[758] Hritsko, interview.

[759] Ibid.

[760] Ibid,; and Brickson, 7.

[761] Theron Mickelson.

[762] Ibid.

[763] Ibid.

[764] Ibid.

[765] Ibid.

[766] Elva Mickelson

[767] Ibid.; and Theron Mickelson.

[768] Laandal.

[769] Ibid.

[770] Ibid.

[771] Brotouski.

[772] Ibid.

[773] Uecker.

[774] Ibid.

[775] Meyer.

[776] Bartow.

[777] Ibid.

[778] Marshall McLean; and AnnaMarie Mclean.

[779] Ibid.

[780] Ibid.

[781] De Jager, interview.

[782] Harriet Laird; and James Laird.

[783] Ibid.

[784] Lyon.

[785] Ibid.

[786] Ibid.

[787] Ibid.

[788] Ibid.

[789] Ibid.

[790] Ibid.

[791] Ibid.

[792] Mueller.

[793] Ibid.

[794] "History Shots" (http://www.historyshots.com/usarmy/backstory.cfm, accessed 9 August 2011); and "World War II Statistics" (http://www.angelfire.com/ct/ww2europe/stats.html, accessed 9 August 2011).

[795] Nesbit, 248.

[796] Nelson, 165-166.

[797] Laandal.

[798] "Lafayette" (http://www.history.navy.mil/danfs/l1/lafayette.html, accessed 4 December 2009).

[799] "Lafayette County LST-859" (http://www.historycentral.com/NAVY/LST/lafayette%20county.html, accessed on 4 December 2009).

Index

B

B-17 (Flying Fortress) 32, 139, 145, 170,
    175–177, 197
B-24 (Liberator) 170
B-25 (Mitchell) 170
B-29 (Superfortress) 199, 218
B-52 (Stratofortress) 234
Babler, Beah 212
Babler, Christine 213
Babler, Curley 212
Babler, Edmond "Ed" xv, 16, 25, 27, 30,
    32, 41, 43, 45, 52, 61, 62, 76, 83,
    101, 107, 111, 121, 130, 152, 163,
    192, 202, 205, 211, 216
Babler, Ferdinand 16
Babler, Jeanette 245. *See also* Rochon,
    Jeanette
Babler, John 212
Babler, Joseph 212
Babler, Katheran (Goetz) 16
Badger Ordinance 235
Bad Noon Hour 182
Bahia, Brazil 146
Bal, Bessie 4
Bal, Dorothy 4, 33, 56, 68, 70, 104,
    105, 124, 132, 199, 218. *See*
    also Vroman, Dorothy
Bal, Martin 4
Bartow, Arthur 230
Bartow, John 230
Bartow, Robert 230
Bartow, Shirley 242. *See also* Karmann,
    Shirley
Bataan Death March 60, 77, 79, 163,
    204
Bataan Peninsula, Philippines 42, 43,
    45, 46, 60
Bataan, Philippines 42, 43, 45–48, 52,
    53, 60, 61, 77, 79, 163, 204, 241
Bataile, Commander (French Navy)
    160, 162
Battle Creek, Michigan 221
Bay of Seine 148
Bayonne, New Jersey 118

Bazooka 90, 91
B Company, 1st Battalion, 4th Marines
    (U.S.) 17
Beaver Dam, Wisconsin xi, 19, 33, 106,
    190, 199, 214, 218–220, 224, 229
Belem, Brazil 146
Belgium 21, 151, 171, 172
Bemidji, Minnesota 22
Berlin High School 24
Berlin, Wisconsin 18, 24, 218
Berra, Yogi 109
Betio, Island of 121
Biggs Field, Texas 145
Big Red One (1st Infantry Division)
    (U.S.) 164
Bilibid Prison, Philippines 78, 107, 111
Bizerte, Tunisia 110
Black Tuesday 1
Blue Lake, Wisconsin 16
Bohnert, Alfred "Al" 4, 17, 81, 82, 85,
    94, 115, 118, 121, 125, 154, 179,
    202, 205, 216
Bohnert, David 242
Bohnert, Doris xv, 33, 55, 103, 104, 124,
    198, 216, 217. *See also* Daniels,
    Doris
Bohnert, Joseph "Joe" 2, 125, 170, 190
Bohnert, Katherine 217
Bohnert, Linda 2, 3, 170
Bohnert, Lois 4, 56, 70, 104, 105, 109,
    124, 132, 190, 209, 216. *See*
    also Schleicher, Lois
Bohnert, Marion. *See* Brown, Marian
Bohnert, Ralph 4, 170, 171, 217
Bohnert, Vergeana 245. *See also* McNeil,
    Vergeana
Bon Ton Tavern 208
Bottomside 48
Boyle, Dan 125, 245
Boyle, Elizabeth. *See* Jagdfeld, Elizabeth
Boyle, Henry 12
Boyle, Howard H. Jr. 12, 19, 106, 107,
    118, 125
Boyle, John 12
Boy Scout 17

Vroman, Frank 218

W

WAAC 85, 130
WAC 85. *See also* Women Army Corps
Wagner, Nova xv, 7, 17, 30, 31, 49, 63,
    67, 70, 98, 115, 131, 198. *See
    also* Vellema, Nova
Wainwright, General Jonathan (U.S.
    Army) 46, 62
Wales 145
Walker, Lieutenant M (U.S. Navy) 160
War Price and Rationing Board 68
Washington 21, 22, 26, 31, 52, 108, 115,
    120, 210, 219, 241
Washington, D.C. 26, 31, 115, 219, 241
Washington Elementary School 210
Washington High School 22
Washington Treaty, 1922 21
Waukesha, Wisconsin 11
Waupun Bottling Works 17, 33, 217
Waupun Canning Company 132, 188,
    189, 209
Waupun District Number Eleven
    Mapledale School 65, 140
Waupun High School 6, 17, 18, 33, 73,
    104, 105, 211, 232, 234
Waupun Historical Society xi, 26, 245
Waupun Memorial Hospital 229, 232
Waupun Senior High School 232, 236,
    285
Waupun Supply 214
Waupun, Wisconsin xi, xv, xvi, xvii,
    xviii, xix, 2–10, 12–15, 17–19,
    21–24, 26, 27, 31, 33–35, 40, 41,
    49, 50, 55, 56, 58, 63–65, 73, 74,
    81, 86, 98, 104–106, 111, 114,
    131–134, 140, 142, 144, 165, 172,
    173, 186–189, 197–202, 205,
    207–212, 214–219, 221, 222, 224,
    228–237, 245, 285
Wayne, John 167
Weber Dairy 122, 227
Wehrmacht 191
Weimar, Germany 184

West, Charles 54
Western Pacific 1, 26, 31
Western Pacific Rim 26
Western Task Force Southern Attack
    Group 88
Western Union 24
Whitewater State Teacher's College 80
Whitewater, Wisconsin 80
Whiting, Harriet 40, 58, 65, 68, 70, 74,
    75, 100, 111, 140, 144, 166, 185,
    232
Whiting, Janet Isabel (Hyslop) 40
Whiting, Ralph Ethan 40
Wiesbaden, Germany 231
Wiesel, Elie 185
Wilcox, Seymour xvi
Williams, Ted 109
Will Rogers Field, Oklahoma 131
Wilson, President Woodrow 30
Winnebago (Indians) xvi, 138
Wisconsin xi, xv, xviii, xix, xx, 2, 4–6,
    8–21, 23–25, 28–30, 31, 33–36,
    40, 45, 51, 53–59, 63, 65, 68, 71,
    79, 80, 82, 85, 93, 97, 98, 103,
    104, 106, 111, 115, 118, 122,
    131–135, 140–142, 150, 155, 156,
    159, 165, 172, 188, 190, 191, 198,
    199, 202, 205–207, 209–212,
    214, 216–220, 222, 224–229, 231,
    232, 236, 237, 241, 242, 285
Wisconsin Aluminum Foundry
    Company 54
Wisconsin National Guard 35
Wisconsin Rapids, Wisconsin 19, 20,
    214
Wisconsin State Child Center 55, 85,
    216
Wisconsin State Maximum Security
    Prison 212, 216, 219
Wittenberg, Germany 187, 193
Wolfen, Germany 186
Women Army Corps 52, 85
Wood County, Wisconsin 19
Woodland Grade School 24
Woodland, Wisconsin 24

282

About the Author

Robert C. Daniels grew up in Waupun, Wisconsin. After graduating from Waupun Senior High School with the class of 1976, he joined the Navy to see the world. Upon his eventual retirement from the service as a chief petty officer, and after indeed seeing quite a bit of the world, he attended and graduated from Tidewater Community College in Virginia Beach, VA, Old Dominion University in Norfolk, Virginia, and the American Military University in Manassas Park,  Virginia, earning an AA in Liberal Arts, a BA in History, and an MA in Military Studies, respectively. He currently lives in Chesapeake, Virginia, with his wife and their cherished pets where he teaches adjunct history at Tidewater Community College.

He is the author of *1220 Days: The story of U.S. Marine Edmond Babler and his experiences in Japanese Prisoner of War Camps during World War II* and numerous essays and articles on World War II and other military conflicts.

CPSIA information can be obtained at www.ICGtesting.com
Printed in the USA
BVOW030102311012

304243BV00001B/7/P

9 781477 236840